WALKING IN THE HAUTE SAVOIE:
Book 2 (South)

Annecy–Chamonix
(Faucigny/Haut Giffre, Aravis/Borne)

About the Author

Janette Norton has lived with her physicist husband, Alan, in the Geneva region for over 30 years, raising four children and working in the marketing field. Her love of mountain walking dates from the time she was a guide in her twenties, and the proximity to her home of the Alps and the Jura has enabled her to continue her passion. Now her family has grown up, she has branched out to walk in other areas of France such as Provence, the Cevennes and the Dordogne. This is Book 2 of the two-volume second edition of her first book, *Walking in the Haute Savoie*.

Other Cicerone guides by the author
Walking in Provence
Walking in the Cevennes
Walking in the Dordogne
Walking in the Haute Savoie: Book 1 North

WALKING IN THE HAUTE SAVOIE:
Book 2 (South)

Annecy–Chamonix
(Faucigny/Haut Giffre, Aravis/Borne)

by
Janette Norton

CICERONE

2 POLICE SQUARE, MILNTHORPE, CUMBRIA LA7 7PY
www.cicerone.co.uk

© Janette Norton 1996, 2005
ISBN 1 85284 411 6

First edition 1996
Second edition 2005

A catalogue record for this book is available from the British Library.
This book was originally published as part of Walking in the Haute Savoie, 1996,
ISBN 1 85284 196 6

Acknowledgements

For this second edition of part of Walking in the Haute Savoie, I would like to
thank my many Geneva friends who redid the walks with me and gave helpful
advice and criticism, especially Janeen Allen, Renée Fevrat, Pamela Harris, Janet
Locke, Jean and Dany Mason-Davids, Catherine Mills, Vivien Nathan, Jennifer
Raper, Geneviève Rieger, Lorraine Ruffing, Isobel Shaw and Alexa Stace. Thanks
are also due to members of the Grand Lancy cross-country ski club (Club des
Pingouins).

A special thank you to my husband who, as usual, read it all before it went
to the publishers and helped me with my computer problems, to my four grown-
up children for criticism and advice, and last but not least to my granddaughter
Clara, who crawled all over my papers and made me realize that actually being
a granny is far more important than writing a book.

I am also extremely grateful for the information provided by the various
tourist bureaux and syndicats d'initiative of the Haute Savoie region.

Advice to Readers

While every effort has been taken to ensure the accuracy of this
guidebook, readers are reminded that changes may occur rapidly in any area, which could make some contents incorrect. It is
advisable to check locally on transport and accommodation.

The author would be glad to hear of any modifications, such
as new signposting or diverted paths. Please write to or e-mail
Janette via the publisher, Cicerone Press. Further information on
walks and updated walk directions are available on the author's
website at **www.janette.freesurf.fr**.

Front cover: *Walking up the Môle (Walk 13)*

CONTENTS

Map Key 7
Haute Savoie: Area Map 8
Haute Savoie: Location of Walks 9
Preface 11

INTRODUCTION
Walking in the Haute Savoie 13
Using the Guide 14
Some Important Walking Rules 18
How to Get There 19
When to Go 21
Equipment and Clothing 22
Accommodation and Refuges 23
Savoyard Food and Drink 28
Flowers and Butterflies 30
Wildlife 33
A Short History of the Haute Savoie 36
The Regions of the Haute Savoie 39

WALKS
Faucigny/Haut Giffre Region
Overlooking Chamonix Valley
1 The Plateau d'Assy 53
2 Refuge du Moëde d'Anterne 58

Overlooking Cluses
3 Pointe de Chevran 65

Samoëns/Sixt Area
4   Lac de Vogealle 70
5   Lac de Gers 77
6   Lac d'Anterne/Refuge de Sales 81
7   Chalets de Criou 93
8   Tête de Bostan 98

Taninges/Praz de Lys Area
9   Pointe de Marcelly 105

10   Pointe d'Uble...110
11   La Haute Pointe 115

Near St-Jeoire
12   Pointe des Brasses...119
13   Le Môle 125

Aravis/Borne Region
La Clusaz Area

14   Boucle des Confins...129
15   Le Trou de la Mouche 137
16   Le Circuit des Annes 143
17   Boucle du Lac de Lessy 147
18   Boucle de St-Jean-de-Sixt...153

Thônes Area
19   La Pointe d'Orsière 157
20   Tour de la Tulle...163
21   Tour de Sulens 170
22   Tour de l'Aiguille de la Tournette 177
23   Boucle des Tervelles 181

Near La Roche-sur-Foron
24   La Roche Parnal...187
25   Montagne de Sous-Dine 192
26   Plateau des Glières 199

Lake Annecy Area
27   Le Parmelan 205
28   Cascade d'Angon 210
29   La Tournette..215
30   Taillefer Ridge and Le Roc des Boeufs 219

Appendix 1 Maps used in the Guide...227
Appendix 2 Tourist Offices and Syndicats d'Initiative 228
Appendix 3 Market Days...231
Appendix 4 Glossary of Useful French Words 232

Map key

———————	road
━━━━━━━	route on road
··············	vehicle track/non maintained road
———————	grassy track
─ ─ ─ ─ ─ ─	route
─ ─ ─ ─ ─ ─	alternative route
———————	footpath
━·━·━·━·━	route on vehicle track
─ ─ ─ ─ ─ ─	route on footpath
⊞	cemetery
P	parking
■	habitation
⚲	church
✦	monument
✳	viewpoint
▲	summit
†	statue
⬆	refuge
❶	walk number
⟶	route direction arrow
D41	road number
○	water
～	river
⌇	rocks/cliffs
⋊⋉	bridge
☆	orientation table
⊢——⊣	cable-car or ski-lift
Ⱥ	pylon
═══	pylon cables

7

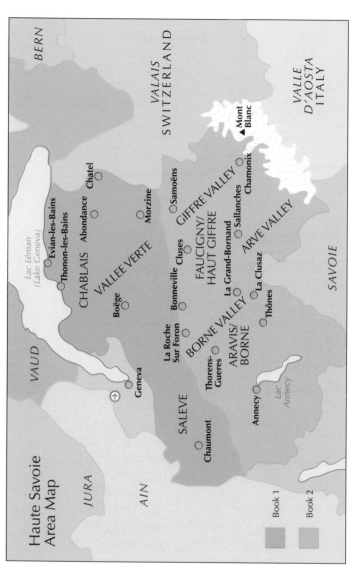

Haute Savoie Area Map

8

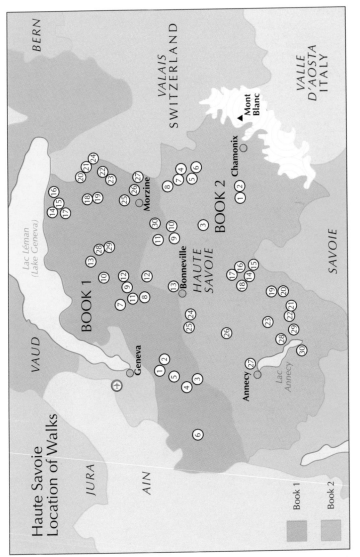

Haute Savoie
Location of Walks

BOOK 1

BOOK 2

JURA

AIN

VAUD

Geneva

BERN

Lac Léman
(Lake Geneva)

Morzine

Bonneville

HAUTE
SAVOIE

VALAIS
SWITZERLAND

Chamonix

Mont Blanc

VALLE
D'AOSTA
ITALY

SAVOIE

Annecy

Lac
Annecy

Book 1

Book 2

PREFACE

It is hard to believe that ten years have passed, seemingly in a flash, since I wrote *Walking in the Haute Savoie*, of which this new edition was a part. At that time I was working and looking after a growing family. Now I am retired, and the family has grown, flown and come back with grandchildren, so the process is starting all over again, and I am busy looking after toddlers who do not quite appreciate that granny might want to do something other than entertain them.

Between the flight of one generation and the return of the next, I managed to flit away to other areas of France and discovered a tantalising chequerboard of different types of terrain and vegetation, each fascinating and challenging in its own way. In every region I left a part of my heart, and vowed I would go back and settle, away from the hustle and bustle of international life, but family and other ties always drew me back to the Haute Savoie and the Alpine region. Then I realised that the original edition of *Walking in the Haute Savoie* badly needed an update, as so much has changed in the intervening years.

When I first did these walks it was quite an adventure, as there was limited signposting and sometimes inadequate maps. Now there are signposts just about everywhere (as in other areas) and they have the same style all over the country. In some instances paths have been rerouted, jeep tracks appear where there were none before, housing estates have mushroomed on beautiful unspoilt meadows, the trees have grown taller or been chopped down and replanted – it is amazing how in 10 years a landscape can change to become, in some cases, unrecognizable; nowhere is this more evident than in the Haute Savoie. Unfortunately, many maps have not been updated to follow the evolution of the landscape.

Somehow, redoing (often more than once) all the 60 walks that appeared in the first edition, and which are now being published in two volumes, has seemed to take longer than it did in the 1980s and 1990s. Many of the gradients seem steeper than I remember, the time taken to get there longer, and the weather more changeable – this could all be put down to being 10 years older and, I hope, wiser! Nevertheless, it has been an exciting time rediscovering mountains that are like old friends – unmoveable and, underneath the changes, just as enjoyable.

Janette Norton

Lac de Lessy (Walk 17)

INTRODUCTION

Most people associate the French Alps with the town of Chamonix, dominated by Mont Blanc, the highest mountain in Europe, and the dazzling array of challenging peaks that surround it.

Visitors flock to the Chamonix area to walk and explore, but they do not always realise that the Mont Blanc range is only part of the Haute Savoie region. Not far away there are dozens of other interesting villages and mountains to discover, less frequented, steeped in history, and crisscrossed with delightful walking trails.

If you look at a detailed map of France, you will see that the Haute Savoie is in the southeast, below Lake Léman (also called Lake Geneva). To the east is the mountainous Valais area of Switzerland and to the west the Rhône valley. The gentler mountains of the pré-Alps to the north give way to the high mountain ranges of Mont Blanc in the southeast and the beautiful, mountain-ringed stretch of water to the southwest that is Lake Annecy. Until quite recently many of the local paths (as opposed to the long Grande Randonnée walks) were badly signposted, but this has changed in the last few years as smart new signposts have been erected and the tourist offices have marked out

local walks, and in many cases issued maps to attract the summer visitor.

Originally published in one volume, the 60 walks have now been split into two books.

Book 1
- Northwest Haute Savoie – the Salève and Vallée Verte.
- Northeast Haute Savoie – known as the Chablais, which is just south of Lake Léman.

Book 2
- Central and east Haute Savoie – the Faucigny and Haut Giffre.
- Southwest and central Haute Savoie – Lake Annecy and the Aravis/Borne range.

Walks in the Mont Blanc region of the Haute Savoie are not included. They are impressive and worth doing, and are covered in Cicerone Press's *Mont Blanc Walks*, by Hilary Sharp.

When describing each area more fully, the towns and villages where overseas visitors might want to stay are given, but most walks are within easy reach of a central base. Under Accommodation and Refuges (later in this introduction) a description of the choices available is given, but without specific names, as each town and most of the larger villages has a tourist office or syndicat d'initiative (see Appendix 2, List of Tourist Offices) where up-to-date information can be found. The choice is usually wide ranging, from first-class hotels to camping sites in the bigger towns, though smaller villages may have only one hotel. For years the Haute Savoie has been a tourist area, so there are usually plenty of restaurants and cafés, with no lack of good shops and supermarkets.

USING THE GUIDE

Walk Grading

Walks are graded Difficult, Medium and Easy, and there are comments after each grading to give the walker a good idea as to whether the walk is suitable.

None of the walks described is at very high altitude (usually below 2500m) and all are possible during the summer months. Many are even low enough to tackle in the spring-

time, but it is worth remembering that snow may linger on the higher northern slopes until the beginning of June and sometimes longer, so it is wise to either watch the weather forecast or speak to the tourist office before you set off. It is very difficult to estimate how tough a walk is, but I have tried to give an honest assessment with extra details, such as 'steep and over scree' or 'not for those who suffer from vertigo', etc. One important indicator of the walk difficulty is the overall gain in altitude, and any walk that has a height gain of over 800m is graded either difficult or difficult/medium, regardless of the timing.

Timings

The timings correspond to the average walking pace of a reasonably fit person, but this is very approximate as everyone has a different rhythm. It

Waterfalls on the way to the Pointe du Dérochoir (Walk 6)

is also important to leave plenty of time for looking at views, taking photos and stopping for a picnic. As a rough guide you can expect to walk 3km in one hour if there are no steep gradients. Four centimetres on a 1:25,000 scale map equals 1km (for quick measurement put three fingers sideways on the map – this equals roughly 4cm, which is 20 minutes walking).

Height Gain

When reading the walk details, look carefully at the height gain. Extra altitude equals extra walking time, and steep gradients can tire you rapidly if you are not used to them. As a rough estimate, with a light rucksack (6 to 7kg) you should be able to climb 400m in one hour (250–300m with a weight of 15kg). The descent is quicker, approximately 500m in one hour.

Maps

Although each walk is accompanied by a sketch map, it is recommended that you buy the 1:25,000 IGN maps listed in the information box at the beginning of each walk. These show the paths in detail.

The 1:50,000 maps, though useful, only show the main paths. The Didier & Richard IGN 1:50,000 maps which were used for the original book have now been phased out and are unobtainable in the shops, although they are still perfectly usable, as little has changed – on the maps anyway!

They have been replaced by the IGN orange series, which are also quite difficult to find. There are also new IGN 1:60,000 maps, which are available in local shops. A good map that gives an overall picture of the Haute Savoie region is the Cartes IGN No. 45 Annecy/Lausanne–Parc Naturel Régional du Haut-Jura, Série Verte 1:100,000.

A complete list of maps can be found in Appendix 1, together with details of where you can buy or order them in the UK. However, it is easier to buy them in the region, and they are sometimes cheaper in local supermarkets.

The numbers on each sketch map show key reference points, especially where there are major changes in walk direction, and correspond to a numbered section in the text. However, please read the route instructions carefully, as there may be additional turnings that are not numbered and where the path is not indicated on the IGN map. Bear in mind that things are still changing in this region, and you may find that there are new ski-lifts, roads and jeep tracks which are not yet on the maps.

Access to the Walks

Access to the walks always starts from Geneva. Since the publication of the first edition of this book, a ring road has been built around Geneva that makes it easier to avoid going through town if you live outside it. I have also given the nearest village or town to

Pointe de Bajulaz, La Tournette (Walk 29)

the start of the walk to help those coming from other directions. Where possible the walks start from points where there is a car park or good roadside parking.

Signposting

Most of the walks in the Haute Savoie, as in other areas in France, have been newly signposted with smart white signs clearly showing the various destinations and time taken to get there (the latter depending on who did the signposting!). There are also green plastic squares with yellow arrows, either nailed to trees or on posts and/or yellow splashes. In many places the original signposting remains, though the splashes are somewhat faded. In some cases the

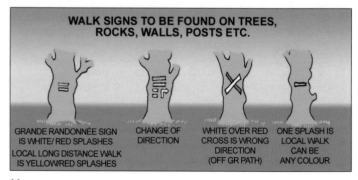

WALK SIGNS TO BE FOUND ON TREES, ROCKS, WALLS, POSTS ETC.

GRANDE RANDONNÉE SIGN IS WHITE/ RED SPLASHES LOCAL LONG DISTANCE WALK IS YELLOW/RED SPLASHES

CHANGE OF DIRECTION

WHITE OVER RED CROSS IS WRONG DIRECTION (OFF GR PATH)

ONE SPLASH IS LOCAL WALK CAN BE ANY COLOUR

local tourist office has gone overboard with their signposting, but better than nothing at all.

If you see white and red horizontal paint flashes on trees, rocks or posts, this means you are on a long-distance Grande Randonnée path. Said to be the finest walking network in Europe, it consists of over 40,000km of footpaths crisscrossing the country. For example, the GR5 starts from the small town of Gingolph on Lake Léman and travels all the way to Nice. The GR4 starts from Nice and goes all the way to the east coast, south of La Rochelle, and so on. However, there are also long regional walks, coloured yellow and red, such as the Balcon du Léman, a path round the mountainous crests of Lac Léman (also called Lake Geneva).

On some walks you will see tree trunks painted with a red stripe in a white square, or with numbers. This may confuse you into thinking they are different GR signs, but in fact they are indications to the foresters that the tree has to be cut down, or else they serve as boundary marks. When following a GR route, it is useful to know that a white/red cross means you are about to go in the wrong direction.

All the hikes included in this guide have been done at least twice,

Example of the new white signposts in the Haute Savoie

New signposting in the Haute Savoie – posts with yellow arrows on green background

SOME IMPORTANT WALKING RULES

- Read the walk description carefully and look at the map before you go.

- Give yourself plenty of time by setting off early.

- Listen to the weather forecast and do not set out if there is a danger of fog, storms or snow.

- Never deviate from the marked path – if there is a short cut, it is usually shown. If you are lost, go back the way you came if possible. Avoid going across patches of scree or snow, and watch out for slippery grassy slopes.

- Be careful not to dislodge stones or boulders – they can gather momentum as they roll down the mountain and hit other walkers.

- Be sure that you have enough warm clothes and food, and especially water if it is a hot day.

- If you are not used to the sun at altitude, remember to put on a high-protection sunscreen and to wear reliable sunglasses.

- Never walk alone, even if you know the route, and always tell someone where you are going.

- If you get caught in a thunderstorm, get off high, exposed ground immediately and take shelter, but not under an isolated tree or rock. When lightning strikes, remove any metallic objects you, might have on you and if necessary, curl up on the ground to avoid being struck.

- If there is an accident, wrap the person concerned in a survival blanket (see equipment list, later in this chapter). Use your whistle – six short blasts means you need help (three short ones means you are all right), or six flashes from your torch if it is dark. If you have to leave to get help, make sure you know where you are located and leave as much warm clothing and food with the victim as possible.

- Take all your litter home with you, and do not pick the wild flowers – leave them for others to enjoy.

- Remember that these mountains are a cultural heritage and should be left unspoilt for future generations – happy walking!

and some more often than that. However, routes and paths do alter, mainly because of the constant foresting that goes on in many of these mountain areas, so some signs or paths may have been altered since this guide was written. If you are walking late in the season, it is also worth remembering that in ski areas the walking signs are normally taken down in mid-September.

Excellent maps giving explanations (sometimes also in English) of the walks that can be done in the immediate area are on sale in many local tourist offices.

Observations

The observations at the start of each walk give useful additional information that is intended to help the reader decide whether or not he or she wishes to do the walk. In this mountainous region some of the walks entail rocky scrambling, hanging on to chains or going down ladders, all of which require dexterity and a head for heights and it is helpful to be aware of this before you start. You will also find anecdotes about the countryside and places of historical interest to visit.

HOW TO GET THERE

By Car

It is not possible to reach many of the walks in this book without a car. For those travelling to the region by train or air, all the main car-hire firms operate from stations and airports, and information about rental can be obtained from your local travel agency.

There are three internet sites which will give you a detailed travel itinerary, namely:

- **www.viamichelin.com** (French site)
- **www.theaa.com/Travel** and Leisure/European Route Planner
- **www.rp.rac.co.uk/Routeplanner** (the official AA and RAC internet sites).

These sites require as a minimum the names of two towns, but you may also add intermediate points. You can also specify fastest/shortest route, avoiding tolls/ferries, etc.

By Air

The nearest airport to the Haute Savoie is Geneva (Switzerland), and many of the walking areas in this guide are within an hour's drive of the city. EasyJet flies to Geneva several times a day from various UK airports, and if you book early you can fly very cheaply indeed. For information about times and prices, go to their website at **www.easyjet.co.uk**. Other airlines that fly to Geneva are British Airways, **www.ba.co.uk**, Swiss (formerly Swissair), **www.swiss.ch** and Flybe, **www.flybe.com**.

By Rail

The UK office of the the French Railways (SNCF), at Rail Europe, 179 Piccadilly, London W1V 0BA, tel 0870 8306030 (brochureline) **www.raileurope.co.uk** will, on request, send a very informative brochure outlining all the different ways to get to France by train, including timetables, cost, car hire, travel insurance information, special hotel/rail packages for short and medium breaks, cross-channel fares, Inter-Rail information for the under 26s, senior citizen discounts, etc. For ticket booking, telephone 0870 5848848 or contact the website.

It is possible to travel by Eurostar to Lille or Paris and then catch a TGV fast train and arrive in Geneva in 3 hours or Annecy in 4 hours. For further information contact Eurostar at **www.eurostar.com**. Also worth asking for is the free booklet entitled *TGV Sud-Est Grandes Lignes, horaire et guide pratique*. This gives destinations, timings and costs of trains leaving from Paris to the southeast, including the Haute Savoie area, and also trains within the region.

One tip for travellers taking TGV trains is that you must have a seat reservation, and before boarding you must validate your ticket by punching it into an orange unit (*composteur*) which you will see before you reach the platform. Also, the price indexes in the booklet are outlined in different colours, which means that different departures are more expensive or cheaper than others. This could be rather complicated for a non-French speaker, but the prices are clearly marked.

By Bus

The most economical way to make the journey from England is by bus from Victoria Station, London, but of course it takes longer. There is a bus to Chamonix, via Grenoble, Chambéry and Annecy, which leaves London at 15.30 and arrives in Annecy at 09.05 (Chamonix 10.25) the next day. Alternatively, you can go to Geneva, via Lyon, leaving London at 15.30 and arriving Geneva at 10.45 the following morning. (These times are subject to change and are an indication only.) For information and booking details, contact Eurolines on the internet **www.Eurolines.co.uk** or telephone 08705 143219.

Local Bus Transport

If you intend to rely on local bus transport, I suggest that you plan your walking programme before you leave home by writing to or telephoning the Annecy tourist office (see Appendix 2) for a free copy of their Haute Savoie bus timetable (Indicateur des Transports Routiers). There is a general information page in English which gives the meanings of the various abbreviations and signs. There are 20 different bus companies serving the region (names, addresses and telephone numbers are included in the book) and the timetables are easily understandable. Bear in mind, however, that many of the walks do not start from the towns or villages themselves, so read the departure explanations carefully. Without a car, a number of the walks will be difficult to do simply because there is no public transport to the departure area and taxis are expensive.

WHEN TO GO

The Haute Savoie climate is more continental than temperate Britain, which means the winters are colder and the summers hotter. The major rains come in springtime and the snow can cling to the higher altitudes and the northern slopes well into May. With the apparent recent changes in climatic conditions there has been a trend towards little snow in the winter months and then a lot in April. The first snowfall of the winter at high altitude may also arrive at the end of August (though it usually melts), when the hot, sticky weather tends to break with heavy thunderstorms.

Since some of the walks in this guide are at lower altitudes, they can be done in late spring, though the weather can be fickle at this time – one day beautiful sunshine and the next cold and rainy. The main advantage is that there are few tourists and the flowers are magnificent.

Summers (July/August) are often hot and humid, though the higher you get the fresher it is. There is also often a heat haze that obscures the view and there are sometimes heavy thunderstorms. The main disadvantages, though, are the crowds of people and the difficulty in getting accommodation. With the growing ecology movement, the mountain areas are becoming more popular than ever. Some of the better-known walks should be avoided during high summer weekends.

In my opinion the best period is September and October, when the school holidays are over, there are very few tourists, and the days can have a balminess and clarity that makes every rock and stone stand out in sharp relief. Although the glory of the flowers is over, you are

View of the Aravis range from Tour de la Tulle (Walk 20)

compensated by a variety of mushrooms and berries, and the trees turning an autumn gold (the mountain rowans with their bright red berries are particularly striking).

Around the start of October the fog sometimes gathers in the valleys, particularly near Geneva where the lake makes it humid, and the weather at low altitude is grey and miserable. You drive up into the mountains and suddenly you pop out of the fog into brilliant sunshine! There is something awe inspiring about walking at altitude and looking down on to a mass of 'cotton wool' where the valley should be. Other peaks stick up out of the plain like islands, and the permanently snow-covered higher ranges such as Mont Blanc look even more impressive with their lower slopes cloaked in fog. If you are walking at this time, be careful to find out what the cloud level is (sometimes it can be quite high and you can be walking all day with the sunshine just a few metres above, if you but knew it). Also, remember that the rocks can be a bit slippery in the morning if the sun has only just reached them, and that the days are drawing in, so there is less walking time. Many of the higher refuges tend to shut around mid-September.

EQUIPMENT AND CLOTHING

As with all mountainous regions, the weather in the Haute Savoie can change rapidly without warning, and a careful choice of clothing and equipment is essential for your safety and security. The best solution is to dress in layers and, even if the forecast is good, to carry a high-quality windproof jacket of breathable material to avoid getting hot and sweaty. As for trousers, lightweight, quick-drying baggy ones are the most comfortable for walking – those that zip down into shorts are very practical. Even on hot days, you may need long trousers to avoid getting scratched by undergrowth. Protection against the sun is important, especially at higher altitudes where ultraviolet rays are more intense.

Sturdy boots are essential for mountain walking, preferably with plenty of ankle support and serrated rubber soles that give a good grip on the rocks. It is worth investing in comfortable, lightweight waterproof boots (e.g. Gore-Tex) and it is very important to break boots in before you start hiking, so that any blisters are suffered at home rather than on a mountainside. Proper walking socks can make an enormous difference to foot comfort – the best ones are made from composite wool–acrylic material with reinforced, cushioned heel and toe areas (avoid cotton as it absorbs moisture and can cause blisters).

For day walks, a light 30-litre rucksack is sufficient, but the ones with a padded, fitted back and a waist strap (which means that the weight goes to the hips rather than the back) are recommended. Make sure there are

View of Mont Blanc from the summit of La Roche Parnal (Walk 24)

several side and top pockets, which are so useful for essentials such as snacks, first-aid kit, money, etc. Some of the larger trekking rucksacks have a big top pocket which can be detached and used as a day pack – this is very useful if you are doing day sorties from a base camp. Even if your rucksack is supposed to be waterproof, you should wrap individual items of clothing in plastic bags to keep them dry. The rustle of plastic bags is a constant background noise when staying overnight in a mountain refuge.

A whistle and a good-quality compass are essential in the mountains, but other gadgets, e.g. altimeter or GPS, are not normally needed for the walks in this guide, although they are useful in bad weather or you get lost (do find out how to use them

before you start). A mobile phone can be life saving if you have an accident (make sure you have the number of the local police station or mountain rescue). Unfortunately, the more remote mountain areas are often out of network coverage.

ACCOMMODATION AND REFUGES

There is plenty of accommodation all over the Haute Savoie, ranging from first-class hotels to primitive mountain refuges. It is all a matter of choice and how much money you want to spend. Remember that many of the hotels in the large ski resorts are shut in the summer. July and August are the high season months, so it is advisable to book in advance if you plan

23

EQUIPMENT LIST

The following is a suggested list for your rucksack on a day walk:

- maps as described in the walk information box
- good-quality compass; whistle (six blows indicates you need help); mobile phone
- basic first-aid kit, including insect repellent and moleskin for blisters
- survival blanket
- sun cream and lip salve, sun hat, sunglasses
- woolly hat and gloves (in cold weather)
- glucose tablets or energy bars; packets of mixed dried fruit and nuts
- Swiss Army knife with as many accessories as possible
- nylon cape/poncho to cover everything, including your rucksack, when it is really pouring (also useful for sitting on when having your picnic)
- lightweight sweater
- lightweight wind- and waterproof anorak
- shorts (if hot)
- extra pair of socks
- water bottle – it is *essential* to take plenty of water; avoid drinking from mountain streams or dubious drinking troughs and fountains
- picnic – buy a crusty baguette at the local bakery before you set off and eat it with fresh cheese or small tins of meat or tuna.

Optional extras include altimeter, GPS, camera, binoculars, reference books.

If you are staying overnight in a refuge, add the following:

- washing things, small towel plus change of clothes
- sleeping sheet (silk ones available in most good camping shops); all the refuges in the Haute Savoie provide blankets
- torch – a head lamp is very useful (especially if there is only an outside toilet)
- track suit for relaxing in the evening (use also as pyjamas)
- lightweight tennis shoes (some refuges provide slippers but this is not guaranteed)
- playing cards and/or paperback book – in case you are holed up by bad weather
- small repair kit with needles, thread, string, buttons, etc.

Check that the refuge supplies meals (most of them do) – if not, take your own. Hot water is available for soup and often you can use the kitchen.

to walk at this time, otherwise it is not essential. A short explanation follows of the different types of accommodation available.

Logis de France

This is a nationwide network of small hotels which offer comfortable accommodation and excellent food at very reasonable prices. The hotels are graded from one to three stars according to their degree of comfort and there are some 200 Logis de France in the towns and villages of the Haute Savoie region (look for their distinctive logo, which consists of a yellow fireplace on a green background). The Logis de France book, listing all the hotels available, with additional information about facili-

ties, is available from good book-shops or the Maison de la France shop in London's Piccadilly (address at the end of this section). Website: **www.logis-de-france**.

Gîtes de France

These are good-value country cottages available all over the French countryside for a weekly rent. They can vary from extremely comfortable to quite basic, so read the small print beside each photo in your brochure carefully. It is a good idea to rent a *gîte* in a central position and then go to a different area every day, none of the walks in this guide being a great distance apart. Gîtes de France holidays are now run in conjunction with Brittany Ferries. For information and booking contact,

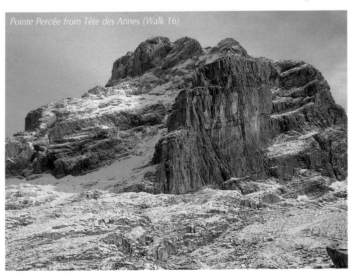

Pointe Percée from Tête des Annes (Walk 16)

www.gitesdeFrance.fr/eng/index.htm.
This website gives information on all
types of *gîtes* and online reservations
are possible.

Gîtes d'Étape

This is a type of youth hostel, usually
with a warden, and open to people of
all ages. They can be reasonably comfortable, with good beds, showers and
a well-equipped kitchen if you wish
to cook your own food, but they can
also be quite basic, with dormitory
accommodation and mainly intended
for cheap overnight stops by walkers
and cyclists. Some of them offer
meals, but if not there is often a
café/restaurant in the vicinity. In the
high season they can be uncomfort-
ably full, but are a wonderful way to
get to know fellow travellers and
share a convivial evening. Out of
season you often have the place to
yourself. A complete guide to the
gîtes d'étape all over France is available from good bookshops, Brittany
Ferries or the bookshop at Maison de
la France, Piccadilly, London, website: **www.gite-etape.com**.

Chambres d'Hôte

This is the French equivalent of bed
and breakfast, though often the breakfast is not included, or may be limited
to coffee and bread (croissants if you
are lucky). These establishments are
increasing in number in French villages (look for the *chambres d'hôte*
sign or enquire in the local café or
shop). The degree of comfort varies

tremendously, but unlike at British
establishments, you will rarely get a TV
or beverage-making facilities in your
room. Most rooms do have their own
shower and toilet, but you could be
sharing with the family. If you can
speak some French it is a wonderful
way to get to know the local people.
The book *French Country Welcome* is
available from the Maison de la France
shop (address at the end of this section) or from the website **www.gitesde
France.fr/eng/index.htm**.

Youth Hostels (Auberges de Jeunesse)

These are rare in France outside the
main towns, but for a complete list
called *Guide des Auberges de
Jeunesse en France* contact the Youth
Hotels Association, Trevelyan House,
Dimple Road, Matlock, Derbyshire
DE4 3YH, tel 01629 592600, fax
01629 592702, website **www.yha.org.
uk**. There are only a few in the Haute
Savoie, namely in Annecy, Chamonix,
La Clusaz and Morzine-Avoriaz.

There is a website, **www.fuaj.
com**, that enables you to book online
up to six months in advance. You can
book for groups of up to nine people
and for a maximum period of six days,
subject to availability. Don't forget that
you have to be a member of the YHA
to stay in a hostel (reductions in membership fees for under 18s).

Camping

Camping sites are graded from one to
five stars and range from those offering shop, hot showers and swimming

pool to sites with basic washing facilities. Camping *à la ferme* is cheap and popular, though the facilities are minimal – remember that some toilets in France, especially on camping sites, are still of the squat variety. Website **www.gites-deFrance.fr/eng/index. htm**. Local tourist offices also have a complete list of camping sites.

Naturefriends (Amis de la Nature)

This is a non-profit organisation, founded in 1895, which has hostels all over Europe offering accommodation to members at reasonable prices. There are branches in most European countries. For full information and details concerning membership there is a website: **www.naturefriends.org.uk**.

Refuges (Mountain Huts)

Details of the refuges on specific walks are given at the end of the walk descriptions. Some are run by the French Alpine Club, but many are privately owned. These refuges are usually above 2000m and mainly occupied by serious walkers and climbers as a base for tackling local peaks. They can be great fun provided you don't mind communal living, such as sleeping in dormitories (men and women in the same room) and often basic cooking and washing facilities. One thing to remember is that they are not cheap, and food is relatively expensive for what you get, as it has to be hauled up on a mountain pulley or dropped by helicopter. Don't forget to take your own sleeping sheet as only blankets are provided (see Equipment and Clothing earlier in this chapter for more information). For a list of Haute

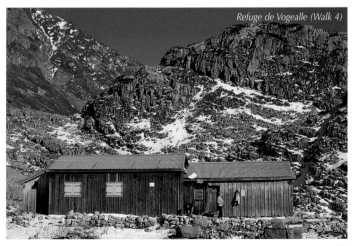

Refuge de Vogealle (Walk 4)

Savoie refuges, telephone the local FAC Club in Annecy: 0450.090.82.09 (no English spoken) or visit the website **www.clubalpin.com**.

For more information concerning the Haute Savoie, contact:

Maison de la France
178 Piccadilly
London WIV OAL
Tel 09068 244123
Fax 020 7493 6594
E-mail info@mdlf.co.uk.
Website **www.franceguide.com**.

If you write, e-mail or telephone they will send the following documentation free of charge.

The Traveller in France Reference Guide. This has a wealth of interesting information, such as: dates to note, how to get there, maps of France, helpful hints, motoring in France, where to stay, hotel groups, package holidays in hotels, special interest holidays, weekends, short breaks, day trips, caravanning and camping, self-catering holidays, maps and guides, and addresses.

Hotels. A brochure which gives a complete list with telephone numbers, prices and other relevant information in the Isère, Savoie and Haute Savoie regions.

Campings. A complete list of all camping sites in the above areas.

There is also a shop selling a wide range of books in English and

French. Fench information line: tel 09068 244123 (affiliated to Maison de la France). Open 10.00–18.00 Monday to Friday and 10.00–17.00 Saturday.

SAVOYARD FOOD AND DRINK

The Haute Savoie is not the most gastronomic area of France. Nevertheless, it has a reputation for high-class dried and smoked meats, a variety of mushrooms, berries and fruits, and more especially the succulent Abondance, Chevrotin and Reblochon cheeses. There is an abundance of freshwater fish, such as trout, pike, crayfish, perch and the *omble chevalier*, a species of Arctic char found mainly in deep mountain waters such as Lake Annecy, but now also artificially farmed near Thonon.

The region of Frangy and Seyssel in the northwestern area produces various white Roussette wines from a type of vine originating in Cyprus at the time of the crusades in the 12th century. There are also vineyards in the region of Lake Léman, as well as near Bonneville, which produce Crèpy, a dry white wine with the smell of hawthorn, and a bubbling white wine called Ayse. And last but not least are the renowned mineral waters from the towns of Thonon-Les-Bains and Evian-Les-Bains.

Since the 14th century Abondance cheese has been made in the farms of the Abondance valley. Based on the milk of a well-known breed of

View up the Giffre valley with Mont Blanc behind, Pointe des Brasses (Walk 12)

cow, it is a slightly cooked, pressed and salted cheese which is produced in the Alpine chalets in summer and in a *laiterie* (dairy) during the rest of the year. It takes three months to ripen and is a round, flat slab like a mill-stone weighing from 7 to 12kg.

Chevrotin cheese is made from fermented goats' milk and has been produced in the Aravis mountains for generations. It is a round cheese, about 10cm (4in) wide by 8cm (3in) high and weighs about 350gm. It only takes three weeks to mature in a cellar after which it is ripe and ready to eat.

Reblochon also comes from the Aravis region around Thônes and Grand-Bornand. It has an interesting history dating back to the time when all the land and cattle in the area belonged to the Catholic church. The peasants used to trick the monks by

pretending that they had finished milking the cows and then, as soon as the monks were out of sight, they would do a second milking (called *la rôblosse*), which was the richest and creamiest. This cheese is first mentioned in the 16th century, when it became recognised and much appreciated by the Sardinian/ Piedmontese court, as it could travel all the way to Turin without getting spoilt. Reblochon cheeses, made from milk slightly warmed till it curdles, are pressed into a wooden mould and a weight put on top. After a while they are taken out of the moulds, salted, washed, brushed, and put in a dry cellar where they are turned every few days until ripe. The finished product is about 15cm (6in) in diameter with an orange rind. It has a very distinctive taste which you either like or you don't.

Tartiflette, one of the region's most noted dishes, is made from Reblochon cheese. It is a relatively simple dish consisting of layers of cooked potatoes garnished with onion and slivers of bacon and then covered with a whole cheese, the rind uppermost. It is then put under the grill till the cheese is crusty and bubbling – worth trying.

You will find regional produce in local markets, which are great fun to wander round, even if you have no intention of buying. (See Appendix 3 for market days).

FLOWERS AND BUTTERFLIES

One of the joys of walking in the mountains, especially in spring and early summer, is the abundance and variety of flowers growing in the Alpine pastures, among rock crevices, and in places where you would think no plant life could possibly take hold. For many it is sufficient to admire and appreciate the blaze of colour, from deep purple to bright yellow, depending on the region and time of year. If, however, you are interested in identifying and knowing the names of the individual species, buy a good flower book and a magnifying lens and keep them permanently in your rucksack (see the end of this section for suggested books). Remember to leave extra time for flower identification, as it is not something to be rushed. One of the advantages of Alpine walking is

that you can enjoy the spring flowers on the lower slopes and then, as the months go by, enjoy them again as you gain height. The type of mountain terrain affects the species you will find, some thriving on granite, for example, while others prefer limestone.

Some of the first flowers you will see in the year, pushing through the melting snow, are members of the bulb and corm family – thousands of little white and purple **alpine crocuses**, **scillas**, **snowdrops**, **blue gentians** and **soldanellas** (snowbells). These are closely followed by **wild daffodils**, sweet smelling **narcissi**, **anemones**, **violets**, **rockroses** and the striking **purple trumpet gentians**.

In May and June come the small, delicate **orchids**, which although different from the large showy specimens you find in tropical countries, are in some ways more beautiful. The most common orchids in the Alps are the **early purple** (which flowers in April), the **green-winged**, the **fragrant**, the **vanilla** (it actually smells of vanilla), the **fly**, the **round-headed pyramidal** and **soldier** or **military**, but there are others, such as the rare **lady's slipper**, which can be found in isolated places. Most orchids have a spike of flowers, often with a sort of helmet behind, and the lower petal is in the shape of a lip.

Yellow **cowslips**, **oxlips** and **primroses** are also in abundance, and watch out for the pretty,

St Bernard's lily on Plateau d'Assy

Purple thistles on the Sous-Dine

lilac-pink **birdseye primrose**, which looks as if it should be growing in a suburban garden rather than in the wild. The prolific creamy and yellow **pasque anemones**, with their attractive yellow centers, strike a vivid note on the dun-coloured Alpine slopes, and the banks of the swollen rivulets cascading down the mountainsides are sprinkled with yellow **marsh marigolds**.

Brightening up bare crevices and clinging to inaccessible rock faces are dozens of different creeping, cushiony rock plants which have lots of tiny blooms, such as the pink and white **saxifrages** and the yellow, white and lilac **rock jasmines**. The **false helloborine**, a delicate, tall, yellowish-green starred flower with six petals is frequently found around Alpine chalets, as it likes the nitrogen-enriched soil. Cattle never touch its poisonous leaves, though these were formerly picked and made into a potion to be used against lice and

Trumpet gentians on the Parmelan

Blue willow gentian – Lac d'Anterne

horseflies. These are just a fraction of the hundreds of different flowers which burst into bloom when the slopes are warmed by spring sunshine and the snows start to melt in earnest.

July, August and September are the time for taller plants such as majestic purple **delphiniums** (larkspur), **monkshood**, graceful, bell-shaped **columbines**, and varied types of the carrot family, including **cow parsley** and the star-like **astrantia**. There is an endless variety of daisies, including the orange splash of the **golden hawksbeard**, purple **asters** and fluffy lilac **adenostyles**, dozens of different white and purple thistles with their prickly, silvery leaves, and the blue **willow gentian** which favours moist woodland areas. Common on high-altitude moorland is the famous **alpenrose** (alpine rhododendron), a bushy evergreen shrub with clusters of pale pink to deep pinkish-red flowers, and of course every walker hopes one day to come across the rare **edelweiss** (I have seen clusters of them in the Swiss Valais but none in the Haute Savoie).

In many of the tourist offices and mountain refuges there are posters indicating which alpine flowers are rare and therefore protected. In the réserves no flowers may be picked. There is nothing more beautiful than a meadow of wild flowers, especially the alpine daffodils or narcissi that can cover an entire mountainside, and nothing more heartbreaking than seeing people walking along with

bunches of wilted flowers in their hands. It is far better to leave the flowers to be admired by others rather than to pick them.

Butterflies can still be found in the meadows, and even at higher altitudes, which are now rare in Britain, such as the graceful, creamy yellow and brown **swallowtails** and the purple **Camberwell beauty** with its striking cream border. Among the commoner species there are plenty of **red admirals**, **tortoiseshells**, **yellow brimstones** and tiny **meadow blues**.

In autumn the flowers die away, but instead there are wild raspberries and bilberries for the picking. In wooded areas there is also a fascinating range of fungi, the edible ones being a real French delicacy. Some of these are quite unlike any found in Britain – they are white, black, grey, purple, and even a chilling green, and can normally be seen clinging to the roots of trees or hidden under mounds of dead leaves. There is also the big round red variety with white spots that reminds one of fairy tales. Many of these fungi are highly poisonous and should never be eaten without checking first at a local *pharmacie* (chemist), where there is usually an expert who will do this willingly.

Suggested books:

Greg Wilson and Marjorie Blamey
The Alpine Flowers of Britain & Europe, Collins. The most comprehensive book on the market.

D and R Aichele and H W and A
Schwegler *The Hamlyn Guide to
Wild Flowers of Britain &
Europe.*

Karl Peter Buttler (consultant editor
Paul Davies) *Field Guide to
Orchids of Britain & Europe*, The
Crowood Press.

WILDLIFE

Thanks to the ecology movement and
the creation of nature reserves, the
animal population of the Alps has
increased in recent years. The various
species which can be glimpsed, if you
are lucky and there are not too many
people, are **deer**, **ibex**, **chamois**,
mouflons, **mountain hares**, **wild
boar**, **marmots**, **grouse**, **buzzards**,
eagles, **ptarmigan** and **bearded vultures**. There are also the more
widespread rodents such as **foxes**,
dormice, **stoats**, **weasels**, **pine
martens** and **squirrels**. **Bears** and **lynx**
may also soon be reintroduced to the
Alps, though the Alpine farmers are
uneasy about the implications for
their livestock. A wolf has already
been spotted as far north as the
Vanoise National Park (southern
Alps), which is a sign that they are
moving in from the Italian mountains.

Ibex (*bouquetins*) are mountain
goats which were hunted to extinction
in the Alps and only fairly recently
reintroduced. They have re-adapted
themselves remarkably and are less
shy than the nervous chamois, often
regarding the mountain climber with
disdain from a near distance as
though knowing they are a protected
species. They have even been known
to knock stones down from above to

Ibex on the Sous-Dine (Walk 25)

33

Walking round Mont de Sulens with Mont Charvin ahead (Walk 21)

deter intruders. Sturdy, passive animals, the ibex has no natural enemies, although the babies have been known to make an eagle's meal. They are usually to be seen in small family groups at an altitude of about 2000m. The males have beautiful long curved serrated horns which they use during the rutting season (December to mid January) to chase away other contenders for their females.

The chamois is a daintier, lighter and more agile animal than the ibex, being the alpine representative of the antelope family. With a pretty, striped brown and cream face, the males having two small curving horns, they are often to be seen in large groups leaping from rock to rock in the most inhospitable places, but you will rarely get near them as they are timid and nervous. Their speed and agility

is due to their hooves which, like small cushions on normal terrain, have the ability to widen and become like crampons on precipitous rocky slopes. The chamois population was greatly reduced by continual hunting after the Second World War, but since 1989 hunting quotas have been strictly controlled and there are now around 40,000 in the Alpine areas.

The mouflon is a species of mountain sheep, originating from Corsica, Sardinia and Cyprus, that was first introduced to the Alpine regions in the 1950s so that it could be hunted and thus solve a food problem. In 1969 about 60 animals were installed in the Roc d'Enfer, Col de Foron region (Faucigny/Haut Giffre) and Mont de Grange National Reserve (Chablais region), and in 1978 a herd were let loose on the

Tournette mountain near Annecy. The males, which weigh around 50kg, have huge curled horns and are also characterised by a white saddle across their backs during the winter. They are passive, slow animals which spend at least eight hours a day peacefully grazing on the upland slopes. There are at present about 300 in the Haute Savoie, although I personally have not seen any. Many ecologists are against animals being introduced into a region where they were never endemic, and there is a certain controversy concerning these Alpine mouflons.

If you come across a large patch of meadowland where the grass has been churned up and the earth turned over, you know that there are wild boar in the vicinity. This is not an animal one would choose to come face to face with (fortunately this is unlikely), since they can weigh as much as 150kg and be very aggressive if cornered. They are really just wild pigs which like to live in small bands, mainly in forest areas (they are more numerous in the wooded Jura mountains than the Alps). They have no enemies other than hunters, and their meat, rich and gamey, is considered a great delicacy.

The most charming of all the Alpine fauna is the cuddly looking marmot. If you hear a piercing whistle echoing across the slopes, stop dead in your tracks and keep your eyes peeled for one of these enchanting creatures, which are usually to be found in rocky grasslands. The whistle is the alarm call from the marmot on sentry duty telling his fellows that there is danger in the vicinity so that they can rush back into their holes. But they are not really shy creatures, and if you stay quiet, curiosity will overcome their fear and you will see a furry head pop out again to look around and survey the slopes. During the winter months, marmots hibernate in their deep, grass-lined holes, living off accumulated fat until they emerge thin and hungry in mid-April. The marmot has few enemies, except for eagles who like to snatch the babies, and they have never been seriously hunted for food. They are prolific in the Alps and the walker has a good chance of seeing them on many occasions.

Of all the Alpine birds of prey, the most impressive is the **golden eagle,** which, having been protected for a number of years can be seen more frequently. The more recent newcomer is the **bearded vulture** (*gypaète barbu*), which was reintroduced into the Alps in 1978 and of which there are now around 100 couples. Since 1987, 19 young birds have been introduced into the Haute Savoie region where they are heavily protected. With a wing span of 3m they are an awe-inspiring sight as they circle majestically among the high peaks.

One of the most interesting of birds to be found at around 2000m is the shy **ptarmigan**. The size of a pigeon, the ptarmigan can only fly for short bursts, preferring to stay on the ground pecking around for grass and berries. In summer its plumage is brown, a perfect camouflage against the rock and scree where between May and July the females will raise from four to eight chicks in a nest in a rocky hollow or long grass. In winter ptarmigans turn white, merging with the snowy environment, and they protect themselves against the arctic cold by building an igloo in the snow with their claws. They can remain there for days without food. Unfortunately, their numbers have been much reduced as they are often disturbed by skiers or caught in the overhead wires of ski-lifts. The **black grouse**, renowned for its mating displays, is another bird that is fast disappearing due to ski installations and being hunted for the pot. It prefers bushy areas at altitudes between 1400m and 2600m.

Big black **crows** are to be found at the top of many a mountain, especially those frequented by picnickers. You will also find the more interesting **chough** and **Alpine chough**, which look completely alike except that the former has a long, curved red bill and the latter a shorter yellow one. They make a sinister, high-pitched screech that is in complete harmony with the precipitous rocky summits they favour. Look out too for **falcons**, **buzzards**, **hawks**, **larks** and the smaller birds such as the **dipper**, which loves to run along the bottom of rushing Alpine torrents at high altitude.

A SHORT HISTORY OF THE HAUTE SAVOIE

The department of the Haute Savoie did not become a definite part of France until 1860, when Napoleon III crossed the Alps with an army of 130,000 and defeated the King of Sardinia, Victor-Emmanuel. At the ensuing treaty on 24 March 1860, Victor-Emmanuel ceded the Savoie area to the French and it was split into the Haute Savoie (high or north region) and the Savoie (the southern region). Since then the Savoyards have been ardent members of the French Republic.

The origins of the Savoie (or La Sapaudia as it was then called) date back to 443AD with the arrival of a Germanic people called the Burgondes who originated from the Bergen region in Norway. They created the first regional monarchies and the Burgundy kingdom, which stretched roughly from St-Maurice in the Valais in the east, as far as Geneva on Lac Léman in the west, and southwards to St Jean de Maurienne.

For the next few hundred years the Savoie was ruled by a series of counts, dukes and petty kings who divided up the territory into small kingdoms and constantly fought amongst themselves. In 1416 Amadée

VIII (called the peaceful) became the Duke of Savoie and established good relations with the Geneva nobles who had been warring with each other until then.

This peaceful cohabitation lasted until the start of the 15th century, when the evangelist John Calvin arrived and preached a new doctrine of revolt against the Catholic church. He converted the Geneva people to his new way of thinking, known as Calvinism, or later Protestantism, and the Reformation, soon to sweep other areas of Europe, was born. The powerful Geneva bishops fled to Annecy and in 1536 the Bernoise (the people from the Berne area of Switzerland who had just joined the Swiss Confederation) invaded the Geneva and Chablais areas.

In 1564 the Chablais was returned to the reigning Duke of Savoy, Emmanuel-Philibert, but Catholicism had been outlawed and there was cultural and economic poverty. It was a young priest, François de Sales, born in 1567 in the Château de Thorens near the village of Thorens-Glières, who, at the duke's request, went into the Chablais and after four years managed to convert the population back to the Catholic faith. He became a great saint and is particularly revered in the Haute Savoie region. In 1589 war broke out round Geneva, and at the Treaty of Lyon the Pays de Gex (the area between the city and the Jura mountains), the Bugey and the Bresse regions were ceded to France.

The Savoie was frequently a battlefield, as it hung between the great

Typical limestone landscape on the summit of the Parmelan (Walk 27)

European powers of France, Austria and Italy, each country coveting the area as part of its empire. In the 17th century Savoie again came under French influence, successful campaigns being launched by both Louis XII and Louis XIV. However, in 1713 Victor Armadée II shook off this foreign influence and reclaimed the Savoie in the Treaty of Utrecht. He also became king of Sicily, which he was obliged to exchange five years later for the royal command of Sardinia. This was the first of two periods when the Haute Savoie came under Sardinian authority. The village of Carouge (now an attractive part of Geneva) was constructed in 1780 and made the *chef-lieu* (capital) of the province. Clock- and watchmaking developed in the Arve valley (see

Cluses), but the area was still very poor and many of the peasants emigrated to France and Germany. A notable achievement at this time was the first ascent of Mont Blanc in 1786 by Balmat and Paccard.

In 1792 France invaded yet again and the Savoie (including Geneva) became part of the county of Mont Blanc with Chambéry in the south as the county town. This region was transferred to Geneva in 1798 and became known as the Département du Léman. After the defeat of France in the Napoleonic Wars, the Sardinians came back into power in 1815 and this time the Geneva people decided to join the Confederation of Swiss States (Switzerland) and cut themselves off irrevocably from the Haute Savoie.

Refuge de Larrieux, Boucle des Tervelles (Walk 23)

THE REGIONS OF THE HAUTE SAVOIE

This was followed by a relatively prosperous economic and cultural period known as the Buon Governo (1815–47). Many churches and other buildings originate from this time and the clockmaking industry and agriculture became firmly established. During the Sardinian era the French culture and language continued to flourish, and in 1860 Napoleon III crossed the Alps and Savoie history changed again.

And what about the region today? Covering an area of 828 sq km, with a population of 518,000 people spread over 292 villages, the Haute Savoie is one of the richest and most expanding areas of France, yet 100 years ago it was one of the poorest. Tourism has grown tremendously in the last 50 years, especially since the 1960s when skiing became popular and new ski resorts such as Flaine and Morzine–Avoriaz were built, opening up hundreds of kilometres of skiable slopes. In 1962 the important Mont Blanc road tunnel was finished, thus linking France with Italy and placing the Haute Savoie one of the greatest trade routes in Europe. Industry has also expanded, the Arve valley being well known for its precision and mechanical engineering, with 1200 enterprises in a 30km radius. There are many other businesses, such as manufacture of sports equipment (the production of skis and mechanical ski-lifts), and wood related industries such as forestry and furniture making.

Faucigny/Haut Giffre Region (central and east Haute Savoie)

Sandwiched between the Chablais region to the north, the Aravis/Borne region to the south, Geneva to the west and Mont Blanc to the east, it is difficult to describe where this region really begins or ends in terms of exact geographical boundaries. It basically comprises the two main valleys of the Giffre and the Arve and is the most populated and industrialised of the Haute Savoie regions.

The Arve Valley

The Arve river starts in the glaciers of the Mont Blanc range and flows northwards for 105km before emptying itself into the mighty Rhône at Geneva. All along this valley there is now a motorway which goes through the Mont Blanc Tunnel, an important link between north and south Europe. Bonneville is the administrative capital of the Faucigny region and is situated at the entrance to the valley. Further south are the towns of Cluses and Sallanches. Despite the advancing industrialisation of this wide valley, the towns still retain their character and the mountains through which the river winds are some of the most impressive in the Alps.

Much has been written about the Mont Blanc and Chamonix area, which is where the valley starts, but east of Sallanches, where the westward-flowing Arve turns north

39

toward Cluses, is the Plateau d'Assy. This is a place of great beauty from which there are more extensive views of the Mont Blanc range across the Arve valley than if you were walking round the mighty mountain itself.

Due to its high, sunny position facing south, the plateau was once a tuberculosis treatment centre, and its many sanatorium buildings are still used as convalescent homes for people being treated for depression, alcoholism and other disorders. The commune of Passy stretches from the Arve valley to the Chaine des Fiz and includes the Aiguilles Rouges and Tête Noire mountain ranges. A nature reserve was created in this region in 1980 consisting of 2000 hectares between altitudes 1347m and 2723m.

To the north, the peak of the Aiguille de Varan and the desolate rocky ridges of the Désert de Platé separate the Plateau d'Assy from the extensive skiing area of Flaine. Built during the 1960s by Marcel Breurer, a well-known architect, it is in a natural bowl in the mountains and also houses a modern art centre (the serried ranks of Lego-like concrete apartments can only be appreciated by connoisseurs and ski enthusiasts). The 140km of superb ski slopes called Le Grand Massif link the ski resorts of Les Carroz, below Flaine on the same access road, Morillon and Samoëns. Undeniably the scenery is magnificent, but for the walker to explore the region a better

base would be Samoëns or Sixt (see below).

Passy, Plateau d'Assy and Plaine Joux: Walk Numbers 1 and 2

The commune of Passy consists of four hamlets: Les Plagnes on the west slopes, Chedde (in the plain), Passy and the Plateau d'Assy, with the ski station of Plaine Joux 300m higher. The latter three villages are the more convenient places to stay, as they are geared to tourism and offer eight hotels, two campsites and plenty of apartments. In Plateau d'Assy there is the modern church of Notre Dame de Toute Grâce, constructed between 1937 and 1945 by the local architect Novarino. It has a vividly painted façade by Fernand Léger, and inside there are stained glass windows by Chagall, Matisse, Lurcat, Léger and Bercot. Also on the road from the village of Passy to Plaine Joux you will see modern sculptures by well-known artists. Many walkers may find this area too crowded for their liking in the high season, though it is amazing how quickly people melt away in the mountains.

Cluses: Walk Number 3

This town is situated where the Arve valley narrows, and is dominated by the Pointe de Chevran, one of the author's favourite walks. The first references to Cluses were in the 13th century, when it was already an important communications centre. In

Looking down at Cluses from the Pointe de Chevran (Walk 3)

1844 a fire destroyed much of the town, which was completely rebuilt on Sardinian lines. Recent modernisation has resulted in an attractive pedestrian centre with easy parking facilities and good shops. Cluses was formerly renowned for its watch- and clockmaking (it houses a watch museum), but this has been replaced by precision engineering and other small industries. Historical buildings include the 15th-century Eglise des Cordieliers, an ancient convent chapel with a particularly striking 17th-century font, the 18th-century church of St Nicholas, parts of the old town and the fountain in the Place Allobroges (1791). Cluses is more of a town to visit than to stay in, although it does have hotels and an all-year-round caravanning/camping park. The walker might prefer the villages in the vicinity and between the two valleys (nearer other walks), such

as Châtillon sur Cluses (on the D902 which goes north to Taninges), St-Sigismond, La Frasse, and Arâches and Marignier on the D26 where the Giffre flows into the Arve. These villages are small, however, and accommodation is limited.

Bearing west of Cluses and through the satellite town of Scionzier, the D4 takes you to the Alpine village of Le Reposoir, which has a flourishing 800-year-old monastery called La Chartreuse du Reposoir, taken over from the Carthusian monks in 1932 by the Carmelites. The D4 winds over the Col de la Colombière to Grand-Bornand facing the Chaine des Aravis.

The Giffre Valley
The River Giffre, springing from glaciers beneath the mighty Buet mountain in the Fer-à-Cheval mountain region near the village of Sixt,

41

flows through a softer, less commercialised valley with spectacular mountain scenery. It passes through the pretty villages of Samoëns, Taninges and Mieussy before bearing south at the Pont de Giffre and spilling into the Arve north of Cluses. The valley continues northward, passing by St-Jeoire with the distinctive peak of the Môle mountain to the left, and through Viuz-en-Sallaz before reaching the Pont de Fillinges and later Annemasse on the outskirts of Geneva. On both sides of this main artery are extensive walking areas and subsidiary valleys worth exploring. From the 15th century, the people of the Giffre were well known as stone engravers and builders. The houses, churches, fountains and wayside shrines of local grey stone are a testament to their craft. Many of the buildings in Geneva, Lyon and other big towns were built by these stalwart valley people, who were forced to practise their craft further afield in order to earn a living.

Sixt: Walk Numbers 4–6

Voted one of the most beautiful villages in France, Sixt is at the head of the Giffre valley and 6km from the larger resort of Samoëns. The region is a walker's paradise. Drive a few kilometres further up the valley and enter a breathtakingly dramatic amphitheatre of rock walls which rise straight out of the flat valley floor. You are looking at the Fer-à-Cheval

('horseshoe') mountain peaks, which must be visited if you are exploring the Haute Savoie region. This became more difficult in December 2002 when a dramatic rockfall obliterated the last two kilometres of the access road. Two years later it is still not clear when the road will be reopened, so there is a temporary parking area and a half-hour of extra walking to reach the huge main car park, with picnic areas, a café and a very interesting exhibition explaining the geological phenomena of the Fer-à-Cheval. This is an extremely popular spot so it is wise to avoid weekends in summer when there are literally hundreds of visitors. Take time to walk into the horseshoe to the Bout du Monde ('end of the world') and admire the dozens of rushing streams which course down the gigantic slopes to end in magnificent waterfalls (see Walk Number 4).

This area became a nature reserve in 1977, covering three-quarters of the Sixt commune. The village itself is grouped around an ancient abbey built in the 11th century by the same monks who founded the Abondance abbey. (It is now a hotel with a classified 17th-century dining room.) The church has an interesting 13th-century nave and houses Les Trésors des Moines (valuable monastic chalices, etc.), which can be seen on request. On a wall is a plaque dedicated to Jâcques Balmat, who in 1783 was the first person to conquer Mont Blanc, and who died mysteriously in 1831 in the Fer-à-Cheval mountains, at the age of 72, while looking for gold. Many days were spent searching for his body, which was never found.

If you turn left in the village of Sixt you will pass through the hamlet of Salvagny. Further up is the start of the two-day walk to the Lac d'Anterne and the Refuge de Sales – this area connects with the region around Flaine, mentioned above, and the impressive Désert de Platé (see Walk Number 6).

Samoëns: Walk Numbers 7 and 8

In spite of the fact that Samoëns is full of tourists in summer and winter, and has a wealth of hotels, apartments to rent, two *gîtes d'étape* and two camping sites, with its ancient stone houses and streets it manages to retain a certain charm. The centre of the village is now restricted to pedestrians. The inhabitants are called Septimontains in memory of the seven alps that were given to the people by Amadée VIII (the local chief) in 1438, and since then the

Septimontains have gone to all corners of Europe as stone engravers and masons. The village was well known in Napoleonic times, as Bonaparte said that he would not visit it without a boat – referring presumably to the hundreds of waterfalls in the region. Samoëns also had its patron in the form of Louise Jaÿ. Born of a modest family in a nearby hamlet, she made her fortune in Paris and, not forgetting

Church at Samoëns (Samoëns/Sixt area)

her roots, came back to Samoëns in her old age to create an alpine garden, restore the 17th-century church in 1917 (restored again in 1975), and build a house for the local doctor.

There are many beautiful little villages and hamlets to explore around Samoëns, such as Les Vallons (Walk Number 7), Les Moulins, Le Bérouze, Verchaix and Mathonex. Samoëns connects with Morzine by the winding D354 over the Col de Joux Plaine. If you start up this road and branch off at the sign Les Allamands you reach the walking area of the Dents Blanches (see Walk Number 8).

Taninges/Praz de Lys: Walk Numbers 9–11

Taninges, situated 12km down the valley from Samoëns, is a pleasant small town, its distinctive feature being the Pointe de Marcelly, a mountain that juts out above the town and has a cross at the summit (Walk Number 9). The places to see are some quaint old streets, the Chapel of St Anne (1583), which is now a private house but has retained its old bell tower, the 18th-century Sardinian-style church of St Jean Baptist, and the Chartreuse de Meylan, built in 1283, which has some interesting 16th-century cloisters. Taninges has four hotels, a camping site, the usual apartments to rent, and is connected to the ski resorts of Les Gets and Morzine by the D902.

If you turn left 7km up the D902 at the Pont des Gets, you arrive at the ski resort of Praz de Lys, alt. 1518m, after 6km. Praz de Lys has a beautiful setting, sitting in a wide, open plateau surrounded by the jagged peaks of the Pointe de Marcelly, Pointe d'Uble and Haute Pointe (Walk Numbers 9, 10 and 11), and with lovely views of the Mont Blanc range. However, it is not an original Alpine village and the buildings, dating from the 1960s, are a scattered hotchpotch of apartment blocks and chalets. In winter there is a lot of life as the plateau is a perfect cross-country ski area, but in summer it is all rather dead. There are four hotels, one youth hostel, numerous apartments for rent, but no camping ground.

The village of Mieussy, not far from Taninges, which connects with the cross-country skiing area of Sommand and, by the Col de Ramaz, to Praz de Lys, is a more attractive choice for a base, though accommodation is limited.

St-Jeoire: Walk Numbers 12 and 13

Continuing down the Giffre valley, you come to the pleasant village of St-Jeoire (also called St-Jeoire-en-Faucigny). Set back from the road at the confluence of the Risse and Giffre rivers, St-Jeoire is dominated by the small, beautiful Château de Beauregard. If you go into the village itself and take the D26 up the Risse valley you will be driving through one of the most unspoilt valleys in the

Landscape around St-Jean-de-Sixt

region, despite its relative proximity to Geneva. It takes you to the popular cross-country skiing area of Les Brasses. There are six villages in the Les Brasses area, apart from St-Jeoire, namely Megevette and Onnion (two hotels, one open in summer), both on the D26 which continues to Bellevaux and the Hirmentaz skiing region, and Viuz-en-Sallaz, Bogève and Villard.

Aravis/Borne Region (southwest Haute Savoie)

As with the other three areas, there is no well-established definition of this region, and enquiries in various tourist offices and other information centres have resulted in maps with conflicting boundaries. For example, on one map Annecy is in the Genevois region, on another in the Lac d'Annecy region, and on a third it is in the Aravis/Borne.

Georgraphically, the Aravis/Borne is the area east of the Arve valley, bordered to the north by Geneva and the Salève, to the west by the Rhône valley and to the south by the Savoie. For convenience I have included Lake Annecy.

Aravis

The Chaine des Aravis is a jagged line of peaks, 25km long, stretching south–west north–east, starting at the eastern end of Lake Annecy with Mont Charvin, alt. 2407m and culminating in the distinctive Pointe Percée, alt. 2752m, west of Sallanches in the Arve valley. The Aravis pass, alt. 1486m, cuts through the range south of La Clusaz and was formerly an important link between the Annecy and Mont Blanc regions.

La Clusaz: Walk Numbers 14 and 15

La Clusaz is a bustling and popular ski resort at the foot of the northern end of the Chaine des Aravis on the D909 coming from the town of Thônes, and the last village before the road goes over the Col des Aravis. The name La Clusaz derives from Via Clusa, meaning 'road confined between two mountains', and it was a tiny, unknown agricultural hamlet until the Col des Aravis was opened in 1902 to become a fashionable spot for the people of Annecy to spend their summers. Somewhat overbuilt, with numerous apartment blocks straggling over the slopes, the only structure worthy of note is the church with its tall, onion-style steeple. This is worth a visit as the interior was strikingly renovated in the 1970s. Although the village already had a skating rink, the first sophisticated ski-lifts were not built until 1945, after a primitive, toboggan-type lift had crashed, killing six tourists. Two local ski champions, Guy Perillat and later Edgar Grospiron, helped to put La Clusaz on the map. The village is also full of life in the summer (market day is Monday morning), which is not always the case with ski resorts, and offers a wide variety of sporting activities as well as a good selection of mountain paths. There are plenty of hotels, apartments to rent, a youth hostel and a caravanning park (no camping). Just up the road is the very pretty Lac des Confins and the start of some tougher walks in the Chaine des Aravis.

Le Grand-Bornand: Walk Numbers 16 and 17

Bridging the Borne river in the valley of the same name, Le Grand-Bornand is the last village on the D4 before the road goes over the Col de la Colombière towards Cluses. Although also a well-known ski station (a cable car links the ski slopes which are further up the valley towards the pass), it has not lost its traditional agricultural activities, such as raising Abondance dairy cattle from whose milk the famous Reblochon cheese is made (see Savoyard Food and Drink). Every week there is a lively market (Wednesday morning). This used to be held in the ancient covered market hall, but has now moved to the central square in front of the church, with its classic onion-shaped steeple. If you follow the sign Vallée de Bouchet, keeping to the Borne river out of the village, you will come to a cross-country skiing area, and at the end of this road is the departure point for the popular walk up to the Pointe Percée. Worth visiting is the old hamlet of Chinaillon, just off the road up to the pass, which has some traditional old chalets and a charming little chapel. Le Grand-Bornand has all the attributes of a tourist resort, namely 15 hotels, flats to rent and two camping sites.

St-Jean-de-Sixt: Walk Number 18

Down the D909 towards Thônes, and on the crossroads between Le Grand-Bornand and La Clusaz, is the smaller village of St-Jean-de-Sixt. This is a much quieter place to stay, with only two hotels and a camping site. Although the village does not have much to offer architecturally, the surrounding valley countryside has some splendid old chalets and farms, many with roofs made out of traditional *tavaillon*-style tiles. There are numerous sawmills on the Non torrent, which runs all the way along the valley bottom to join the larger Fier river south of Thônes. It was a sawmill owner, Jean-Marie Favre Lorraine, who built many traditional chalets, and two architecturally different farms for himself and his brother in the hamlet of Les Lombardes, south of the village. Dated 1903 and 1907, they are beautifully embellished with intricate woodcarvings, but, more extraordinary for those days of no central heating, they have enormous windows, indoor toilets (unheard of then) and separate bedrooms for the children.

Thônes: Walk Numbers 19–23

Thônes sits at the entrance to the Aravis region in a junction of three valleys: the Non coming in to the east, the Fier to the west and the Sulens to the south. This big village (hardly a town) has always been strategically important. In 1889 a tramway was built (subsequently closed in 1930) linking it to the town of Annecy, which considerably boosted the economic development of the area. Thônes has managed to

retain the quaint stone bridge over the Non river, and the arcaded shops looking on to a pleasant square with the parish church of St-Maurice opposite. If you appreciate baroque interiors, this church has the best example of such work in the whole Savoie area, the altar having been sculpted and decorated by the Italian Pierre Jacquetti in 1721. There is also a fascinating museum, Le Musée du Pays de Thônes, which gives an interesting insight into the life of the local people past and present.

On the D909 towards Annecy is the Musée de la Résistance, which is dedicated to the Resistance movement during the Second World War. It commemorates the battle of the Free French Army in March 1944 on the nearby Plateau des Glières, when a few hundred men held out for two months against a German army of 7000 trained Alpine troops. The battle became the symbol of the French resistance against the Germans and the survivors were able to play an important part in the liberation of the Haute Savoie a few months later (see Walk Number 26). Thônes is also the 'capital' of Reblochon cheese, which is made in the adjacent valleys (you can visit the cheese cooperative on the road to Annecy), and because of the proximity of so many woodmills, the site of the Mobalpa fitted kitchens factory.

Thônes has four hotels and there are another six in nearby villages, plus four camping sites in the region and various gîtes – it is a centre to be recommended. The local walks in this guide start from the beautiful valleys south of Thônes: the Manigod valley running southwest along the Fier river, which goes over the Col de Fry and joins the D909 south of La Clusaz, the Sulens valley behind the mighty Tournette mountain (see Annecy area), which joins the Manigod valley south of Thônes, and the narrow valley to the hamlet of Montremont along the Mainant river. These valleys, until recently victims of the rural exodus to nearby towns, are breathtakingly unspoilt, with bright-green fields, beautiful old farms and lots of chapels and wayside shrines. They are still mainly agricultural, the large farms producing cheese and milk from their extensive

herds of Abondance cattle. Of course times are changing, and the ageing population is selling its unprofitable land to larger enterprises. The farms, which have often been in the same family for hundreds of years, are then sold and renovated into holiday homes. Manigod is the only village in these valleys which has a syndicat d'initiative (see Appendix 2, Tourist Offices). It also has four hotels. There is skiing further up at the Col de Fry which is linked with La Clusaz.

Borne is the plateau area south of the Salève mountain (including the Plateau des Glières) and includes the pré-Alpine mountains of the Sous-Dine, La Roche Parnal and the Chaine du Bargy – in fact all the countryside southeast of the Annecy region and bordered by the Chaine des Aravis.

Looking towards the Sous-Dine (Walk 24)

Flowing from the snows of the Pointe Percée, the Borne river passes through the village of Le Grand-Bornand before swinging north and cutting a sinuous, gorge-like passage through the mountains, eventually to empty itself into the Arve at Bonneville 33km later.

La Roche-sur-Foron: Walk Numbers 24–26

West of the Arve valley on the River Foron, and almost opposite the town of Bonneville, La Roche-sur-Foron is situated on the Plateau de Borne under the shadow of the first range of mountains (pré-Alps). La Roche (as it is called locally) has long been an important regional centre, second only to Annecy in its historical heritage, but far less well known. Despite industrial development, the centre has retained a medieval aspect, with picturesque cobbled streets and old houses from the 15th and 16th centuries. The ruins of a tower perched on the top of a tall rock are all that remain of the château/fortress of the Counts of Geneva, built in the 12th century and destroyed in the 15th during the Savoyard wars – hence the name La Roche-sur-Foron ('rock over the Foron'). Somewhat off the general tourist route, La Roche is a delightful place to stay, with four hotels, apartments for rent and four camping sites. There are another 10 hotels in the surrounding villages of La Chapelle-Rambaud (one), St-Laurent (one), St-Pierre-en-Faucigny (four) and St-Sixt

(four). Orange is the nearest village to the start of the two walks in this guide and has one hotel and a camping site.

Thorens-Glières, on the D2 road going southwest towards Annecy from La Roche, is famous as the birthplace in 1567 of St François de Sales. He is still venerated throughout the region and was responsible for the extreme Catholicism of the entire Savoie area – in contrast to the Calvinism of Geneva to the north. The 12th-century château was restored in 1873 by Count Eugène de Roussy de Sales and is still owned by the de Sales family. The château museum was opened to the public in 1960 (visits in season only). A further 14km from the village is the historic Plateau des Glières, with an impressive white stone monument dedicated to the men of the Resistance who fell during the Second World War (see Thônes, earlier, and Walk Number 26). There are three camping sites in the vicinity, several restaurants and one hotel. In winter the plateau is a popular cross-country ski area. The village of Le Petit-Bornand, in the narrow winding Borne valley, is 7km by road from the plateau and has one hotel, a *gîte d'étape* and a camping site.

Annecy Area: Walk Number 27

Annecy is unashamedly beautiful, situated between the Bornes and Bauges pré-Alps with the Parmelan mountain as a backdrop (Walk Number 27), and at the end of the

From the Parmelan, looking down the valley towards Thônes (Walk 27)

cleanest lake in Europe. Pretty little ports and villages hug the lake shore and a diversity of mountain scenery rears behind, culminating in the grandiose Tournette peak at the southern end (Walk Number 29). Annecy must be visited, preferably out of season, but is only a place to stay if you appreciate a very touristy environment. Capital of the Haute Savoie region, with a population of around 120,000, Annecy has a rich historical past and was an important centre even in Roman times. The castle was built by the Counts of Geneva in the 12th century and still dominates the old town, which has remained almost intact, with narrow, cobbled streets bordered with deep arcades alongside the flower-lined Thiou canal and lock. The Palais de l'Isle, said to be one of the most photographed places in France, is an old building jutting

out into the fast-flowing canal like the prow of a ship. Originally constructed in the 12th century, and used later as an administration centre, it was only saved from demolition in 1952 at the eleventh hour by the people of Annecy, who purchased it for a symbolic sum of 1000 French francs.

There is much else to see: the Basilica of the Visitation, built in 1922, which is the mother house of the St François de Sales order, also overlooking the town and beautifully illuminated at night; the Cathedral of St Peter, built originally as a chapel by the Franciscans in the 15th century, but afterwards to become the cathedral for the Bishop of Geneva when he took refuge in Annecy during the Reformation; the churches of St-Maurice (dated 1422), Notre Dame de Liesse (16th century) and St François (16th century), to name but a few.

The Annecy tourist office has a brochure in English with descriptions of places of interest and a map of the old town. It also has full details of hotels, camping sites (most of these are round the lake) and a youth hostel. If you are going to stay in the Annecy lake area in high season, it is advisable to book your accommodation well in advance.

The lakeside is swarming with people in the summer months of July and August, but in spring and autumn it is reasonably peaceful. There are lots of sporting possibilities, including swimming, sailing, water-skiing, wind-surfing and pedal-boats for hire. You can also relax and take a boat trip round the lake, calling in at the various lakeside villages. The first tourist paddle steamer was built in 1839, as Annecy was a popular tourist town even then!

Talloires: Walk Numbers 28 and 29

Situated on the western side of the lake where it begins to narrow, Talloires is an ancient village with lots of charm. It has a 17th-century abbey, which can be visited but is now a hotel, and a 13th-century priory (now an international centre). Talloires is rather upmarket, with well-known restaurants and numerous hotels. There are eight camping sites in the vicinity and all the usual sports facilities on offer. North of the village is the Roc de Chère nature reserve and a lovely, easy waterfall walk (Walk Number 28). Just before the village you turn off on the D42 for the Col de Forclaz (worth going to see for a fab-

Lake Annecy from the waterfall walk (Walk 28)

ulous view right down the lake) and the start of the walk up the splendid Tournette peak (Walk Number 29).

Duingt: Walk Number 30

Almost facing Talloires on the opposite shore is the equally ancient but unspoiled village of Duingt, with its beautiful old houses and château jutting out into the water. Just off the busy lake road, and therefore protected from mainstream traffic, it has been inhabited since Roman times.

The church was originally built in 1370, then newly constructed in 1831 and again in 1900. The château is medieval and was the seat of the local overlords – in the 1400s it belonged to the Count of Geneva. The present building with its tower dates from the 18th century and is privately owned by the Certeau family (it houses some beautiful Italian paintings). In the Duingt region are seven hotels and three camping sites.

The Resistance monument on the Plateau de Glières (Walk 26)

OVERLOOKING CHAMONIX VALLEY

WALK 1

The Plateau d'Assy
Alt. 1620m (Overlooking Chamonix valley)

Difficulty	Medium balcony walk with fantastic views of the Mont Blanc range
Time	4hrs
Height gain	563m
Maps	Editions Didier & Richard IGN No. 8 Massifs du Mont Blanc/Beaufortain 1:50,000
	Cartes IGN 3530 ET Top 25 Samoëns/Haut Giffre 1:25,000
Depart from	Le Coudray – 1127m
Signposting	Follow the Tour du Pays du Mont Blanc signs until Charbonnière – after that the signposting is sporadic (**Note** The path from No. 7 to No. 8 is not marked on the IGN 1:25,000 map, so follow directions carefully.)

This walk is ideal for someone fit who wants to do some hiking but has never really been in mountainous country, as you get magnificent views of the Mont Blanc range across the valley for a moderate effort. There is the added attraction of the world-famous modern church in Plateau d'Assy, Notre Dame de Toute Grâce. Here there are dramatic stained glass windows by famous artists such as Chagall, Matisse, Lurcat, Léger and Bercot. There are also modern sculptures on the road from Passy to Plaine Joux. Beware, this is a popular part of the Chamonix region and on weekends in high season you risk meeting a lot of people.

Access (from Geneva)
Take the motorway, direction Chamonix, and exit at No. 21, Passy/Le Fayat. Follow briefly the D339

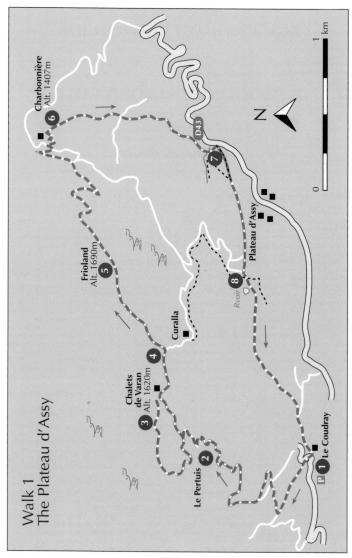

Walk 1
The Plateau d'Assy

and D39 signposted Passy/Plateau d'Assy. At Passy turn right on the D43 and continue on towards Plateau d'Assy for about 4km until you see a chapel on the left. At this point take the signpost left saying Bay, Le Coudray and Refuge de Varan. Continue to the hamlet of Le Coudray (Chemin de Coudray) at the end of the road and park in the car park. (**Note** If this car park is full there is a further parking area 100m up the road.)

The Route

(1) Start up the tarmac road beyond the chalets. Follow all signs to Varan/Chalets de Varan and red/yellow splashes, ignoring the sign Raccourci Varan to the immediate right (*raccourci* means short cut). After the second car park the road deteriorates into a wide jeep track going up through woods. After 15mins you see a sign left indicating Varan Sentier. There are a few wooden steps and then a narrow path upwards through woods. This is a short cut, but if you keep to the jeep track all the way up you get there anyway. You reach Le Pertuis, alt.1360m (40mins).

(2) Follow the signpost to Chalets de Varan 35mins and Charbonnière 1hr 50mins. On the jeep track to the left there is a rock painted in different colours which looks quite hideous.

At this stage we saw an eagle circling above us in the air currents. It looked very impressive with the imposing

Aiguille de Varan behind. This was only the second eagle I had ever seen in the Alps so it was an exciting moment.

The track becomes stonier as it comes out of the woodland into open meadowland. On one side there is a beautiful view down to the Arve valley and its little lakes, with the entire Mont Blanc range beyond, and on the other the dramatic rocky peak of the Aiguille de Varan. Behind is the Chaine des Aravis with Mont Percée rearing up at the end. Keep on the jeep track (or alternatively, look out for another short cut to the right on a steep, narrow track that cuts across a wide corner – this is 5mins shorter and reaches the signposts below the chalets), to arrive at the Chalets de Varan, alt. 1620m (1hr 15mins).

Sculpture 'La Porte de Soleil', Plateau d'Assy

(3) This is a popular overnight and refreshment spot as the chalet is situated on an open ledge with magnificent views of the Mont Blanc range. It is also the start of the walk up the Aiguille de Varan, which is a tough climb of nearly 1000m. Go round the refuge to meet signposts (the way you came up if you took the short cut) and follow the sign to Charbonnière 1hr 15mins (Tour du Pays du Mont Blanc) – this is not the official Mont Blanc circuit, but an offshoot. The path is defined and at first goes down through scattered woodland. It levels out and then goes uphill again and along to reach further signposts where the path divides (1hr 30mins).

(4) Continue straight, direction Charbonnière par Frioland (right goes down to the hamlet of Curalla). The path crosses some shale – follow the red circles carefully and, where there is a red arrow on a stone, go left upwards and over open hillside rather than straight into the woods. The path curls up and round the mountain – the views across to the Mont Blanc range are spectacular. After 30mins you reach Frioland, alt.1690m (2hrs).

(5) This is a dip in the mountainside and the highest point of the walk. The grassy hump to the right is an ideal place for a picnic. The path, still defined but eroded in many places, winds medium steep down the hillside. In front is the impressive rock wall of the Désert de Platé and the

Dérochoir (Walk Number 6), with the Rochers des Fiz beyond. You come into scattered and then dense woodland, where there is an old mule trail with a wall on one side, to arrive at Charbonnière, alt.1407m, at a large rock covered in splashes and signposts (2hrs 30mins). (**Note** Ignore the wooden sign to the right, before you get to the chalet, saying Sans Issue. This is the higher path you can see on the map, now closed due to rockfalls.)

*This used to be a hamlet where they made charcoal (*charbonnière *means charcoal burner in English), but it is now just one renovated chalet with outbuildings.*

(6) Careful – just before you reach the renovated chalet, take an unmarked grassy path going sharp back right. This becomes a wider track descending through beech wood and then lesser woodland, crossing a stream.

Vetch on the Plateau d'Assy

Paintings on the façade of Notre Dame de Toute Grâce, Plateau d'Assy

Keep on the main path which widens into a country lane as it descends towards the village of Plateau d'Assy. After a yellow arrow the track crosses a stream by a slatted wooden bridge and shortly after reaches the road at some chalets (3hrs).

(7) Go up right following old wooden signs indicating Curalla/Balcon d'Assy and a VTT No. 7 sign (mountain bike path, so watch out for them). This is a jeep track going upwards. **Careful** – on the first turning, bear to the left on a grassy track downwards which soon becomes more defined to reach a sign saying Balcon d'Assy. At a fork go straight (do not go up right to Curalla/Varan) and continue on a flattish path to reach a T-junction. Turn up right, and then bear left along the hillside where there are occasional views through the trees down to the village

of Plateau d'Assy below, to reach meadowland at a grassy T-junction. Go up right to meet a defined track. Bear left (signpost indicating Petit Balcon) and continue on this narrow pleasant path with a small rivulet flowing on the right, to meet a jeep track by a concrete water reservoir (3hrs 30mins).

(8) The track descends to the left, and a few minutes later at a fork go up to the right, signposted Cran/Le Coudray, on a narrow path following the contour of the hill through mixed woodland and clearings. Go straight on at a crossroads following the sign Cran/Le Coudray, over a stream and than later a manmade concrete waterfall. At a T-junction, where there is a field in front, go right (signposted) through open meadowland to reach the hamlet. Retrace your steps to the car park (4hrs).

WALK 2

Refuge du Moëde d'Anterne

Alt. 2003m (Overlooking Chamonix valley)

Difficulty	Difficult – moderate up to the refuge, but the way back along the gorge is tricky (marked with dots on map), so if you are not used to heights, go back the way you came
Time	5hrs, plus 15mins walking round Lac Vert
	(detour to Lac de Pormenaz 20mins)
Height gain	748m (to refuge)
Maps	Editions Didier & Richard IGN No. 8 Massifs du Mont Blanc/Beaufortain 1:50,000
	Cartes IGN 3530 ET Top 25 Samoëns/Haut Giffre 1:25,000
Depart from	Plaine Joux – 1360m, or Le Châtelet – 1418m
Signposting	Excellent – this is a very popular walking area

This is a magnificent area for walking. It is not far from Mont Blanc, but tends to be crowded with tourists in summer so should be avoided at weekends. However, the further you walk the fewer people you find. The jeep track up to the Chalets d'Anterne is eroded and does seem to go on and on, although though there are obvious short cuts, but the exciting way back along the narrow ravine makes up for it.

The word *moëde* means 'between two waters' in patois – the waters being the Souay stream and the Diosaz to the south. The name Anterne was given to the area by the inhabitants of Sixt who owned it until 1313, and could come from the Latin *internus*, meaning 'insular'.

Don't forget to visit the church, Notre Dame de Toute Grâce, in the village of Plateau d'Assy (see Walk Number 1).

Access (from Geneva)

Take the motorway, direction Chamonix, and exit at No. 21, Passy/Le Fayat. Follow briefly the D339 and D13 signposted Passy and Plateau d'Assy before turning on to the D43 in Passy to Plateau d'Assy. At Plateau d'Assy follow the signposting to Plaine Joux, which is a large open area and the start of various ski-lifts.

Continue on and follow signs right down to Lac Vert where there is a large car park and a restaurant.

The Route

Before setting out on the walk, it is a good idea to walk round the very attractive Lac Vert, which is to the left of the car park, though you cannot see it. The lake, nestling in the woods, is a beautiful deep green (for clearer reflections go in the morning) with five rocks in the middle. There are noticeboards on the path giving details of the varied vegetation and birdlife to be found here.

Long ago, according to legend, this lake was frequented by beautiful fairies who liked to play on the shore and bathe in the transparent water. The bad spirits who lived in the mountain caves higher up observed them at play and decided to come down and seduce them. However, the fairies repulsed their advances which made the spirits angry. In revenge they sent down an avalanche of rocks which blocked the lake and the fairies had to leave. The lake became silent and sinister. Years later some young girls from Passy were laughing

and singing in the region. The joyful sound reached the mountain spirits, who thought the fairies had returned and sent down another avalanche of rocks. But the fairies were watching and managed to send the rocks in another direction. Above the Ayères Chalets there is to this day a round green fairy circle called the Pré des Dames ('circle of women'). It was here that the girls escaped a tragic death.

Lac Vert start of Walk 2, Refuge du Moëde d'Anterne

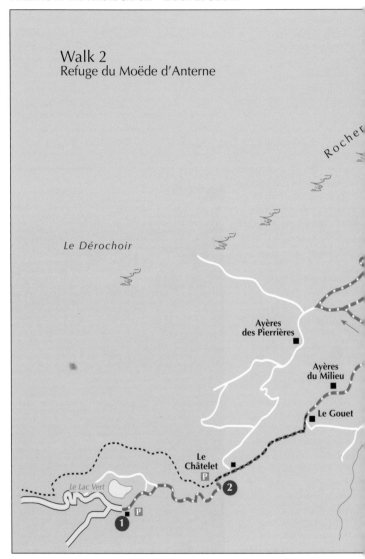

Walk 2
Refuge du Moëde d'Anterne

Rocher

Le Dérochoir

Ayères
des Pierrières

Ayères
du Milieu

Le Gouet

Le Châtelet
P

Le Lac Vert

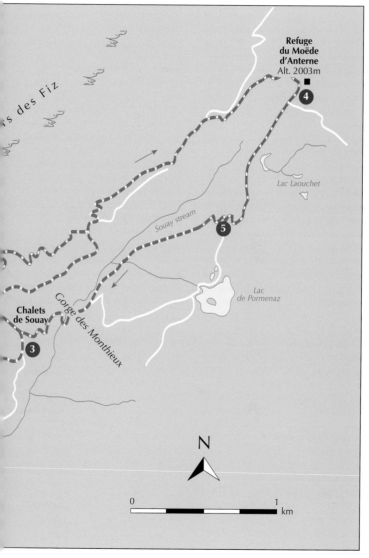

(1) From the car park follow the sign Le Châtelet up a wide jeep track through woods. You come to a large clearing with a concrete water course to the left where you continue following signs straight (left goes back to Plaine Joux). The jeep track continues through beech wood and gains height steeply in places to reach the unpaved road from Plaine Joux and further signs (30mins).

(2) Turn right and 100m later you pass the hotel/restaurant Le Châtelet d'Ayères. (**Note** You can also park your car here by continuing straight after the sign right to Lac Vert – see Access.)

On the left are the impressive white limestone cliffs of the southern end of the Rochers des Fiz, and to the right incredible views down the valley to the Col d'Aravis with the Mont Blanc range on the other side. Continue on the jeep track, following the sign Lac de Pormenaz/Les Ayères/Lac d'Anterne, to reach another small parking area.

Shortly after there is a sign to Le Souay/Ayères and you continue on the track reaching Le Gouet, alt.1430m, an attractive huddle of small chalets (no signs here). The wide jeep track continues upwards with pine trees on the left and, behind, the impressive rock wall of the Rochers des Fiz. It seems quite a long way, passing scattered chalets, before you reach the Chalets de Souay on a corner where there are signposts (1hr 10mins).

(3) Continue on the wide track signed Col d'Anterne/Lac de Pormenaz. To the right is another sign, Lac de Pormenaz/La Corde, which is the narrow path you will emerge from on the return journery. (Ignore wording Sentier à Risque ('difficult path') as this is not the path you will be taking.)

Keep to the main track, which is fairly steep and completely exposed. When you reach a small sign Réserve Naturelle, take the obvious short cut that slices off a large corner. If you look back you can see that the jeep track also goes to another huddle of chalets which is Ayères des Pierrières (there are three Ayères marked on the map). You reach the main jeep track again and turn right to continue towards a low ridge. There is another short cut over the ridge, and depending on the time of year, you can see impressive waterfalls to the right. There is a third short cut by a fountain and, as you gain height, you can see your return path going along the other side of the gorge on the right. You meet the main jeep track again and continue towards the refuge which you can see ahead. You pass a track on the left, which goes over the Col d'Anterne and down to Lac d'Anterne on the other side, and continue to reach the Chalet/Refuge du Moëde d'Anterne (2hrs 40mins).

Chalet/Refuge du Moëde d'Anterne, tel 0450.93.60.43, fax 0450.78.02.09.

Rooms and dormitory accommodation. Open from 15 June to 15 October.

This is a pleasant, privately owned refuge, built at the turn of the century and with an almost Victorian look about it. (There is now a new refuge alongside which was being built when I first did the walk in 1992.)

(4) For the return, take the path down from the refuge towards a long grassy shoulder. Go right where it forks (**careful** – no sign). (Left is the Tour du Pays du Mont Blanc which goes eventually to Le Brevent.) You are on a narrow, open path past Lac Laochet, a tiny patch of water fringed with incredibly flat white plants, and undulating over a lovely grassy ridge with the lake to the left and an impressive view of the Rochers des Fiz to the right. Follow the yellow splashes carefully as they go left off the shoulder. After 20mins you come to more signposts (3hrs 15mins). Go right in the direction of Ayères/Plaine Joux (3hrs 15mins).

Alternative You can go straight on to the very pretty Lac de Pormenaz, alt. 1945m, situated in a rocky glacial depression of 4.6 hectares with an attractive island in the middle. This is a popular fishing spot as the pure waters are stocked with rainbow trout. Retrace your steps to the signpost, but **do not take the short cut right from the lake**, as this path is difficult (add 20mins for this detour).

(5) Continue on an open grassy path with little streams and pools, and

Crossing streams on the way back from the Refuge du Moede d'Anterne

Walking back along the gorge – Möede d'Anterne

yellow splashes to guide you. After about 15mins the path runs parallel to the Souay stream, and then climbs high above it, crossing the stream just below a waterfall where the water gushes down quite swiftly. **Careful** – the rocks can be very slippery early in the season or after heavy rain. The path continues along the Gorge des Monthieux. This is a rocky, twisty section, quite steep in places, and you have to watch your feet. For about 100m there is a drop on the right, but there are ropes on the left to give support where necessary. (**Note** This part of the walk is marked on the map with little dots, meaning tricky, and is not for anyone suffering from vertigo.) Later on you meet the path coming down from Lac de Pormenaz, marked Passage Difficile. The path eventually winds down out of the narrow gorge back to the river, where you cross on a wooden bridge and then over rocks to reach the jeep track at the Chalets de Souay (No. 3) where you come out of the reserve (4hrs 10mins).

Retrace your steps back to the car park near Lac Vert (5hrs).

OVERLOOKING CLUSES

WALK 3

Pointe de Chevran
Alt. 1150m (Overlooking Cluses)

Difficulty	Medium – the way up is steep
Time	3hrs 15mins
Height gain	684m
Maps	Editions Didier & Richard IGN No. 3 Massifs du Chablais Faucigny & Genevois 1:50,000
	Cartes IGN 3430 ET Top 25 La Clusaz/Grand-Bornand 1:25,000
Depart from	Cluses – 485m
Signposting	There are green/red splashes and signposts (**Note** Some of the green/red splashes are difficult to see or have been obliterated by grey paint. This applies particularly to the way up.)

A really attractive walk at all times of the year, especially on a hot day in summer as much of the walk is in shade. Although this walk is called Pointe de Chevran (pointe meaning 'point' or 'summit'), it is in fact just a circular walk round the mountain. On the noticeboard at the alternative start (see No. 2, below) it looks as if there is actually a path to the summit, but after two futile attempts to reach the pointe, and abortive telephone calls to the tourist office in Cluses, who did not seem to know much about it, I was put in touch with someone from the Forestry Commission. He assured me that there is indeed no path to the pointe, and that this is a circular walk round the mountain. So that solved the mystery, and the walk is lovely anyway.

Access (from Geneva)

Take the motorway, direction Chamonix, and exit at No. 19, Cluses centre. Turn left on the N205 and make for the centre of Cluses. Turn right immediately before the mairie onto the Rue de l'Hôtel de Ville (also says Clinique d'Esperance). Continue straight, crossing the railway and passing the cemetery on the right.

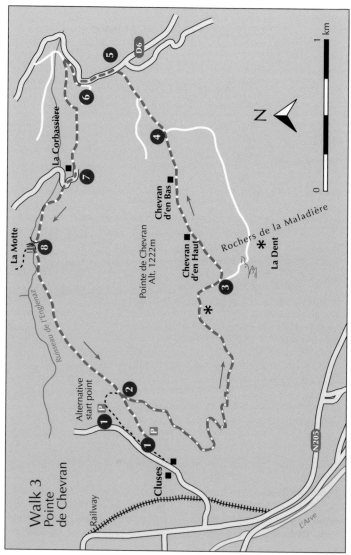

Walk 3
Pointe
de Chevran

Here the name of the street changes to Blvd de Chevron. You will see a building beyond with Imprimerie Monterrain, Micheal Vaillant Livraisons written on it. There is a small parking place before the building to the right where there is a narrow road.

Alternative If there is no room here, drive slightly further on the Blvd de Chevron and you will see a narrow road up right (Chemin du Sigismond). Go up this stony road until you come to a rough parking area. On the main road there is a noticeboard with a map of the walk.

The Route

(1) Walk up the jeep track between the store and the parking area, passing some rather shabby tin shacks on the right with houses down on the left, before the path narrows and becomes stony to reach a crossroads (10mins).

(2) Turn right through a metal barrier where there is a red/green splash – do not go straight where there are signs Tour de Chevran, St-Sigismond (you will come from here on your return).

Alternative Start Go straight upwards on the stony track (no signs or splashes) which bends to the right to meet a crossroads. Go straight towards a metal barrier where there are red/green splashes. Ignore the sign up left indicating Tour de Chevran, St-Sigismond (you will come from here on your return).

There are red/green direction splashes (though not always very visible) for the entire walk on rocks, trees and wooden arrows.

Continue along the wide track. On the right there is a beautiful view over the town of Cluses with the Môle behind, and the dramatic Pic de Marcelly back on the right. The path passes under a small grey limestone cliff called Fontaine aux Oiseaux ('fountain of the birds') before curling round the left of the mountain. At an intersection, just before the track starts to descend, bear up left, still on the jeep track (ignore the steep, narrow path on the immediate left) (30mins). Continue upwards on the main path and ignore any paths branching off. Here the red/green splashes are not easy to see and some are covered with grey paint.

Careful –10mins later look for a narrow path up left where there are no signs or splashes, though there are red/green splashes later on. You are winding up steeply through tall bushes, mainly wild raspberries (this used to be a coniferous forest but the trees have all been cut down), till you come to a small bushy plateau (1hr).

From here the path becomes steep and zigzags through the woods for approximately 30mins (look out for a carved wooden cross up on the left).

In late April and early May there are some magnificent specimens of early purple orchids, and in autumn you can see the flowers of the delicate pink cyclamen.

Continue until the path reaches a high shoulder and levels out at alt. 1190m. For the best view, bear up right through trees (there is no defined path) until you come to the edge of a sheer cliff face called Rochers de la Maladière, where there is a metal chain used for rappelling (it says Le Grand Cric on the rock). This is a good picnic spot while you contemplate the wonderful view down the Arve valley with the motorway and river running through it. On the other side you can see the road winding up the slopes to the little villages of La Frasse and Nancy-sur-Cluses. Retrace your steps to the track, which starts to go down before emerging into a clearing with a signpost (1hr 30mins).

(3) Alternative You can go straight on and then up a path to the right (not signposted) which takes you nearer the cliff edge and eventually to a lookout spot called La Dent, alt. 1196m. Before the lookout there is a path down to your left, through the forest, which eventually joins up with the path that has come through the combe (shallow valley) (see No. 4, below).

Follow the sign left to La Croix Verte on a grassy path, down the centre of an attractive open combe and through some stately fir trees. This takes you by Chevran d'en Haut (on the door it says Chez Doux Jésus) and then 5mins later Chevran d'en Bas. These are lovely old farms which have now been renovated. In spring the surrounding fields are covered with yellow dandelions and other meadow flowers.

After Chevran d'en Bas continue along the combe for a few minutes before entering the forest again and

Pic de Marcelly seen from the Pointe de Chevran

going down, gently at first, and then on a more steep and stony path to reach a junction at a stony clearing where there is a signpost (1hr 50mins).

(4) Go straight following the usual red/green splashes. The way you've come is marked Pointe de Chevran and to the right is Chevran par St-Jean (this is where the alternative described at No. 3, above, comes out). Continue down, keeping to the main track till you see a road (D6) below and a car park. You can see the villages of La Frasse and Treydon nestling in the valley to the right. Just before you get to the car park, bear left on to a narrow path to reach a tall wooden cross by the side of the road. This is called the Croix Verte, inscribed with the date 1976 (2hrs 5mins).

(5) Turn left on the road towards St-Sigismond (another good view here of the cross on the top of the Pointe de Marcelly straight ahead) and a few metres along there is a path down on the left with signs La Corbassière 15mins/La Motte 20mins/Cluses 30 mins and green/red splashes on a rock.

(6) Go left down through woods, where the road runs parallel up on the right for a short while, to reach a T-junction where you bear left following red/green splashes and yellow mountain bike signs. Continue down steeply, ignoring any paths branching off, through coniferous and beech woods, crossing a dry streambed, to

the hamlet of La Corbassière, alt. 797m, which is at the end of an asphalt road (2hrs 30mins).

(7) Walk down the road for a short while and then turn off left on the corner (green/red flashes and yellow mountain bike markings). You are now on an attractive path through woodland and meadows with a stream called the Ruisseau de l'Englenaz flowing down on the right. Beyond the stream there is an upward sweep of meadowland with the occasional old chalet and fruit trees.

(8) Before reaching the hamlet of La Motte you cross a bridge made of flat slabs of stone, and then a few metres later turn left over a bigger bridge.

An idyllic spot where one has to dawdle and gaze down at the water as it gurgles around the weedy rocks. If tired and hot, you can dip your feet into the shallow, icy stream.

Continue on the path round the side of the hill with a ravine on the right, and in places quite a drop. Suddenly you are in the open and there is another spectacular view of the town of Cluses.

The path reaches the crossroads at the start of the walk (No. 2 on map). Turn left and follow the smaller track for about 5mins till you reach your car (3hrs 15mins). (If your car is at the alternative start, keep straight on the main path.)

SAMOËNS/SIXT AREA

WALK 4

Lac de Vogealle

Alt. 2001m (Samoëns/Sixt area)

Difficulty	Difficult – the way up is very steep and not for anyone suffering from vertigo, although one can always go up and down by the return route, which is longer but easier
Time	7hrs 30mins
Height gain	1046m
Maps	Editions Didier & Richard IGN No. 3 Massifs du Chablais Faucigny & Genevois 1:50,000
	Cartes IGN 3530 ET Top 25 Samoëns/Haut Giffre 1:25,000
Depart from	Plan du Lac, near Sixt – 955m
Signposting	Good – new signposting

This is a superb walk best done in late spring when the waterfalls and lake are more impressive, but beware of snow. The flowers are also varied and abundant at this time. The Fer-à-Cheval is a horseshoe of high, dramatic mountains ringing a flat valley, and because of its beauty and easy accessibility it is very popular with families, so if possible avoid weekends in the high season. There are a lot of picnic areas, kiosks, cafés and also a riding school. When we arrived early on a Sunday in August there was not a soul about, but when we got back the place was crowded. However, fewer leave the valley floor and once you start climbing you are relatively on your own. I have also rewalked this route in late autumn and seen nobody all day, except a lone chamois.

Access (from Geneva)

Take the motorway, direction Chamonix, and exit at No. 15, Boëge/St-Jeoire. Then turn left briefly on the D903 and watch for the D9 right, signposted Fillinges, Samoëns and Vallée Verte. Follow this road to the Pont de Fillinges and then turn right on the D907, direction Taninges/Samoëns. (**Alternative** Go through Annemasse and take the D907, direction Taninges/Samoëns.)

At Samoëns follow signs to Sixt. Go straight through the village of Sixt (do not turn at the bridge) and continue through the hamlets of Les Curtets, L'Echarny, Le Molliet and Nambride till you come to a parking area on the right. (This is a new new starting point because on 16 December 2002 there was an important rockfall which destroyed part of the D907 leading to the Plan du Lac, which was the large parking area for the Fer-à-Cheval walks. But as the road has had to be closed, you must park here, further down the valley, which makes the walk longer. It is not as yet known when the road will reopen.)

The Route

(1) Cross the road and go left for a few metres till you see a signpost indicating Buvette de Prazon 1hr, which takes you across a wooden bridge over the Giffre river (there is a large noticeboard here explaining about the rockfall in 2002). Follow a wide track through woodland with the river down on the right – where the wood thins you can see where the rockfall has gone right across the road. Go past an arrow to the right, indicating Fer-à-Cheval/Chalet de la Réserve, and a large chalet to reach another sign indicating Refuge de Vogealle/Buvette de Prazon. Continue straight on a pleasant, undulating path through woodland, and then out into the open with tall cliffs left and the river rushing along on the right.

You pass a bridge over the river on the right and a sign Pas de la Samosse, alt. 1012m. Continue on the path following the sign Refuge de Vogealle to reach another bridge to the right and beyond the Buvette de Prazon (40mins).

(2) Take the path which goes left of the *buvette* ('café') where there are signs, and further on a wooden cross dated 1968. This is a narrow, stony path which goes gently upwards towards the end of the open valley, marked Réserve Naturelle, and across a dry

Crossing a stream in the Fer-à-Cheval valley

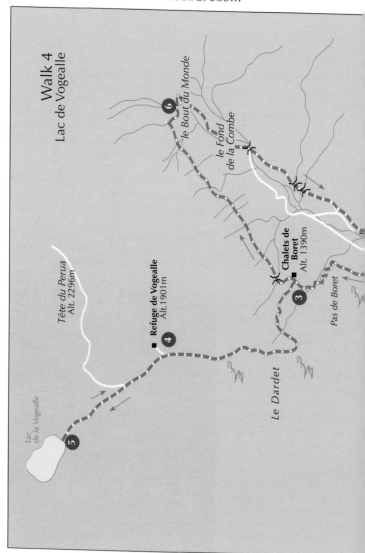

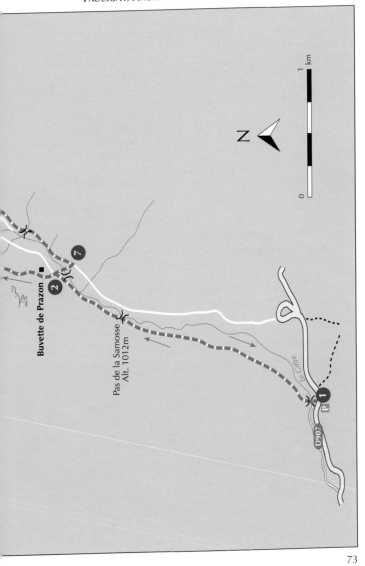

Buvette de Prazon

Pas de la Samosse
Alt. 1012m

Le Giffre

D907

N

1 km

0

riverbed following red splashes. You start to climb up the side of the valley where there are chains to hang on to, passing a small commemoration stone to Hubert Ducroz, with the inscription *'et sa vie dans ces montagnes'* ('and his life in these mountains'). After scrambling across several rushing streams the path becomes steeper and rockier. Be careful to follow the red arrows and splashes.

This is a very impressive path called the Pas de Boret. It winds up the left-hand side of the incredible horseshoe of towering cliffs with countless streams coursing downwards, often ending in dramatic waterfalls in the valley below. The path gets steeper and is very exposed. In the more vertiginous places there are lengths of wire hawser to hang on to. A stone dated 1826 is evidence that this is an ancient pathway (1hr 10mins).

After the date stone the path becomes less exposed and there is no longer a huge drop on the right. The grassy, rocky path seems to go into the mountain, undulating through woodland and bearing round to the right before passing ruins and arriving at the newly renovated Chalets de Boret, alt. 1390m, on a grassy shelf. In the high season this is a welcome *buvette* with benches and tables from where you can enjoy the magnificent views (1hr 30mins).

(3) Go up to the left of the hut following the signpost to the Refuge de Vogealle – straight on indicates Fond de la Combe (this is the high path to the end of the valley by which you will return). There is a shrine, dated 1848, with an empty stone niche which obviously once held a statue. The path goes through meadowland and stunted vegetation and then becomes more exposed again, with some patches of flat rock and scree and a number of dry streambeds to cross. It becomes

Walking towards Lac de Vogealle

steeper and rockier as it zigzags up and you have to watch where you are heading. Keep checking for the red/orange flashes on the rocks.

You pass under a high rock face and across riverbeds before coming to a new cross dated 1991, with a sign saying Refuge de Vogealle 45mins. The path becomes less steep, though still rocky and strewn with big boulders, as it clings round the mountain underneath an impressive cliff face called Le Dardet. This is followed by another fairly steep climb negotiating rocks and boulders. You do not see the Refuge de Vogealle, alt. 1901m, until you are almost there, as it is tucked back in a grassy area (3hrs 15mins).

(4) It is better not to stop at the hut (which is off the path to the right) until you have visited the lake, which is another 25mins on the same path climbing upwards for 100m with a stream down on the right. The path is not so rocky, which is rather a relief, and climbs medium steep, flattening out after around 10mins and reaching a magnificent hanging valley (a hanging valley is a valley you have to climb up into). Walk straight down the valley past a signpost till you reach the lake.

This lake is impressive when full of water, but in late summer it can be practically dry and rather a disappointment. The best time to visit is early June (snow permitting), when all the streams are cascading down the mountains.

(5) Retrace your steps to the refuge where you can stay the night and also get food (4hrs 10mins).

> Refuge de Vogealle (privately owned), tel 0450.89.77.59. Dormitories for 40 people. Toilets, cold water, no showers. Overnight 10 Euros, half-board 33 Euros. Open 1 July to 15 September.

Take the same path back to the Chalets de Boret at No. 4 (5hrs 10mins). At the hut go left, following the signpost Fer-à-Cheval par la Fond de la Combe 2hrs 45mins. This is an easier path, undulating through Alpine pastures, intermittent woodland and rocky places, into the head of the valley. If you look back you get an impressive view of the track you came down from the refuge. A few minutes from the Chalets de Boret you cross a stream with lots of boulders by a wooden bridge, past a further signpost. The path, marked with occasional faded pink splashes, is well defined but may be muddy and slippery after rainfall. It crosses a number of streams and dry riverbeds and goes through some lovely stunted beech woods. After 25mins you cross a wide gully where there has been a landslide, so pick your way across with care (there used to be a sign saying La Combe, but it has disappeared.) As the path wends round to the head of the valley, you cross a number of streams and can hear the constant sound of gurgling water as they cascade down to the valley floor. You come to a large slab of rock with streams coursing over it – this is easy to cross in good weather, but could be tricky if it is raining or there is a lot of water. The path descends slightly to reach the head of the valley (6hrs).

(6) You are now at the Bout du Monde ('end of the world'), but there is no sign except a red arrow on a large rock. The path starts to wind down towards the end of the valley, with some flashes which now seem to have turned pink, but the path is self-evident as you can see it from above. The gradient is fairly steep, and you pass a large boulder on the right with a house painted on it and Boret written

underneath (referring to the hut above), on the way to the Giffre river on the valley floor (6hrs 15mins).

The Giffre is quite a torrent in all seasons, and in spring the banks are a profusion of flowers, including white alpine anemones (pasque flowers), lily of the valley, globe flowers and butterwort.

Keep to the left on a wide path crossing several bridges, some made of wooden slats. The path goes along the dry edge of the riverbed, which is very wide, but I would imagine there are times of the year when it is full of water. The streams are rushing down off the cliffs and there are some fantastic waterfalls. After more scree and riverbed you cross the river at an easy point and take the wide path on the left-hand side of the valley (signposts here) with the river on the right. Continue down the valley on the defined path. If you look up to the right you can see the steep path taken up the cliffs on the Pas de Boret. You reach a sign right which says Buvette 2mins (6hrs 50mins)

(7) Turn right and cross the river to reach the path you came in by just before the *buvette*. Turn left and retrace your steps to the car (7hrs 30mins).

Fer-à-Cheval valley from Le Bout du Monde

WALK 5

Lac de Gers

Alt. 1533m *(Samoëns/Sixt area)*

Difficulty	Medium – steep walk up to the lake
Time	4hrs 30mins
Height gain	765m
Maps	Editions Didier & Richard IGN No. 3 Massifs du Chablais Faucigny/Genevois 1:50,000
	Cartes IGN 3530 ET Top 25 Samoëns/Haut Giffre 1:25,000
Depart from	Le Fay, near Sixt –768m
Signposting	Adequate, though could be better – difficult to find the alternative path down from the lake, though the choice is signposted on the way up

This is a delightful walk at any time of the year, but especially dramatic after lots of rain when the Gers stream rushes impressively down the wooded mountainside, over rocky boulders and narrow gorges, on its way to join the Giffre river. There is plenty of shade on a hot summer's day, but I prefer late autumn just before the first snow, when the mountains seem to rise out of the mist like illustrations in Chinese paintings, and the precipitous waters are muted by glistening icicles. (**Note** It is possible to make this walk much longer by continuing from the lake through the Combe de Gers to the Col de Pelouse, alt. 2227m, then circling back under the Téléski de Gers past minuscule Lac Parchet and the Chalets de Foges on your right.)

Access (from Geneva)

Take the motorway, direction Chamonix, and exit at No.15, Boëge/St-Jeoire. Then turn left briefly on the D903 and watch for the D.9 right, signposted Fillinges, Samoëns and Vallée Verte. Follow this road to the Pont de Fillinges and then turn right on the D907, direction Taninges/Samoëns. (**Alternative** Go through Annemasse and take the D907, direction Taninges/Samoëns.) At Samoëns follow signs to Sixt. At Sixt turn right across the bridge and then right again at the *bureau de tourisme*, which is the old railway station. Turn left at the next intersection (a sort of crossroads) and you will arrive at the hamlet of

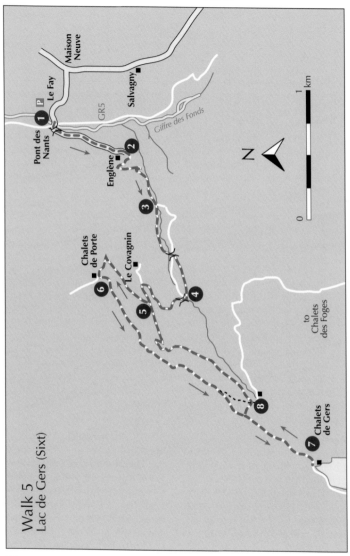

Walk 5
Lac de Gers (Sixt)

Le Fay. Leave your car just before the bridge (Pont des Nants).

The Route

(1) There are signposts at the bridge indicating straight on to Lac de Gers on the GR96, and left for the Tour du Giffre Haut on the GR5. Walk across the bridge over the River Giffre, which is a rushing torrent, and up the asphalt road. On the left you can see the village of Salvagny and behind you are the dramatic mountains of the Fer-à-Cheval ('horseshoe') beyond Sixt, with the tops of the pylons which disfigure the Lac d'Anterne area. You reach Englène, a cluster of attractive chalets with a big old stone cross and a fountain (15mins).

(2) Continue straight on a wide stony track, winding up fairly steeply through pretty, mossy woodland consisting mainly of birch. You can hear the sound of water all the way from the Gers stream coming down from the lake. Keep to the main path, passing a shrine set in the side of the rock and then an attractive watery *grotto*.

At the shrine and grotto are some intriguing white crosses with two parallel white lines across instead of the usual one. I was told that this is the cross of the French Resistance, but the tourist office assures me that nobody was killed in the Sixt area during the war and that this is the Cross of Lorraine, although why they are there is a mystery.

As you turn a corner you can see the fencing of a new ski piste, which goes from the Chalets de Foges all the way down the hillside. Shortly after, the track forks (30mins).

(3) Go up right with the stream rushing along down on your left (if you turn left and over the stream you will reach the new ski piste, which then goes up steeply to reach the same track you are on). There is a rock to the left on the track, with GR96 painted in red, just before you cross a bridge where there is an attractive waterfall. Shortly after, the ski piste joins from the left and you stay on this track for a while as it goes upwards through woodland. Ignore a narrow path coming in from the left just before a corner (there is a small wooden sign here on a tree on the other side of the track indicating Lac de Gers) and continue on. You can now hear the stream again down on the right, and then it levels with the track by a further bridge bordered by netting (red/white cross on the bridge) to protect skiers from falling in. The ski piste goes up steeply left, but keep straight on a stony path (1hr).

(4) The track crosses the stream on an iron bridge and, just after the ski piste joins again, there is a tall rock face on the left with water trickling down and a waterfall further on. (If you happen to do the walk after a frost, the icicles on this rock face are very impressive.) Eventually the path comes out of the forest and you can see a lovely chain of mountains on the right and a little hut on the left with slopes of coniferous trees behind. Ignore a rather undefined junction where the grassy path right goes to the scatttered wooden chalets of Le Covagnin, and stay on the wider track bearing left.

(5) Continue on upwards round a sharp right-hand bend where a wide grassy track comes in from the left (this is where you join on your return). The track continues along the contour of the mountain, with steep slopes of dense coniferous woods to the left and dramatic views down to the right into the valley. The track bears round left to reach a T-junction at the three wooden buildings of the Chalets de Porte, alt. 1470m, and a signpost (2hrs).

(6) Go left, following the sign to Lac de Gers par Porte (the path to the right is signposted Samoëns and eventually joins the GR5 at the Giffre river in the valley). You go through lovely woodland on an easy, undulating path which doubles back round the mountain.

The path comes out into a beautiful, wide valley, apparently unspoilt until you see the top of a ski-lift on the skyline to the right. This is one of the lifts coming up from the ski resort of Flaine, just over the brow – higher up the valley. There is another ski-tow coming down, but it is not visible. The path turns into a wide track, passing a large noticeboard outlining Forestry

Commission work in the region, and continues on to reach the lake where there is a refuge and a café which also sells goats' cheese (2hrs 30mins).

> Gîte du Lac de Gers, tel 0450.34.44.83. Meals/snacks available. Four rooms for four and one room for six, with showers. Open 1 June to 15 October and during the ski season.

(7) This is an attractive lake with mountains all around and little habitation to spoil the natural beauty of the area. It is worthwhile strolling round the lake to select a picnic spot (preferably away from the chalets where there are lots of goats and goat droppings!). You can see the path at the end of the lake, which continues up to the Col de Pelouse.

(8) Go back down the valley for approximately 10mins and turn right on a grassy path (no sign) towards some scattered chalets – you can see the signpost ahead in front of one of the chalets. Bear left following the sign Sixt/Fer-à-Cheval (to the right goes to the Chalets de Foges). This is a narrow, grassy path which becomes rockier and steeper as it meanders through woods, bracken and raspberry bushes, with the river down on the right. You pass an old chalet on the right before reaching the turning (No. 5) you took on the way up (3hrs). Retrace your steps back to the bridge (4hrs). (At Le Fay there is a *gîte d'étape*.)

WALK 6

Lac d'Anterne/Refuge de Sales
Two Day Hike: **Day 1** – *alt. 2104m,* **Day 2** – *alt. 2220m*
(Samoëns/Sixt area)

Difficulty	Medium – a rather long haul up from the Chalets des Fonds the first day and a short, steep climb to the Pointe du Dérochoir the second day
Time	**Day 1** – 4hrs direct to the refuge, or 5hrs 45mins via Lac d'Anterne
	Day 2 – 7hrs 15mins
Height gain	**Day 1** – 1093m
	Day 2 – in three stages, 480m down, 840m up, 1115 metres down
Maps	Editions Didier & Richard IGN No. 3 Massifs du Chablais Faucigny & Genevois 1:50,000
	Cartes IGN 3530 ET Top 25 Samoëns/Haut Giffre 1:25,000
Depart from	Les Fardelay – 1054m
Signposting	Good – a number of signs as this is a popular walking area

A wonderful and varied two-day walk in a beautiful Alpine area which is a very popular summer weekend walk, so you will meet a fair number of people. It is possible to split the walk into two separate one-day hikes. Another alternative is to make a complete circle by continuing past the Lac d'Anterne and over the col to the Refuge d'Anterne, where you can spend the first night. You then continue on a variant of the Tour du Pays du Mont Blanc before turning up right to the Passage du Dérochoir and then spending a second night at the Chalets de Sales. This option is only for experienced walkers, however, as not only does it involve two long days, there is a tricky section (Passage du Dérochoir) which involves chains and ladders.

Access (from Geneva)

Take the motorway, direction Chamonix and exit at No.15 Boëge/ St-Jeoire. Then turn left briefly on the D903 and watch for the D9 right, signposted Fillinges, Samoëns and

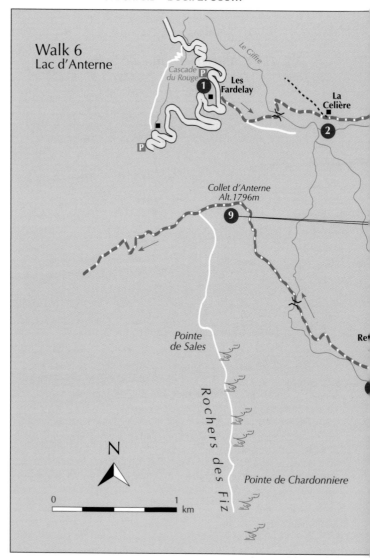

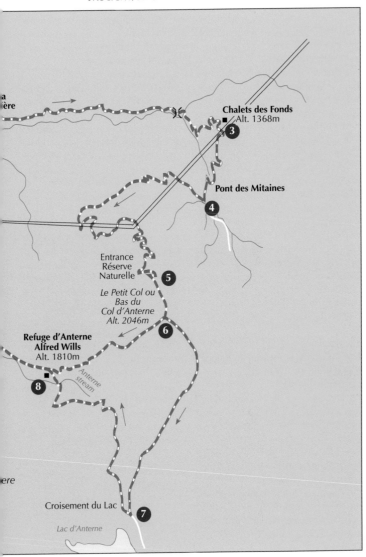

Vallée Verte. Follow this road to the Pont de Fillinges and then turn right on the D907, direction Taninges/ Samoëns. (**Alternative** Go through Annemasse and take the D907, direction Taninges/Samoëns.) From Samoëns follow all signs to Sixt. At Sixt turn right across the bridge, go through the village of Salvagny and turn right again where it is signposted Cascade de Rouget. The road winds up past the Rouget waterfall (worth stopping to look at) and reaches the Chalets de Fardelay, a small group of old chalets above the road. **Careful** – it is easy to drive by the chalets without noticing them. Park in a wide clearing to the left beyond the chalets, or near the signpost Les Fardelay beyond on the left. (**Note** The road continues to Le Lignon, a popular parking area for the walk up to the Chalets de Sales.)

The Route
Day 1 Chalets de Fardelay to Refuge Alfred Wills, Lac d'Anterne

(1) Follow the signpost Les Fardelay on the left, alt. 1040m, indicating Refuge/Cirque des Fonds 1hr 45mins. At a fork soon after, keep straight following posts with yellow arrows. You are on a wide and stony path descending through woods, with the rushing Giffre stream, which starts in the nearby Le Buet mountain, down on the left, and high rocky cliffs beyond. Cross the river on a bridge at a pretty ravine called Creux d'Oua (15mins).

Continue straight up the path, crisscrossed with tree roots, which starts to climb gently upwards with the rushing stream falling away on the left. This is the start of a 330m climb up to the Chalets des Fonds, and the path initially goes through beech and coniferous forest with some clearings and little huts. It meets a jeep track coming from Salvagny at La Celière and another signpost (30mins).

(2) Go right, following the sign Les Fonds, on a wide track up the side of a gorge with the stream flowing down on the right. You negotiate several rivulets trickling off the rock on your left and spilling across the path to cascade into the river far below. Further on cross another bridge above a ravine where the river crashes impressively over big boulders (55mins).

Continue up to some small chalets which are set in a circle of imposing peaks. This is the Cirque des Fonds. The large old chalet on the left is called the Nid d'Aigle ('eagle's nest') and was built in 1858 by an Englishman called Alfred Wills (see below). Just after is the Refuge des Fonds, alt. 1380m (1hr 30mins).

Refuge des Fonds (privately owned), 74740 Sixt Fer-à-Cheval, tel 0450.34.44.05.

Accommodation for 40 people (dormitories); food available.

(3) From the refuge bear round to the right on a wide stony track through coniferous trees until you come to another signpost. Keep straight (left goes back to Salvagny), indicated Anterne/Buet/Chamonix.

In August or early September you will see big bunches of blue willow gentians which, unlike their spring flowering dwarf counterparts, are tall with lots of blooms on one stalk.

The track comes out of the forest and into a gorge with the Giffre stream still flowing nearby. It continues on under pylon wires and across the Pont de Mitaines, where the track deteriorates into a narrow path going steeply upwards to reach another signpost Les Mitaines, alt. 1145m (1hr 45mins).

(4) Go right, direction Anterne, on a path curling up round the hillside and under pylon wires for the second time. You can see the Chalets des Fonds below on your right – it is about 400m up to the Chalets d'Anterne and another 200m to the lake. The path is mossy and wet, with lots of tall gentians, pink adenostyles, blue alpine sow thistles and ferns growing on the banks, depending on the time of year, and there are lovely views down into the Samoëns valley. Leaving the trees behind, the path winds round through open pasture with glorious views to left and right.

One feels diminished by the sheer immensity and height of the mountains in this area, which contrasts with the more graceful, friendly Chablais peaks to the north.

The path continues upwards through dwarf alder bushes, and in summer the red alpenrose bushes are in bloom. It passes by a big fir tree on the left, and goes under the wires of the big electricity pylons that march across this magnificent landscape. Looking back you can see the entrance of the valley to the Chalets de Sales and Pointe du Dérochoir, where you will be walking the following day. Still with a good view down to the Chalets des Fonds huts and the impressive amphitheatre of the Cirque des Fonds to the left, the path continues zigzagging upwards, passing a tiny pond to reach a signpost at 2076m (3hrs).

(5) The sign says you are entering a Réserve Naturelle – Chiens Interdit ('dogs not allowed'). Continue on, following the sign Pas d'Anterne/Lac d'Anterne. You are now right on top of the mountain where the terrain is open, undulating and boggy, with lots

Grass on the Lac d'Anterne

Lac d'Anterne

of heather, bilberry bushes and white bog cotton flowers. You reach another signpost at the Petit Col d'Anterne, alt. 2046m (3hrs 30mins).

(6) (**Note** Here you can go to the right, which says Refuge 30mins. If it is foggy it is wise to do this, as it is easy to lose your way on the path to the Lac d'Anterne.)

If you wish to see the Lac D'Anterne and then go to the refuge (1hr 45mins), go left and follow the obvious path through open grassland, over some black shale, and over rocks, pools and riverbeds which may be empty in dry weather. The long, towering rock wall of the Rochers des Fiz, 800m high, is over on the right. When the lake finally appears below, shaped rather like a whale, one is agreeably surprised at how large it is. Ahead you can see the path winding up and over the Col d'Anterne, alt. 2257m (4hrs 5mins).

(7) Go down to the signpost near the lake which says Croisement du Lac, alt. 2163m, and then right, following indication Refuge 40mins. You are now on the long-distance footpath of the GR5, so follow the red/white GR splashes carefully as the path is not obvious. There are lots of marmot holes, so look out for these furry creatures, which you can often see bounding over the countryside. There is always a marmot on sentry duty and he will give a piercing whistle to warn the others of danger.

After you pass a cairn, you can see the refuge nestling below in a grassy Alpine plain with the huge Rochers des Fiz behind. The path snakes down for about half-an-hour and is irritatingly stony and steep. You can see from above that this used to be a small Alpine hamlet, as there are traces of broken-down walls where crops were grown. Just before arriving at the chalet, cross over the

Ruisseau d'Anterne, which runs right through the valley, with signposts to Chamonix back towards the lake and Chalets des Fonds to the right. There is a signpost before the hut indicating you are at alt. 1810m (5hrs 45mins).

> Refuge d'Anterne Alfred Wills, Plaine d'Anterne, 74740 Sixt Fer-à-Cheval, tel 0450.34.91.63 (privately owned).
> Situated on the GR5 between Sixt and Chamonix, this is a small refuge, clean but fairly rudimentary, with dormitories housing 50 people. There are no showers, and only one small basin with cold water in the toilet. However, there is a pipe outside with running water. The food is copious and good. Demi-pension 30 Euros. Open June to October.

The Refuge d'Anterne is dedicated to Alfred Wills, an Englishman who lived from 1828 to 1912. A brilliant magistrate and founder of the London Alpine Club, he was also an accomplished mountaineer and the first person to climb the Wetterhorn in 1864. He came to the valley of the Giffre, fell in love with it and constructed a large chalet, Nid d'Aigle, in 1858 in the Cirque des Fonds. There is a picture in the refuge of Alfred standing in front of his chalet in 1877.

The present guardians of the refuge (which is private) got very excited when they heard my name

Refuge d'Anterne Alfred Wills

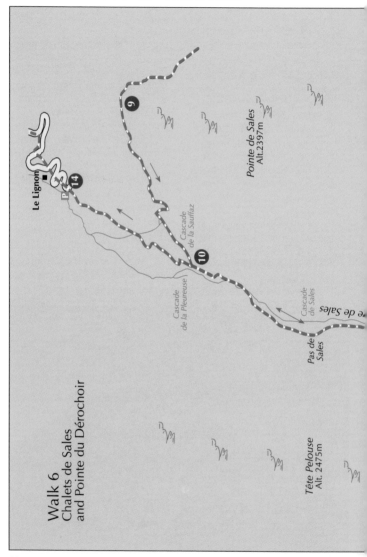

Walk 6
Chalets de Sales
and Pointe du Dérochoir

Le Lignon

Pointe de Sales
Alt.2397m

Cascade
de la Sauffiaz

Cascade
de la Pleureuse

Cascade
de Sales

Pas de
Sales

Tête Pelouse
Alt. 2475m

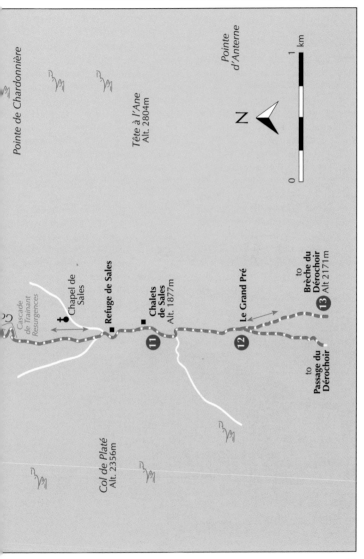

(Norton). The daughter of Alfred Wills married a Norton and lived in the Nid d'Aigle for many years. The family, according to hearsay, lost their fortune in India and so sold the chalet to the Lucas family who still own it.

Day 2 Refuge Alfred Wills, Lac d'Anterne, to Chalets de Sales and Pointe du Dérochoir

(8) Walk down the valley with the high, flat wall of the Rochers des Fiz on your left. The valley floor is boggy, with flattish rocks on the left from an ancient glacier formation. You are on the GR5 which goes all the way from Sixt to Chamonix. Cross a small river by a wooden bridge. The path goes by large rocks and is well defined, winding up round the mountain to the base of the electricity pylons. You

quickly lose sight of the refuge round the corner, but there is a good view back down the valley with the snowy Mont Blanc range rearing up behind the Col d'Anterne. You can see the path you went up the day before over on the right. The Fiz escarpment ends dramatically at the Collet d'Anterne, alt. 1796m, where there are signposts and a first view down to the Samoëns valley beyond (45mins).

(9) Continue on down the path winding round the end of the Fiz mountain, going gently downwards at first and then much steeper, crossing dry riverbeds and in and out of woodland. The path is sometimes quite rocky and, in wet weather, slippery and muddy. There are wonderful views down to the valley and village of Salvagny. Follow the GR red/white

Refuge Alfred Wills near Lac d'Anterne

signs carefully all the way until you finally reach a T-junction and signpost at alt.11440m, with the spectacular waterfalls of Cascade de la Sauffraz and Cascade de la Pleureuse in front (1hr 35mins). (**Note** Here you can go right and walk back to the car (30mins) – route details below.)

(10) Turn left and follow the sign to the Refuge de Sales – you are now on the GR96 which is a variant of the GR5. Follow the stony path, which goes quite steeply up for 100m along the side of a ravine with the stream rushing below on the right. This is a watery boulder area with two rock faces each side, making the ravine narrow before it opens out. On the left is the other side of the sinister Rochers des Fiz.

After 20mins you reach a plateau level with the stream and then cross the stream before starting to climb up along the other side of the ravine. This walk is characterised by flattish stretches and then steepish climbs with dramatic waterfalls. The interesting thing about these waterfalls is that the riverbed may be empty in dry weather, and the water tumbling down the boulders seems to come from an underground source. At the first waterfall (Cascade de Sales) the path becomes a ledge going under a cliff as the gorge narrows (Pas de Sales on the map) – however, there is a solid protection rail so it is no problem. At the next waterfall (Cascade de Trainant) the path deviates to the right

Refuge de Sales, 74740 Sixt Fer-à-Cheval (privately owned), tel. 0450.34.47.01.

Accommodates 60 people in various dormitories – no showers. Demi-pension 30 Euros.

following a *resurgence* (a waterfall coming out of a spring) cascading down to meet the main river (after a period of no rain this is often dry).

You reach the final plateau at a cross with a small chapel on the left – Chapel de Sales, built in 1642 and dedicated to St François de Sales, a local saint. The path reaches a signpost at alt. 1870m. Continue straight (right goes to Chalet des Foges/Col de Pelouse/Lac de Gers), and shortly after you reach the Refuge de Sales, alt. 1886m. This is an ideal place to stop for a refreshing drink before starting to climb up to the Pointe du Dérochoir (2hrs 40mins).

(11) Follow the sign Brèche du Dérochoir/Passage du Dérochoir. The path is fairly flat for a while, and goes between renovated huts which must have originally housed the shepherds guarding the huge flocks which were kept up here during the summer months. After 10mins you go past an old stone water trough (hewn out of the rock in 1869) and up over rocks onto a slightly higher plateau in a wide, grassy valley called Le Grand Pré. This valley is very attractive, with two small ponds and cows and horses grazing in summer. You come to another signpost at Le Grand Pré, alt. 1914m (3hrs 10mins).

(12) Keep left towards the Brèche du Dérochoir, which takes you to the col but no further. The right fork goes to the Passage du Dérochoir, which is a difficult way down to the Passy valley (involving ladders and chains – best done the other way round), Col de la Portette and eventually to the Chalets de Platé, another refuge in an area called the Désert de Platé, a desolate region of flat, creviced rock.

Continue over a series of grassy, rocky humps, like giant steps, before going steeply to the col on a defined path. The top (alt. 2171m) comes as a surprise, as it is a narrow ledge with a steep drop over cliffs on the other side and magnificent views. You can see right down the Chamonix valley with Lac Vert far below, and the glistening, snowy peaks of the nearby Mont Blanc range (4hrs 10mins).

This is a walk which is really worth the effort, as the view is one of the most dramatic in the region. What

a spot for a picnic! The only snag is that in summer the col is often crowded.

(13) Retrace your steps to the Chalets de Sales and then the Cascade de la Sauffraz at the junction where you arrived from the Col d'Anterne (No.10 on the map). Continue straight down for 30mins until you reach the Chalets de Lignon, alt. 1180m. The path is wide and stony, and seems endless at the end of the day as it goes steeply down through spaced coniferous woods with lots of larch trees (6hrs 20mins).

(14) Keep right when you get to the Chalets de Lignon, where there is a car park, café and lots of signposts, one stating that you are entering the Sixt National Reserve. Continue down the tarmac road, making use of the obvious short cuts to avoid the bends, until you reach the car parking at the Chalets de Fardelay (6hrs 50mins).

WALK 7

Chalets de Criou
Alt. 1664m (Samoëns/Sixt area)

Difficulty	Medium/difficult walk with quite a height gain – steeper if you go on to the Aouille
Time	4hrs 45mins
Height gain	953m
Maps	Editions Didier & Richard IGN No. 3 Massifs du Chablais Faucigny & Genevois 1:50,000
	Cartes IGN 3530 ET Top 25 Samoëns/Haut Giffre 1:25,000
Depart from	Near Vallon d'en Bas – 711m
Signposting	Good new signposting

Considering these little villages are very near the bustling ski and summer resort of Samoëns, they are curiously unspoilt, maybe because they are off the main road. It is obviously an area with a lot of history, as the chalets are old, some as yet untouched by renovation. Vallon d'en Bas is a charming hamlet of weathered Savoyard farms with few modern chalets.

We did this walk in high summer and saw very few people. It is also a good choice on a hot day, as much of it is in shady woodland, and the way up, although long, is not too steep. The views down the Giffre valley and of the nearby Mont Blanc range are superb, even more so in early winter when there are no leaves on the trees. I thought that the French word Aouille (de Criou) might have a specific meaning, but the tourist bureau at Samoëns assures me it does not.

Access (from Geneva)

Take the motorway, direction Chamonix, and exit at No.15 Boëge/St-Jeoire. Then turn left briefly on the D903 and watch for the D9 right, signposted Fillinges, Samoëns and Vallée Verte. Follow this road to the Pont de Fillinges and then turn right on the D907, direction Taninges/Samoëns. (**Alternative** Go through Annemasse and take the D907, direction Taninges/Samoëns.) Drive through Samoëns (note the village itself is closed to traffic but the way round is clearly marked). Follow all signs to Sixt, turning right at a T-junction and then taking

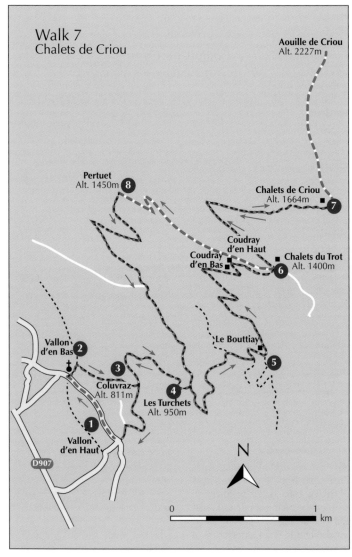

Walk 7
Chalets de Criou

Aouille de Criou
Alt. 2227m

Pertuet
Alt. 1450m **8**

Chalets de Criou
Alt. 1664m **7**

Coudray
d'en Haut

Coudray
d'en Bas

Chalets du Trot
Alt. 1400m **6**

Vallon
d'en Bas **2**

3

Coluvraz
Alt. 811m

Le Bouttiay

5

4

Les Turchets
Alt. 950m

1

Vallon
d'en Haut

D907

N

0   1
                    km

the first turning to the left marked Vallon d'en Bas. Go through the village and park on a grassy verge to the right just beyond a *colonie de vacances* called L'Hermitage (do not park in their parking area!).

The Route

(1) Walk back down the road into the village of Vallon d'en Bas and take the stony path, signposted L'Alpage du Trot, which goes up to the right of the little chapel (5mins).

(2) The path goes up initially between mossy stone walls. After a few minutes turn sharp right following the sign to Criou. Keep to the main track, which goes up through woods with the Samoëns valley down on the right to reach a T-junction at Coluvraz, alt. 811m – this is where you will continue straight on your return (20mins).

(3) Turn up left, following signs to Chalets de Pertuet/Chalets du Trot/Criou, on a wide, defined jeep track through deciduous and coniferous forest. You pass an attractive wooden trough fountain called Fontaine du Vin Blanc to reach a fork at Les Turchets, alt. 950m.

(4) Bear up right, following signs Chalets du Trot/Criou (to the left is where you come out on your return). Keep on the main path (ignoring all paths branching off), passing small wooden huts to reach further signs at Le Bouttiay, alt. 1130m (1hr).

(5) Continue up left (right goes to Chalets les Basses/Le Mont), passing high rocks and further wooden chalets at Coudray d'en Bas and Coudray d'en Haut. Finally the woods give way to attractive, open Alpine pasture, covered in bright blue forget-me-nots and early purple orchids in springtime, just before you reach a collection of wooden huts signposted Le Trot, alt. 1400m. (Left is signed Chalets de Pertuet, which you will take on your return). At the chalets there is a sign saying Boissons/Buvette (only open in high season). If you have time, take a drink and buy some of the delicious goats' cheese (the goats are all around you) (1hr 50mins).

(6) Go straight past the chalets on the left, passing another sign and continuing on the path, winding up round the mountain with the odd hut dotted here and there. This is probably an old mule track, as it appears manmade, hewn out of the mountain, with intermittent low stone walls. The slopes are partially covered with a flat, fissured rock formation, this ancient, glacier-type terrain being fairly common in the Samoëns area.

In summer there are lots of butterflies, particularly the tiny blue ones which cluster round dried goat dung. I have also seen swallowtails, mottled whites and the rarer Camberwell beauty.

You reach another huddle of wooden huts by a large rock, with a green plastic square and yellow arrows, and a sign saying Criou, alt. 1664m. (It is interesting to note that all over the region the painted arrows, which are now fading, are being replaced by small plastic squares – how they remain fixed to the rocks is a mystery.)

(7) Walk through the chalets, skirting a big, round, modern water tank, until you come to an attractive old stone trough higher up, which must have been the original source of water for the cattle and goats. The chalets look old and unspoilt, apart of course from the inevitable corrugated-iron roofs, and they are surrounded by high nettles in summer. Above the water trough is a large rock with Criou painted in red. This rock is the highest point of the walk – there is a splendid view of the Giffre valley below, with

the rearing peak of the Roc d'Anterne beyond at the end of the impressive Rochers des Fiz ridge; to the left is the Mont Blanc range. Straight ahead on the horizon are the tops of the ski-lifts coming up from the ski resort of Flaine (2hrs 30mins).

From the rock there is a path going steeply upwards to the Aouille de Criou, alt. 2227m, which takes about 1hr 30mins. However, the path peters out and you have to find your own way to the top (not done by the author).

Retrace your steps, passing the Chalet Corbet up on the right, until you come to the second sign at Chalets du Trot (No. 6 on the map) (3hrs 10mins). Go up right, following the sign Chalets de Pertuet, on a narrow path over meadowland where you can see the chalets on the horizon. Just before the chalets there is a sign saying Pertuis alt. 1450m.

Fountain at Vallon d'en Haut, Chalets de Criou

(**Note** It says Pertuet on the map, but Pertuis on the signpost.) (3hrs 30mins.)

These small chalets now look rather rundown and neglected, and all have iron roofs, whereas 10 years ago some of them had the original wooden slatted roofs called tavaillon. In summer, when we did the walk, there were a number of rather evil-looking cows with enormous horns chewing the cud amongst the stinging nettles.

Passing the Chalets de Criou

(**8**) Go down left towards Vallon on a rocky, open path, where you get further extended views up the Giffre valley with, from left to right, the Môle, Pointe de Chevran and Pic des Mémises. Keep up right at a small fork and soon the path widens into a jeep track as you reach woodland. There is now a long descent through beech and fir woods with, at times, a steep drop on one side before you eventually reach the signpost at Les Turchets (No. 4). Bear down right to reach the signpost at Coluvraz (4hrs 20mins) where you continue straight on the jeep track (you came from the right on the way up). It takes 10mins to reach the village of Vallon d'en Haut. Here there is a charming fountain with water coming out of duck heads, and a notice saying 'Fontaine de Chernieux, Oeuvre [designed by] François Mugnier 1820 to 1900'.

It is worth taking a look at the beautiful wild garden of the old farm opposite. In July it was ablaze with purple and pink and the rare yellow Mongolian variety of clematis, plus clusters of highly scented white stocks. The old farmer's wife was delighted to show us around.

Turn right and walk along the road for about 10mins, flanked by some dilapidated Savoyard farms, till you get to Vallon d'en Bas (4hrs 45mins).

WALK 8

Tête de Bostan

Alt. 2406m (Samoens/Sixt area)

Difficulty	Difficult – the walk to the Col de Bostan is long and steep, and the way back is airy at the start
Time	6hrs 30mins
Height gain	1308m
Maps	Editions Didier & Richard IGN No. 3 Massifs du Chablais Faucigny & Genevois 1:50,000
	Cartes IGN 3530 ET Top 25 Samoëns/Haut Giffre 1:25,000
Depart from	Plan aux Arches – 1098m
Signposting	New signposting – red/white GR markings

The Dents Blanches is the first high mountain range rising from the lower slopes of the pré-Alpine region – it is separated from the main Mont Blanc peaks by the Chamonix valley. This is a long, challenging walk at a fairly high altitude, but with no technical difficulty. It is very popular, so you risk meeting quite a number of people in the summer season. There are magnificent views into the Rhône valley and over the Vaud and Valais peaks in Switzerland. It is interesting to note that the Col de la Golèse is one of the two main migrating routes for birds flying north–south over the Alps, and every year thousands of birds are ringed and checked by ornithologists here. It is also traditionally a great smuggling area, and the legend goes that one Christmas eve a Swiss customs officer met a heavily laden Frenchman coming from the direction of Samoëns. When challenged as to what he carried, the Frenchman replied that he was the Archangel Gabriel!

Access (from Geneva)

Take the motorway, direction Chamonix, and exit at No. 15 Boëge/St-Jeoire. Then turn left briefly on the D903 and watch for the D9 right, signposted Fillinges, Samoëns and Vallée Verte. Follow this road to the Pont de Fillinges and then turn right on the D907, direction Taninges/Samoëns. (**Alternative** Go through Annemasse and take the D907, direction Taninges/Samoëns.)

The main street of Samoëns is a pedestrian precinct, so follow signs to Sixt which will take you round the village. Then turn left where it is signposted Col de Joux Plaine and Morzine. Take the first turning right (D354) to Les Moulins/Morzine on a narrow uphill road, and then at a left-hand bend take the still narrower road straight ahead, signposted Les Allamands/Les Chavonnes/Refuge de Tornay (this is easy to miss, so be careful). Continue up this road by two car parks and through the hamlet of Les Allamands (just over 4km) till you get to a third car park where you leave your car.

The Route

(1) At the entrance to the car park there is a noticeboard which says Plan aux Arches alt. 1098m, with a map showing the Tour des Dents Blanches and signs to the Refuge and Col de Bostan. The way up is at the end of the car park to the left, where there is no sign, but red/white GR marks on a rock and tree. The wide, stony path goes up through woodland, climbing gradually. After 10mins ignore the sign to the right which says Bostan Palatieu (according to the map this could be a shorter way, but the author has not tried it). Continue straight on and over a cattle-grid where there is a sign Forêt de Bostan, alt. 1444m. A few minutes later you are out in the open in a sort of narrow valley which never really opens up fully. Here you get your first uninterrupted view of the imposing rock face of the Dents d'Oddaz to the right. This magnificent wall of fissured rock accompanies you all the way to the Col de Bostan.

Continue upwards through Alpine pastures, passing the old cattle hut of Chalet de Bostan, alt. 1602m, on your right with another signpost and, shortly after, an old stone water trough which is in a very strategic spot for a drink on hot day (1hr 15mins).

Keep going past a more modern chalet, with the Refuge de Tornay/Bostan visible ahead (the refuge is known as both Tornay and Bostan), to reach a signpost at Le Ramble, alt. 1796m, indicating left to the Col de la Golèse (this is a short cut across, which can be used if you do not wish to go all the way to the Tête de Bostan).

(2) Continue straight and you see the Refuge de Tornay/Bostan, alt. 1763m, down on the right, a fairly recent building and a popular overnight stop for people doing the Dents Blanches circular walk, which takes about six days (1hr 45mins).

Refuge de Tornay/Bostan (French Alpine Club), 74340 Samoëns, tel 0450.90.10.94.
Open summer and winter seasons, plus weekends and holidays.

Following signs and the red/white splashes the path gains height steadily. Here you are crossing flat,

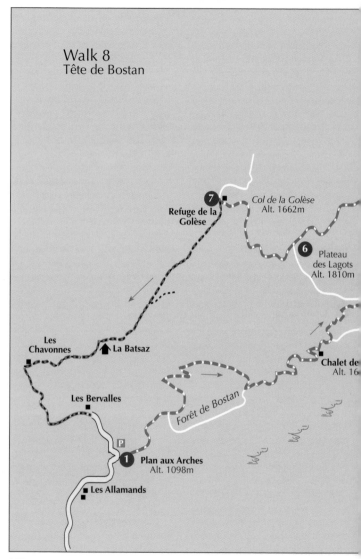

Walk 8
Tête de Bostan

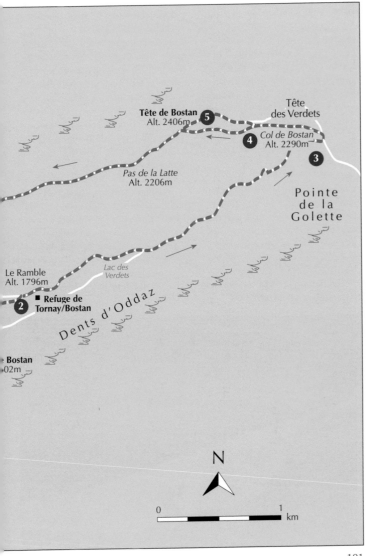

rocky terrain, indicating that hundreds of years ago the valley was covered by a glacier. After 15mins you get your first view of the Col de Bostan on the horizon. When you come to the Lac des Verdets down on your right (it shrinks to a muddy puddle in summer) the path crosses over and joins another path coming up from the right. You are now climbing more steeply through a jumble of big boulders.

In July and August you will see lots of tall purple monkshood, lilac-coloured hairy adenostyles with their big leaves, and clusters of forget-me-nots, amongst a profusion of other flowers.

Take time to turn round and appreciate the magnificent view down the valley. Where there is a path going off right, stick to the main one with the red/white GR splashes. You think that you are nearly at the summit, but the path goes over a hump and you see that there is another steep climb ahead! You need a lot of puff for the last part, which is steep but defined and not technically difficult. It is nevertheless a relief to reach the Col de Bostan, alt. 2290m (3hrs 30mins).

Here you are rewarded by sweeping views on all sides. In front is Planachaux, the top of the ski resort of Champèry in Switzerland, with the Rhône valley beyond. On the skyline are the Vaudois Alps with the ski resort of Leysin nestling halfway up. To the right are the daunting peaks of Les Dents Blanches (meaning white teeth), from the Pointe de la Golette,

Col de Bostan

View of the Dents Blanches from the Col de Bostan

alt. 2638m, to the Dent de Barme, alt. 2756m, and to the left is the green mound of the Tête de Bostan. (This is the obvious place for a picnic before tackling the rather airy way back.)

(3) Go left at the signpost indicating Tête de Bostan/Refuge Col de la Golèse. (Right goes to the Refuge de Vogealle and Refuge de Folly. This is the path you would take on the difficult way round the Dents Blanches – it is often covered in snow, even in summer, and should only be attempted by experienced walkers). The col is on the French/Swiss border and there is a yellow signpost to the Swiss destinations of Luibrome/Pas de Bide and Barme.

The return path goes round the back of the Tête des Verdets ridge and is quite exposed and rocky, with a steep slope down on the left as you approach the Tête de Bostan.

(4) After 15mins you come to an undefined fork. The left fork takes you round the bottom of the Tête de Bostan and the right one up to the summit, so take your choice! Be careful, as there are various sheep trails which are confusing. (**Note** All along the ridge there are no markings.) It is worth going up to the top, alt. 2406m, as you get a good view of the peaks around Morzine and Les Hauts Forts ridge (the highest point in the Chablais region). You can now see the top of the Mont Blanc range behind the Dents d'Oddaz (*dents* meaning 'teeth'), which is a magnificent sight, the glistening, snow-covered peaks

103

contrasting with the sombre d'Oddaz ridge, which from here really does look like a row of teeth. The path continues along the top of the wide, exposed ridge, passing three cairns, gradually losing height and then going down steeper. Down on the right are interesting rock formations, and the valley of the Dranse river down to Morzine. Towards the end of the valley is a small, attractive lake, the Lac des Mines d'Or, where the Hôtel/Refuge Mines d'Or is situated (see Walk 27, Book 1), a popular stopping-off place for tourists (4hrs 15mins).

(5) There are glorious views in all directions as you pick your way down the slope to meet the lower, alternative path and descend to the Pas de la Latte. Keep going straight, always walking along the top of the wide ridge where you get better views (on two occasions you can go left on a lower path). After a while you start to wind down the shoulder to reach signposts at the Plateau des Lagots, alt. 1810m (5hrs).

(6) Continue straight, signposted Refuge/Col de la Golèse. (If you go left, signposted Refuge de Bostan – a conflict of names, as it is also called Tornay – you get back to No. 2 just below the refuge. It is a narrow, rocky path, but quite easy. You then continue down on the original upward route.)

As your path curls round the hillside you can see down to the refuge at the Col de la Golèse and the long jeep track going up to it. Pick your way down to the refuge, as there are a number of paths and it can be con-

Refuge de la Golèse, Col de la Golèse, 74340 Samoëns, tel 0450.34.43.80. Accommodation for 60 people in three dormitories.

fusing. The building is not very attractive, having a new corrugated-iron roof with a modern extension stuck on the end. However, when it is open there are tables and chairs outside and it is a welcome stop for refreshment (5hrs 15mins).

(7) You have now joined the GR5 on a jeep track going down through open pastures, passing large barns down in the shallow valley to the left with herds of cows. Keep on the main track and ignore a sign left saying Les Allamands/Samoëns. The stony track seems to go on and on as it descends through open meadowland, finally reaching woodland where it continues down past two signs saying Les Chavonnes, and becomes a tarmac road about 5mins from the carpark (6hrs 30mins).

TANINGES/PRAZ DE LYS AREA

WALK 9

Pointe de Marcelly
Alt. 1999m (Taninges/Praz de Lys area)

Difficulty	Medium/difficult – this is a ridge walk so some places are somewhat airy and not for anyone suffering from vertigo – there is a tricky stretch at the end where there are cables, but there is an alternative path round to avoid these
Time	4hrs
Height gain	470m and 69m
Maps	Editions Didier & Richard IGN No. 3 Massifs du Chablais Faucigny & Genevois 1:50,000
	Cartes IGN 3429 ET Top 25 Bonneville/Cluses 1:25,000
Depart from	Praz de Lys – 1510m
Signposting	Some signposts and posts with green arrows, but not always where needed; orange and turquoise splashes along the ridge

The Pointe de Marcelly is a dramatic walk, as the long ridge with its enormous cross at the summit dominates the town of Taninges and is a landmark for the entire region. It is very popular, as the views from the ridge are magnificent, especially of the Mont Blanc range. Although an airy ridge walk, it is within the capabilities of most walkers with a head for heights, but it should not be attempted in wet weather when the rocks are slippery. As this is a classic walk of the region it is best to avoid the inevitable crowds on Sundays in July and August.

Access (from Geneva)

Take the motorway, direction Chamonix, and exit at No. 15 Boëge/St-Jeoire. Then turn left briefly on the D903 and watch for the D9 right, signposted Fillinges, Samoëns and Vallée Verte. Follow this road to the Pont de Fillinges and then turn right on the D907, direction Taninges/Samoëns. (**Alternative** Go through Annemasse and take the D907, direction Taninges/Samoëns.)

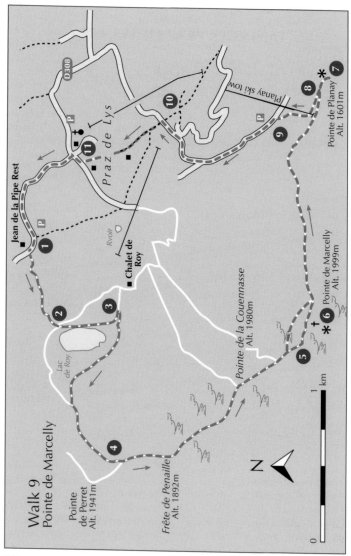

Walk 9
Pointe de Marcelly

From Taninges take the D902, sign-posted Les Gets, and at Le Pont des Gets (7km out of Taninges) turn left on the D328 and then left again on the D308, signposted Praz de Lys. Go through the ski station in the direction of the Col de Ramaz (at an intersection you can go either left or right as the roads join up later), following signposts to the Restaurant Jean de la Pipe at Les Molliettes. Park your car opposite the restaurant.

The Route

(1) Walk up the road from the restaurant and on the first corner take a defined path (no signpost) which climbs up fairly steeply over bare hillside, crossing a stream to a crest. Here there is a signpost indicating straight, Pic de Marcelly (a more direct way to the ridge), and left, Pic de Marcelly par La Couennasse, which is a more interesting route round the side of the Lac de Roy (20mins).

(2) Turn left, recrossing the stream, and take the path round the side of the lake where there is an intriguing notice at the edge of the water saying Beware of Vipers. Where the path continues round the end of the lake, go straight until you see large chalets over the crest and a defined grassy track coming up from the chalets.

(3) Bear right on this track and continue upwards towards the path you can see ahead coming up from the signpost. Turn left when you get to the wider track and continue climbing for a few minutes. **Careful** – on a corner watch for a narrow path up to the left (there is a post with green arrows, but not immediately visible) which takes you to the top of the ridge and a signpost saying you are at the Frête de Penaille, alt. 1892m (1hr). (**Note** The actual Frête de Penaille peak is further along the ridge.)

(4) Bear left towards the Pointe de Marcelly (the path on the right goes to the Pointe de Perret, alt. 1941m, and Pointe de Haute Fleury, alt. 1981m). You are now walking along a wide ridge with impressive views of the surrounding peaks on either side. Down on the right you can see the road you came up and the valley of the Giffre with Taninges, and on the left are the peaks of Pointe d'Uble, Pointe de Chalune and the Roc d'Enfer with the Lac de Roy and Praz de Lys in the valley below. About 10mins along the ridge look for a path down to the right (no signpost and **not on the map**), dropping steeply for a short distance, and then turn left at a T-junction (post here) back up to the original path. **Careful** – if you continue you come to a rather difficult short scramble down some rocks with a steep drop on the right – this is not recommended.

Shortly after you reach the Frête de Penaille, alt. 1892m (the one on the map), which is the first peak along the ridge, and 15mins later you come to the second peak, the Pointe de

Couennasse, alt. 1980m, at a cairn. (The name is marked faintly in red on a rock, so you know you are there!) You can now see the Pointe de Marcelly in front – a towering rock with a large cross on top and a magnificent view of Mont Blanc beyond (1hr 30mins).

(5) Warning If you suffer from vertigo, watch for a path off to the left (signposted) just before you reach the airy scramble to the top. This path goes down steeply and round to meet a T-junction. Turn up right and continue upwards, steeply over boulders, to reach the cross at the top. This path is longer but avoids the more vertiginous direct route (and is the way you will return). Otherwise the path becomes quite precipitous, and at the end you are scrambling over rocks for about 40m while hanging onto steel cables. The climb is not difficult for those who like doing this sort of thing (I find it exhilarating), but do not attempt it otherwise. From the top of the cables there is a short walk to the summit marked by an tall, ugly iron cross painted yellow and held down by long wires (2hrs).

(6) There is an incredible view from the pointe, alt. 1999m. The peak juts out over and dominates the town of Taninges, and beyond you have a magnificent, uninterrupted view of the entire Mont Blanc range and the Dents du Midi. (This is a good place to have your picnic if it is not too

108

windy and you are there on an uncrowded week day – otherwise you could find that there are lots of people up here and it is not exactly peaceful.)

Do not go down via the cables, but take the rocky path which comes up from the back which is the same as the easier way up. You descend steeply to the T-junction where you turn down right.

Continue down, picking your way over the boulders carefully and gradually losing height. The surroundings are open, with glorious views on either side and lots of low alpenrose bushes. Where there is a choice of path, just before a rocky outcrop, go down to the left as this is easier than the path over the top. As you descend you go through patches of low woodland, and pass a large wooden cross on the left which is a memorial to Marc Claude who died here on Christmas Day 1974 (one wonders how, as it is not a dangerous place) (2hrs 40mins).

The path loses height as you walk on, passing the top of the Téléski de Planay. Ignore any paths branching off until you reach the Pointe de Planay, alt. 1601m, which is a hump at the very end of the ridge and a popular jumping-off spot for parapenting (3hrs 15mins).

(7) There is a convenient bench for contemplating the extended views of the surrounding peaks. You can see right up the Arve and Giffre valleys from the town of Cluses almost to Chamonix, and from Taninges to Samoëns. Nearby is the distinctive peak of the Môle, which divides the two valleys, and the Pointe de Chevran above Cluses.

(8) Retrace your steps for about 150m and then, following the signpost, take the jeep track down right through some woodland and across an open slope, passing another path joining from the left. The path goes under the Planay ski-tow and then straight at a crossroad before reaching a narrow road going to a chalet with a small parking area opposite (3hrs 15mins).

(9) Turn left down the road and you come to the first chalets of the Praz de Lys area. Continue for another 15mins and just before a new bridge above the road, which you can see from the hill, take the path left (no signpost).

(10) This track crosses the plateau area with ski-tows and various chalets (go straight at a crossroads). It deteriorates just before the end, but continue straight and you will reach the road again by an ugly block of flats with a tiny chapel beyond.

(11) Turn right at the side of the flats and then almost immediately left at a T-junction with a sign to the Jean de la Pipe restaurant. Follow the road for about 10mins till you reach your car (4hrs).

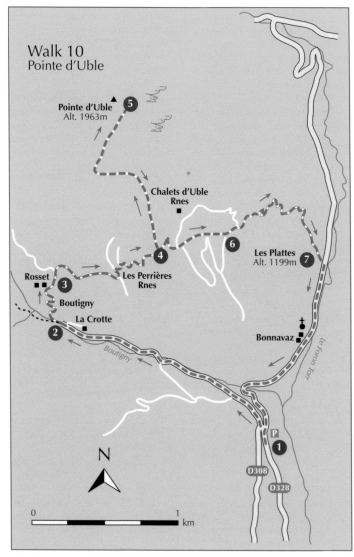

Walk 10
Pointe d'Uble

Pointe d'Uble
Alt. 1963m ▲ **5**

Chalets d'Uble
Rnes ■

Les Perrières
Rnes **4** **6**

Les Plattes
Alt. 1199m **7**

Rosset ■ ■ **3**

Boutigny

La Crotte ■

2

Boutigny

† ●
Bonnavaz ■

Le Foron Torr

P **1**

D308

D328

N

0 — 1
km

WALK 10

Pointe d'Uble
Alt. 1963m (Tangines/Praz de Lys area)

Difficulty	Medium, though steep in places; don't walk along the ridge if you suffer from vertigo
Time	4hrs 45mins
Height gain	798m
Maps	Editions Didier & Richard IGN No. 3 Massifs du Chablais Faucigny & Genevois 1:50,000
	Cartes IGN 3528 ET Top 25 Morzine Massif du Chablais 1:25,000 or Cartes IGN 3429 ET Top 25 Bonneville/Cluses 1:25,000
Depart from	Les Côtes – 1165m
Signposting	Good some of the way – white signposts and posts with yellow arrows on green background

The walk is quite a surprise, because the way up to the pointe is not so interesting, but when you reach the ridge summit there is an unforgettable panorama, especially of the Roc d'Enfer ridge, one of the most impressive mountains in this area. The flowers in springtime are lovely and in the autumn the woods are full of interesting fungi, including the large red variety with white spots.

Access (from Geneva)

Take the motorway, direction Chamonix, and exit at No. 15 Boëge/St-Jeoire. Then turn left briefly on the D903 and watch for the D9 right, signposted Fillinges, Samoëns and Vallée Verte. Follow this road to the Pont de Fillinges and then turn right on the D907, direction Taninges/Samoëns. (**Alternative** Go through Annemasse and take the D907, direction Taninges/Samoëns.) At Taninges take the D902 signposted Les Gets, and at Le Pont des Gets turn left on the D328 towards Praz de Lys. Continue for about 2km to a place called Les Côtes. Look for a small parking area to the right, just after a small chalet, immediately before the D328 goes off to the right, where the D308 comes in from Praz de Lys.

The Route

(1) Walk up the D308 (ignore the D328 to Morzine – this is where you rejoin at the end of the walk) and take the narrower tarmac road which goes straight on at the hairpin and is sign-posted to La Crotte. You are walking along an attractive, narrow wooded valley with the Boutigny river rushing down on the right in a ravine and a wooded hill up on the left. After 10mins the road levels with the stream and becomes flat and easy. You pass a signpost on the left before crossing over a bridge into coniferous trees, where you will find a variety of fungi growing in the autumn. You reach a large wooden barn on the right called La Crotte (25mins).

(2) Take the wide path up to the right, signposted Pointe d'Uble/Les Munes (the road continues on as a jeep track). Just before an iron barrier go right again, signposted Chalets de Rosset, on a narrow, sunken path bordered by pines. A few minutes later you come into open meadowland and zigzag steeply to reach the chalets (35mins).

(3) Go straight past the three huts to reach a signpost indicating Pointe d'Uble. Continue on the rocky path which then bears to the right, going upwards round the contour of the slope through coniferous trees. You go through a wooden barrier and out into attractive meadowland, passing the almost hidden ruins of Les Perrières, to reach a wooden sign with a green spot on it and a post with yellow arrows.

Follow the signs up left, ignoring a path off to the right and, a few minutes later, bear right at a further post. The path zigzags up steeply through another patch of coniferous forest and then comes out out again into open grassland, continuing upwards to reach a humpy ridge where there is a wooden edifice and a signpost. Here there are masses of purple violets in springtime, and you can see ahead Mont Chéry, the top of the ski conglomeration above Les Gets, and the jagged peaks of the Roc d'Enfer to the left (1hr 30mins).

(4) Go left following the sign Pointe d'Uble lhr (straight goes to Bonnavaz, which you take on your return). You are now climbing up to the summit of the pointe over open pastureland on a path which is steep and tiring. The path winds over to the left and become slightly rocky and fragmented, so it is really easier to pick your own way to the top.

(5) The terrain suggests that the pointe will be another grassy hump, but in fact you come on to a ridge, the ground dropping away in front very abruptly, which is most unexpected. This is the Pointe d'Uble, alt. 1963m (2hrs 30mins).

The views all round are impressive, especially the Roc d'Enfer straight ahead with the Pointe de Chalune to the left and the Haute

Pansies on the Pointe d'Uble

Pointe behind. Below to your left is the Lac de Roy and the jagged crest of the Pic de Marcelly above Praz de Lys. If you walk to the end of the ridge, which takes 5mins, you will appreciate the sudden dramatic drop.

Retrace your steps to the signpost at No. 4 on the map and turn left through the barrier following the sign Bonnavaz. You can see the Chalet d'Uble below, but you never actually reach it. The track goes down, passing a small wooden chalet on the right. Follow the wooden posts with yellow arrows carefully here as they are not easy to see and the path is not well defined. At a T-junction (post) go right (left goes to the Chalet d'Uble). Keep on the wide, grassy path which goes down to meet a wider track (3hrs 50mins).

(6) Turn down left and shortly after the path becomes a defined jeep track. You go through a wooden turnstile and into coniferous woods. After 30mins of winding down through the forest you reach the road at a sign Les Plattes, alt. 1199m (4hrs 20mins).

(7) Turn right and walk down the road with the River Foron on the left. On the right you pass the hamlet of Bonnavaz, which has an attractive little chapel with a huge golden weather vane in the shape of a cockerel, and an imposing wooden door. The road crosses the Boutigny stream which rushes attractively over boulders before joining the River Foron. After 25mins you arrive at the hairpin bend and the point of departure (4hrs 45mins).

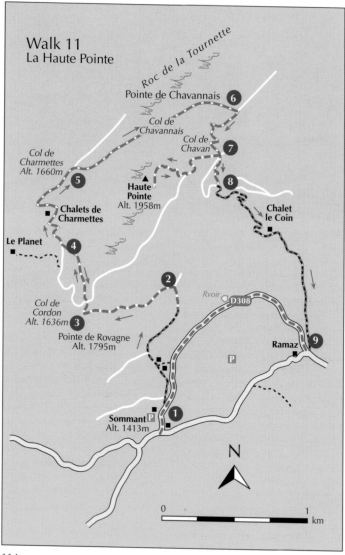

Walk 11
La Haute Pointe

Roc de la Tournette

Pointe de Chavannais 6

Col de Chavannais

Col de Chavan 7

Col de
Charmettes
Alt. 1660m 5

Haute
Pointe
Alt. 1958m

8

Chalet
le Coin

Chalets de
Charmettes

Le Planet 4

Col de
Cordon
Alt. 1636m 3

Pointe de Rovagne
Alt. 1795m

2

Rvoir D308

P

Ramaz 9

Sommant P
Alt. 1413m 1

N

0   1
km

WALK 11

La Haute Pointe
Alt. 1958m (Taninges/Praz de Lys area)

Difficulty	Medium, though steep in places
Time	3hrs 15mins, plus 1hr if you climb to the pointe
Height gain	455m (545m to the pointe)
Maps	Editions Didier & Richard IGN No. 3 Massifs du Chablais Faucigny & Genevois 1:50,000
	Cartes IGN 3429 ET Top 25 Bonneville/Cluses 1:25,000
Depart from	Sommant – 1413m
Signposting	New signposts and posts with yellow arrows, as well as some (faded) splashes, but not always obvious or where you really need them

Once you get round the other side of the mountain, away from Sommant where there are a number of ski-lifts, you come into unspoilt and peaceful mountain scenery. Do this walk in springtime as the flowers are particularly abundant here, especially big trumpet gentians, various orchids, and king cups and marsh marigolds in the valley. However, make sure that the snow has left the north side as too much makes walking round impossible. It is worth the extra effort to go to the Haute Pointe summit if you want a panoramic view of the entire region (don't forget to look out for marmots!).

Access (from Geneva)

Take the motorway, direction Chamonix, and exit at No.15 Boëge/St-Jeoire. Then turn left briefly on the D903 and watch for the D9 right, signposted Fillinges, Samoëns and Vallée Verte. Follow this road to the Pont de Fillinges and then turn right in the D907, direction Taninges/Samoëns. (**Alternative** Go through Annemasse and take the D907, direction Taninges/Samoëns.) Follow this road for 15.6km to Mieussy. Go through the village, and at a roundabout just after take the D308 direction Messy/Sommand/Col de Ramaz. Continue uphill for about 11km to Sommand, a downhill and cross-country ski station situated in an attractive wide bowl in the mountains. Turn left in front of the Hotel du Lac (towards the Col de Ramaz) and leave your car in a small parking lot on the left-hand side, just after a new self-service bar.

The Route

(1) Go right on the road and then take the first left turning after the new self-service bar, on a jeep track, where there is a sign Sommand 1413m/Col de Cordon 40mins. The track goes behind scattered chalets, bending to the right where you see the first post with yellow arrows, and narrows to a grassy path. Continue on straight through open grassland (ignoring a path going off left), with a fence and crumbling intermittent stone wall to the right, until you come to the end of the fir trees (20mins).

(2) Bear left at a further post with yellow arrows and follow the track, marked with faded blue and white splashes, up and back along the hillside, but higher up. Just before the col the path goes through an attractive dell where there are lots of interesting orchids in springtime. Ahead on the left is the rocky pinnacle of the Pointe de Rovagne, alt. 1795m. When you reach the Col de Cordon ridge at alt. 1636m you can see both ways – back to the Mont Blanc range and Col de Ramaz and ahead to the mountains of the Vallée Verte, Les Voirons and the Jura on the horizon (40mins).

(3) Go right on the well-defined path signposted Les Charmettes and ignore the path going straight on. The path

116

undulates downwards round the mountain, with fairly steep slopes descending on the left into a wide, attractive, unspoilt valley where you can see a jeep track and the chalets of Le Planet. Higher up you can also see the Chalets de Charmettes which you are making for. The track goes through rocky, scree-type terrain which is natural marmot country.

If you keep quiet you may well see one of these huge furry creatures running across the rocks. Listen for the piercing whistle which is uttered by the marmot who is acting as sentry to warn the others that danger is approaching.

(4) Continue straight where the path descends to meet the jeep track going up past Le Planet to Les Charmettes (there is a faded white arrow on a rock saying Sommand to the right). The path continues up past the Chalets de Charmettes, alt. 1620m (1hr).

Go past the chalets and, at the next corner, take the narrow, grassy path which goes straight on (there are no markings here). (**Note** This is a short cut, so you can just stay on the main jeep track if you prefer.) You can already see a signpost at the Col des Charmettes on the skyline, so make for this landmark. Eventually you meet up with the main track going to the col (1hr 10mins).

(5) There is a fence, a gate and a signpost at the Col des Charmettes, alt.

1660m. **Careful** – do not go through the gate, which seems the obvious way, but turn right on a narrow, grassy track which curls back the way you came, but higher, marked with yellow/red splashes. Keep a lookout as this area is riddled with marmots.

Every time I have done this walk I have seen a marmot at this spot. It is amusing to watch the antics of these big furry creatures, as they amble around sniffing at rocks and rooting for food (see Wildlife in the introduction for more).

The path goes straight and very steeply up the side of the mountain. About three-quarters of the way up, just before some scree, take a grassy track to the left (well indicated with a red/yellow splash). If you look back you have a good view of the impressive Môle mountain which stands out in splendid isolation.

Walk right along the top of the ridge to the Col de Chavannais. There is a steep drop on the left over the edge of a huge cliff (Roc de la Tournette) and a good view down to the Bellevaux valley. At a grassy T-junction bear right upwards and then left at the next junction which takes you over the col to signposts (1hr 35mins).

(6) Go right, following the indication Col de Chavan, on a path which you can see going along the side of the mountain (straight goes to La Chèvrerie). Where the path forks (red/yellow splash), take the lower path which goes down and then up again, as the higher fork peters out. (**Note** Go back if there is too much snow, as this is the north side of the mountain where snow can linger in thick patches till quite late in the season.)

The path goes over some scree and in places you have to pick your way – at one point it climbs up over some rocky steps. Look for the red/yellow splashes carefully as sometimes they are difficult to see. At a grassy T-junction turn upwards to reach the path from the Col de Chavan going to the Haute Pointe. (**Note** This is a short cut, so if you do not want to go to the Haute Pointe turn left to reach the Col de Chavan, alt. 1157m.) (2hrs 15mins.)

(7) From the col it is possible to follow the sign up to the Haute Pointe, which says 40mins. The path is marked with intermittent blue splashes and is fairly clear until just below the summit, where it could benefit from some direction splashes. At a rather undefined junction take the path down left, which may seem the wrong way, but takes you round the slope and up to the ridge avoiding the rocks. The view from the top is spectacular. Starting from the west in a semicircle: the Pointe des Brasses, the Pointe de Miribel, the Hirmentaz ridge and Les Voirons in the Vallée Verte, the Grand Rocher de

Nifflon and Pointe de la Gay near the village of Bellevaux with La Dent d'Oche in the background; the Pointe de Chalune with the Roc d'Enfer behind, the Pointe de Folly and the Pointe d'Uble near Praz de Lys, the cross of the Pointe de Marcelly ridge dominating Taninges with the nearby Pointe Fleurie, and finally the lone Môle peak. On the southern skyline are the higher Alpine ranges, including Mont Blanc. (It takes about 20mins to descend to the col, making it 1hr in total.)

From the Col de Chavan follow the sign Chalet du Coin/Sommand down the grassy hillside to a new-looking chalet at the start of a jeep track.

(8) Turn right down the jeep track towards the road you can see below heading for the Col de Ramaz. The track goes past another chalet (called Le Coin on the map, but marked L'Escape on the chalet), and then further chalets to reach the tarmac road (3hrs).

(9) Turn right and walk down to the parking spot (3hrs 15mins).

NEAR ST-JEOIRE

WALK 12

Pointe des Brasses
Alt. 1503m (Near St-Jeoire)

Difficulty	Difficult/medium (only due to height gain) – a stony jeep track up and down, but worth it for the glorious views at the top
Time	5hrs
Height gain	823m
Maps	Editions Didier & Richard IGN No. 3 Massifs du Chablais Faucigny & Genevois 1:50,000
	Cartes IGN 3429 ET Top 25 Bonneville/Cluses 1:25,000
Depart from	Entreverges – 680m
Signposting	Signposts and posts with yellow arrows – also blue splashes

Despite the rather long, stony track up and down, this is a really lovely circular walk with magnificent views. The area is very popular for cross-country skiing, hence the number of ski-lifts which rather spoil the landscape.

Access (from Geneva)

Take the motorway, direction Chamonix, and exit at No.15 Boëge/St-Jeoire. Then turn left briefly on the D903 and watch for the D9 right, signposted Fillinges, Samoëns and Vallée Verte. Follow this road to the Pont de Fillinges and then turn right on the D907, direction Taninges/Samoëns. (**Alternative** Go through Annemasse and take the D907, direction Taninges/Samoëns.) Continue straight through the traffic lights at Le Brochet (Viuz-en-Sallaz to the left), and about 2.5km later look for a small sign off to the left saying Entreverges (just before the D26 to St-Jeoire). Go up this narrow road and take the first turning to the left, signposted Les Brons. Go straight to a crossroads and bear left on a stony track (there is a road to flats on the right and straight ahead is a disused quarry). The road becomes stony and bumpy, so it is easier to park on the left before reaching a larger parking area where there are signs and an information board. To the left is a huge quarry reached by a tarmac road, but there are often big trucks going up and down this way, so it is best avoided.

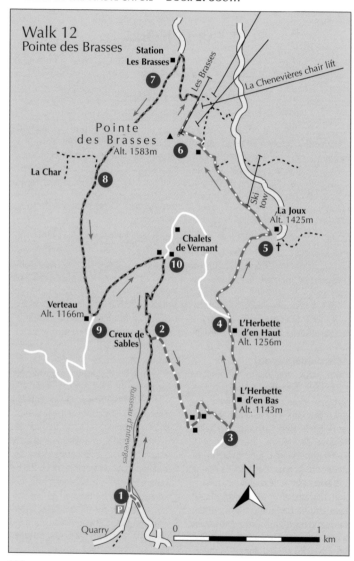

Walk 12
Pointe des Brasses

Station
Les Brasses

Les Brasses

La Chenevières chair lift

Pointe
des Brasses
Alt. 1583m

La Char

La Joux
Alt. 1425m

Ski tow

Chalets
de Vernant

Verteau
Alt. 1166m

Creux de
Sables

L'Herbette
d'en Haut
Alt. 1256m

L'Herbette
d'en Bas
Alt. 1143m

Ruisseau d'Entreverges

N

P
Quarry

0   1
km

The Route

(1) It takes about 5mins from the fork to the information board, which is headed Pointe des Brasses No. 6, and signposts. You start walking up a wide, wooded gorge with the Entreverges stream initially on your right, and then crossing under the path to the left after about 10mins. The jeep track goes up medium steep through beech and coniferous woodland. When you come to an intersection and a track going down left, go straight on as indicated by a wooden post to reach another intersection and signposts at the Creux de Sables, alt. 940m (35mins).

(2) Go up right (left is where you come out on your return), leaving the river down on your left. You initially climb up fairly steeply, and then the path levels out somewhat as it starts curling round the mountain. Through the trees (if there are no leaves) there are tantalising glimpses of the Arve valley below and the village of Viuz-en-Sallaz. At a fork, go left following a yellow splash (the right path goes down to a large chalet which you can see). Here there is a sign saying Réserve de Lièvres ('hare reserve'). Shortly afterwards you come out of the woods proper and into an attractive glade where there is another large chalet. The path is still defined and goes round the building and then winds up through meadowland with occasional trees. Ignore a path to the left just before reaching a newish chalet which you pass behind (1hr 15mins).

(3) Soon after, another path merges from the right (this is the way up from Pouilly) at a sign indicating L'Herbette d'en Bas alt.1143m. Bear left towards L'Herbette d'en Bas which takes you up on to the wide shoulder of the mountain.

Go past the few chalets of L'Herbette d'en Bas on the right (no signs) and then continue upwards towards the chalets of L'Herbette d'en Haut which are visible ahead. The path goes through a fence where there is a noticeboard and then into open pastureland. From this wide shoulder you get your first view of the Arve valley and the magnificent peaks of the Haute Savoie. From left to right: the Haute Pointe, Pointe de Chalune, Roc d'Enfer and the Pic de Marcelly above Taninges, with the Mont Blanc range on the horizon. Behind is the distinctive peak of the Môle.

Continue following the ridge (there is a post here) past L'Herbette d'en Haut, alt. 1256m, which consists of three houses and two outside toilets, one shabby looking and the other distinctly upmarket with a little path to it. (Since the author first did this walk an impenetrable fence has been put round these chalets.)

Near the large farmhouse down on your right there is a smart bath on a platform surrounded by tiles! On the top of the main door of the farm it

View of the Giffre valley from L'Herbette d'en Haut, Pointe des Brasses

says Domaine des Balisiers, Peney, Genève – Caves des Palais de Justice SA. The mind boggles. Is this where the law courts hide their reserves of wine so that they can come up to this relatively hidden spot and drink it? Does the Lord Chief Justice sit in the bath with his wig on and have a nip or two? One really does discover some intriguing places on these mountain walks!

After the farm look up on the right and you will see a small grotto in the rocks with a cross (rather spoilt by a sheet of galvanised iron over it). It is worth going to have a look inside, as there is a charming, natural stone statue of the Virgin Mary with a lovely maternal expression on her face. Normally the statues in these Alpine grottoes are painted, cheap looking and expressionless.

(4) At further signposts go straight, following the sign Pointe des Brasses par la Joux (left says Pointe des Brasses par Verteau). Following blue splashes, keep to the path which curls round the side of the hill through woodland and then into open country again. You pass a sign which says Pointe des Brasses, and then more signs indicating ahead to La Joux and left to Pointe des Brasses (2hrs).

Go straight to La Joux. You can see the top of the chair-lift at Les Brasses up on your left. The path follows the contour of the mountain through occasional coniferous trees. Keep a look out for the cross of La Joux, alt. 1425m, up on your right and either cut up across to it (no defined path to start with) or stick to the path which goes to the first chalet of La Joux itself. Then turn up right to the cross (2hrs 25mins).

(5) From here you get another magnificent view of the surrounding mountain peaks. Below are the half a dozen chalets of La Joux with a jeep track going up to them and a small pond. Following the sign Pointe des Brasses, make your way along the defined path on the grassy ridge, which goes behind a ski-tow. You can see the arrival point of the chair-lift from Les Chenevières, as well as other chair-lifts and ski-tows coming up from all directions.

Keep to the path, which at times is not very evident as you climb up a steepish hill to reach a large new chalet. The path goes in front of the chalet to reach a jeep track. Go right on the jeep track and shortly after you will see a blue splash and a narrow path left. Go left, which is a 15mins steep walk to the top of Les Brasses, alt. 1583m. The actual summit is rather ugly, being the end of a ski-tow and the site of a walkie-talkie transmitting station. However, the view is extensive, as you can not only see all the surrounding peaks, but also into the Vallée Verte down on one side, and on the other Lac Léman (Lake Geneva) with the Salève ridge and the Jura on the skyline (3hrs).

(6) Follow the ski-tow down. Bear left at the first intersection, just above the end of two other tows coming up from below. Do not go down to the defined jeep track further on where the chair-lift ends (there is a further chair-lift on your right). At the turning there are no signs, but a post and blue splashes appear later. At the bottom of the wide grassy track there is a big barn and signposts at a T-junction (3hrs 15mins).

(7) Bear left towards Verteau, past the barn on a wide track, beside an old stone wall where there is a row of stately fir trees. After lovely meadowland the path drops down through intermittent woodland and then levels out somewhat as it starts to curl round the mountain. You come to another T-junction at La Char, alt. 1260m (3hrs 30mins).

(8) Go left, following the sign to Verteau/Vernant, and continue on past a small new chalet on your right. Shortly after you pass another big chalet and a small shrine. Continue straight, ignoring any tracks branching off, on an undulating path which contours the mountain, through woodland to reach Verteau, alt. 1166m, consisting of a large chalet, a rusty old plough and another shrine below (3hrs 50mins).

(9) Following signs to Vernant/ Entreverges, go up left on a medium-steep path which then descends, still going round the mountain, through tall beech forest. (There is a little spring along this jeep track with a padlock on it and one wonders why on earth someone wants to lock up a water supply!) The track reaches Vernant, alt. 1225m, a group of chalets buried in woodland, at an intersection with signposts (4hrs 10mins).

(10) Go down right (straight on would take you back to L'Herbette/La Joux). You now follow the Entreverges stream again, below on the right, as you go down medium steep through woodland on a defined, stony jeep track. 20mins from Vernant you get back to the branch where you went up right to L'Herbette. From here you retrace the path to the car (5hrs).

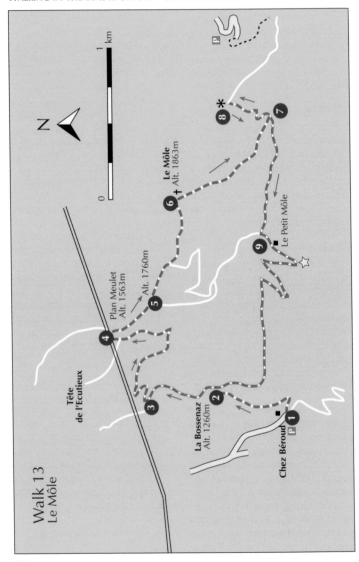

WALK 13

Le Môle

Alt. 1863m (Near St-Jeoire)

Difficulty	Medium/difficult – very steep at the end and somewhat airy coming down off the top (the traditional way is easier)
Time	4hrs
Height gain	703m
Maps	Editions Didier & Richard IGN No. 3 Massifs du Chablais Faucigny & Genevois 1:50,000
	Cartes IGN 3429 ET Top 25 Bonneville/Cluses 1:25,000
Depart from	Chez Béroud –1160m
Signposting	Good – white signs and posts with yellow arrows

From Geneva the lone peak of the Môle stands out clearly in front of the Alps – in fact it is sometimes mistaken for Mont Blanc. Dominating the confluence of the Giffre and Arve valleys, with the splendid panorama of the Haute Savoie Alps all round, this walk is a classic, and if any walk in the region should be done, this is the one. As it is not far from Geneva it is a very popular outing, so avoid sunny weekends in summer if you want to escape the 'madding crowd'. On a golden weekday in September I was alone and 'master of the world' at the top.

Access (from Geneva)

Take the motorway, direction Chamonix, and exit No.15 Boëge/St-Jeoire. Then turn left briefly on the D903 and watch for the D9 right, signposted Fillinges, Samoëns and Vallée Verte. Follow this road to the Pont de Fillinges and then turn right on the D907, direction Taninges/Samoëns. (**Alternative** Go through Annemasse and take the D.907 direc-tion Taninges/Samoëns.) Continue on the D907 and filter right on the D.12 signposted Perillonnex/Bonneville, just before the crossroads and lights in Les Brochets (Viuz-en-Sallaz to the left). At the first roundabout turn left and follow all signs to St-Jean-de-Tholome and Le Môle on the D9, and then turn right on the D20 (also signed Le Môle). At the church in St Jean turn up left (there is a signpost

125

saying Le Môle). Continue upwards for 5.5km through the village of Bovère to Chez Béroud at the end of the tarmac road. On the left-hand side there is a small restaurant, Le Relais de Môle, with parking space.

The Route

(1) At the end of the parking area follow the sign Bovère alt. 1160m, indicating Le Petit Môle/Le Môle/Marignier par les Granges, up a wide, defined jeep track to the right (Cars Prohibited sign). The going is medium steep uphill through shrub and woodland. Shortly after the start another wide track joins the jeep track. Do not go up a steep short cut to the right, but continue round on the main track to reach another signpost, La Bossenaz alt. 1260m (15mins).

(2) Go left, following the sign Le Môle par le Plan Meulet, on a wide forest track.

(**Alternative** The main path bending right, signed Buvette/Le Môle par Le Petit Môle, is the classic route to the summit and the easier way up.) Continue on the forest track, which goes in and out of woodland as it snakes up round the mountain to reach a T-junction in front of a pylon and a post with yellow arrows (30mins).

(3) Bear up to the right, passing underneath the pylon wires. Keep upwards on the main track and ignore any tracks branching off to the right. After going through a cattle fence you

come out on to Alpine pasture, underneath the pylon wires again, at Plan Meulet, alt. 1563m, where there is a signpost. To the left is the hump of the Tête de l'Ecutieux, alt. 1627m (there is a track leading to the top). Straight on is a path down to the hamlet of L'Ecutieux (the signpost says St Jean par La Bossenaz) and a glorious view into the Giffre valley and the town of St-Jeoire. You can see the Môle summit up on your right (1hr).

(4) Go up right, following the sign Le Môle, and keep to the side of the ridge, with the firs on your left, on a grassy path going over a small hump and alongside a fence before going through it. You then start to climb up another steep hump. Keep the fence on your left as the track winds up very steeply through scrubs and raspberry bushes. Keep to the main track till you reach another signpost at alt. 1760m.

(5) Continue up straight on a narrower track going up steeply. (**Alternative** Follow the main path bending right, indicating Le Môle. This easier track goes round the front of the mountain and meets the classical track coming up from Le Petit Môle. You pass another sign which points up left to Le Môle 5mins and down right to Le Petit Môle, which is the way down and back. Continue till you reach a large wooden cross.)

If you continue straight, keep climbing on a steep path up to the ridge. This is quite a tough ascent over

Summit of the Môle

open pastureland (ignore smaller paths off to the right), reaching a crest and a borne at alt.1863m. Keep going along the crest to reach the big wooden cross. The drop on the other side is very abrupt, so be careful (2hrs).

This summit is an enigma. When the author first did this walk in the early 1990s, there were no signposts and no wooden cross. The borne (boundary mark) was thought to be the summit, but in 1994 a cross was erected a few metres further on and this is now considered to be the top of the Môle. But it doesn't really matter, because wherever you are the views are wonderful.

It is worth the rather tough haul up for the magnificent open views on all sides of the surrounding Haute Savoie countryside, which include Lac Léman, with the Jura behind, and the entire Mont Blanc range. You can also see down the Arve valley with the town of Bonneville and, on the other side, the Giffre valley and the town of Taninges. (This is a favourite picnic stop, so there may be lots of people at the weekend.)

(6) If you have a good head for heights, continue along the ridge, if not, go back by the one of the various paths you can see snaking down the bare mountainside to the chalets below. The ridge path is rather airy and rocky, so watch your feet. It descends steeply for about 20mins to a large concrete block dated 1909. There are cows grazing here in summer and a signpost at alt. 1587m (2hrs 20mins).

(7) From the sign, walk along the continuation of the ridge for approximately 10mins to reach its

127

Looking back from the route to the summit of the Môle

end – do not continue on the path which descends to Les Granges.

(8) Take a few minutes to appreciate the strategic site of this magnificent mountain, which stands alone at the confluence of the Giffre and Arve valleys with the Mont Blanc range straight ahead. You can see the Giffre river flowing into the larger Arve, and in front, in the valley below, is the town of Cluses with Mont Chevran (Walk Number 3) behind. Left is the Pic de Marcelly above Taninges, with the Pointe de Chalune and the jagged peaks of the Roc d'Enfer. Return to the signpost at No. 7 (2hrs 40mins).

Following the sign St-Jean par le Petit Mole, you take an easy, undulating path along the front of the mountain through scattered fir trees and shrubs, till you come out into

open pastureland at the Petit Môle chalets, where there is an incredible assortment of animals such as goats, cows, geese and turkeys. There is also a little *buvette* (cafe) where you can buy drinks in summer, and a signpost alt. 1530m (3hrs).

(9) At the signpost skirt the chalet onto a wide jeep track at the side which goes across the open mountain to an impressive orientation table (here you can name all the peaks you are looking at). Carry on to two other little chalets, and then follow the wide, defined path downwards in and out of woodlands with lovely views into the valley below (this is where you join the path you came up, No. 2 on the map). Retrace your steps to the starting point (4 hrs).

ARAVIS/BORNE REGION

LA CLUSAZ AREA

WALK 14

Boucle des Confins
Alt. 1395m (La Clusaz area)

Difficulty	Easy – one stiff climb at the start
Time	4hrs
Height gain	About 300m (undulating)
Maps	Editions Didier & Richard IGN No. 2 Massifs des Bornes-Bauges 1:50,000
	Cartes IGN 3430 ET Top 25 La Clusaz/Grand-Bornand 1:25,000
Depart from	**Departure 1** The Parc parking area on the road to La Clusaz
	Departure 2 La Clusaz itself
Signposting	Good – lots of signposts and also yellow and blue markings; there is one place where there is no sign, so follow walk instructions carefully

A truly delightful walk as the path goes round a beautiful valley with glorious mountain scenery. There is some climbing at the start, but after that the path undulates along the side of the valley and there are no difficulties. It is a good walk for someone fit who hasn't got a head for heights. There are some beautiful farms and chalets to admire and, shortly after the snow melts, the slopes are bright with a myriad of alpine flowers which continue until late summer.

Access (from Geneva)

Take the motorway, direction Chamonix, and exit at No.16 Bonneville/La Clusaz. Follow the N203, signposted St-Pierre-en-Faucigny/La Clusaz, and shortly after

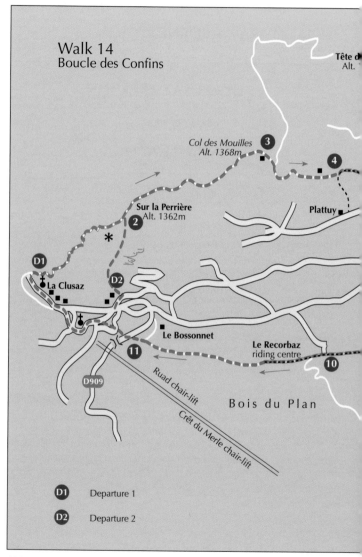

Walk 14
Boucle des Confins

Tête d
Alt.

Col des Mouilles ❸
Alt. 1368m

❹

Sur la Perrière
Alt. 1362m ❷

Plattuy

❋

D1

La Clusaz

D2

Le Bossonnet

Le Recorbaz
riding centre ❿

⓫

D909

Ruad chair-lift

Crêt du Merle chair-lift

B o i s   d u   P l a n

D1   Departure 1

D2   Departure 2

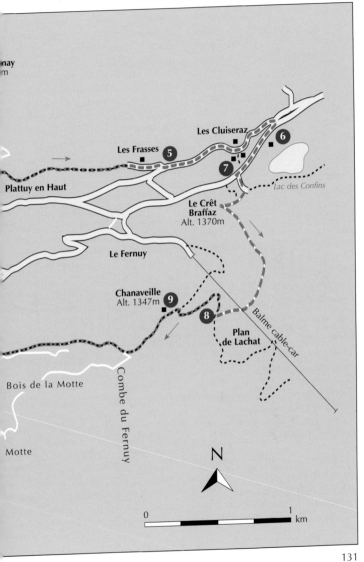

turn left on the D6, direction St-Pierre-en-Faucigny. At the roundabout in the village continue on the D6A over the railway line and then turn right on the D12, signposted La Clusaz. This road takes you up the Borne river valley, a narrow, twisting road through the villages of Petit-Bornand and Entremont. Continue on the D12 to St-Jean-de-Sixt and then take the D909 to La Clusaz.

Departure 1

If you want to park on the road just before you get to La Clusaz, look for a small parking area on the left with signposts and wooden steps going upwards. This is easier if you don't want to bother looking for parking space in La Clusaz.

Departure 2

At the start of the village go straight (do not bear down right, signposted Centre) and you come to a roundabout. Park near here or in the underground parking near the cinema (free parking all the year round). (**Note** Out-of-season parking is free, but otherwise there are parking meters everywhere, so parking could be difficult in July and August.)

The Route
Departure 1

(1) The sign says you are at Parc Parking, alt. 1030m. It also indicates Chapelle du Parc 200m/Col des Mouilles 1hr 30/Les Confins 2hrs 30mins/Tête du Danay 3hrs. Climb

the wooden steps and continue on a wide path to reach a small chapel dated 1615. Just before the chapel the path swings up left. Continue on this wide, wooded path which zigzags steeply up the side of the hill.

After 20mins you come to another signpost. Go up left following the sign Les Confins 1hr 55mins (the sign ahead indicates La Clusaz 20mins). The path continues to climb up through delightful beech woods to reach another signpost at Le Parc, a clearing in the woods. Continue to reach a viewpoint from where you can see over the town of La Clusaz nestling in the valley below, surrounded by the snowy peaks of the Aravis. Shortly after the path comes to Sur la Perrière, alt. 1362m (45mins). (**Note** This is where Departure 2 direct from La Clusaz comes in from the right.)

Departure 2

(1) Walk to the roundabout and then up the road, signposted Piscine (swimming pool). Turn left at the antiques shop (an old chalet) and continue till you see a wooden signpost on the right to La Perrière/Tour de Village/Circuit des Houches/Col des Mouilles. Take the grassy path up between new chalets, marked with yellow flashes, which is medium steep and goes behind apartment blocks. You come to an impressive jumble of huge grey rocks left behind by a massive landslide in the 19th century. Stop here and enjoy a

panoramic view over the valley and village of La Clusaz. The path becomes rocky. At a wooden cross follow a yellow splash and sign to Circuit des Houches/Toutes Directions. Take a right turn at a T-junction called La Perrière at the top of the rockfall – left is to Les Houches. Keep going upwards and ignore a turning shortly after to the right, signposted Clusaz/Nant/Le Bossonnet. (If you are walking in summertime the plants along this path are usually labelled.)

Climb some wooden steps and go left at another T-junction with no signpost (the right turning peters out into nothing). Go through scrubs and trees before coming to yet another signpost. Turn left to Les Confins, following the yellow splashes and arrows on a path climbing gently through dense vegetation and deciduous woodland. You arrive at Sur la Perrière, alt. 1362m, and another host of signposts (45mins). (**Note** This is where Departure 1 comes in from the left.)

(**2**) Directions are now the same for both departures. Follow the signpost to Col des Mouilles. You have stopped climbing and are now on a wide, undulating rocky path, crisscrossed with tree roots, going through tall pine woods, beech wood and clearings.

(**3**) Continue straight, passing further signs before coming out into lovely open meadowland at the Col des Mouilles, alt. 1368m, where there is an old barn. On your right there are lovely views of the outskirts of La Clusaz with ski-lifts on the horizon beyond (1hr 10mins).

At another bevy of signs continue straight to Les Confins. (Ignore a sign

Walking towards Les Confins

to the left indicating Tête du Danay.) You can now see the path going back to La Clusaz along the other side of the valley, below the splendid peaks of the various summits of the Aravis mountain chain. The path becomes a jeep track along the open side of the hill with lovely old chalets dotted around. After passing an old chalet on the left, cross over a narrow rivulet to some more signposts (1hr 15mins).

(4) Take the path up to the left, indicated Les Confins, following yellow splashes (straight on goes to La Clusaz par la Plattuy). Go past two further chalets, one displaying the name Plattuy en Haut (here there is a further sign left to the Tête du Danay). From here you start to descend gradually following yellow splashes towards the head of the valley. You arrive at a lovely old Savoyard farm (La Rousserolle) with chickens, a cat, geraniums hanging from the windows and the wood stacked up at the side ready for the winter. Just past the farm there are other chalets and a sign announcing you are at Les Frasses, alt. 1372m. Keep straight and you come immediately to a tarmac road and then later on to a wider road (1hr 50mins).

(5) Turn down left, signposted Confins, and walk down the road till you come to a signpost Les Cluiseraz alt. 1380m, indicating right to La Clusaz by the Bois de la Motte. This is a possible short cut on a shingly

134

track, through a meadow and past two old chalets, to reach another road at No. 7. (**Alternative** Continue on the road to the hamlet of Les Cluiseraz and a junction by a restaurant (a good place for refreshment).)

For an interesting detour, walk a few minutes further up the road to the little chapel at Les Confins dedicated to the 40 martyrs, St John the Baptist and St John the Evangelist. It was constructed a year after the big freeze of 1833 which, during the night of 2–3 September, destroyed the wheat and potato harvest, causing local hardship. The people of the valley made a petition to God, promising that if he gave them a good harvest the following year they would build a special chapel in thanksgiving – their wish was granted!

Near the door there is a plaque in memory of a young couple, members of the French Resistance in the Second World War, who were killed by Italian fascists in August 1943.

(6) Turn abruptly right at the junction and go down the road, with pretty Lac des Confins on the left, to reach a sign on the left, La Clusaz par le Bois de la Motte. There is also a sign Restaurant du Lac (2hrs).

(7) Go left on the wide track which shortly after reaches a T-junction. Go right, following the sign to La Clusaz par le Bois de la Motte (the track left takes you to the restaurant by the lake). **Careful** – after a few minutes there are further signs at the Crêt Braffaz, alt. 1370m, where the track hairpins left on to a narrower track. This takes you round the head of a valley on a very attractive path giving extended views of the surrounding mountains and down the valley to La Clusaz. The path contours the valley and goes under the Télécabine de la Balme and then up to reach signposts at the Plan de Lachat, alt. 1401m. Continue to follow signs to La Clusaz, passing a rocky area and then climbing over the brow of a hill to reach a wide unmade road and further signs.

(8) Turn down right (left goes to the Chalet de la Balme) and continue on the main track, ignoring all paths going off left or right, to arrive at another junction by the overhead wires of a further ski-lift and a large barn. There is a sign indicating you are at Chanaveille alt. 1347m (2hrs 30mins).

(9) Go left, following signs to La Clusaz, on a wide jeep track through the Bois de Merdassier to reach the Combe du Fernuy, alt. 1328m, a few minutes later at an intersection with signs. Continue straight down to La Clusaz (the GR Tour d'Aravis joins from the left here), going through deciduous and coniferous woods on the edge of the Bois de la Motte. The track passes another sign left to Crêt du Merle just before reaching Le Recorbaz, a big riding centre (3hrs).

(10) Continue straight and shortly after you can see the outskirts of La Clusaz down on the right. The track traverses a number of streams and narrows to a path as it continues through beech woods and open meadows. The path crosses the top of ski-lifts, with the beginner slopes of La Clusaz down to the right (you are quite high above the village). Continue to reach a T-junction.

(11) Here you can turn right to La Clusaz Nord/Bossonnet, which is easier if you have left your car in the village (Departure 2). When you meet the road below, turn right past a grotto with a statue of the Virgin (here there are lots of signs). Walk back to where you have parked your car.

If you started from Departure 1, turn left to Clusaz centre, which takes you along and down past a huge chair-lift (four double chairs) and under further télécabine wires to reach the road at another chair-lift station. Cross over the road and follow signs down a grassy path to reach a bigger road by the Crêt du Merle chair-lift. Turn down towards the church and then down left again to walk along a narrow road by the river (this is much nicer than walking along the main road into the village). This leads to the small car park on the other side where you started (4hrs).

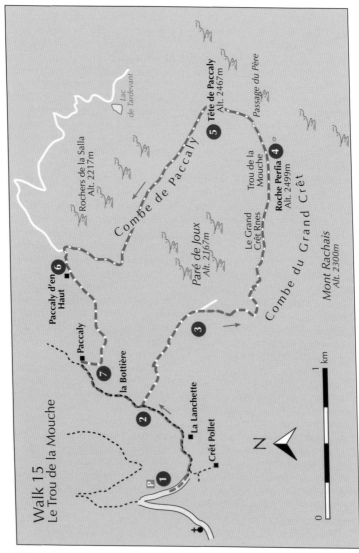

Walk 15
Le Trou de la Mouche

N

0   1 km

Lac de Tardevant

Tête de Paccaly
Alt. 2467m

⑤

Passage du Père

Rochers de la Salla
Alt. 2217m

Combe de Paccaly

Trou de la Mouche

Roche Perfia
Alt. 2499m

④

Le Grand
Crêt Rnes

Paré de Joux
Alt. 2167m

Combe du Grand Crêt

Mont Rachais
Alt. 2300m

⑥
Paccaly d'en Haut

③

Paccaly

⑦
la Bottière

②

La Lanchette

Crêt Pollet

P ①

✝

WALK 15

Le Trou de la Mouche
Alt. 2467m (La Clusaz area)

Difficulty	Difficult – a tough walk (**Warning** Do not do this walk unless the weather is good, you are fit, and above all *do not suffer from vertigo*.)
Time	5hrs 30mins
Height gain	1035m
Maps	Editions Didier & Richard IGN No. 8 Massifs du Mont Blanc/Beaufortain 1:50,000
	Cartes IGN 3430 ET Top 25 La Clusaz/Grand-Bornand 1:25,000
Depart from	L'Arpette, Les Confins (La Clusaz) – 1432m
Signposting	Signs at the beginning and end – some red arrows

This is a really dramatic walk – one that gets the adrenaline flowing, and can be quite frightening (although a friend from England strolled up it in his sneakers and declared it was nothing!). The views of Mont Blanc and the surrounding peaks are unforgettable. The walk can also be done the other way round (this is often shown in guidebooks). The advantage is that you can see the Trou from the very bottom and thus avoid going the wrong way, as we did the first time. However, you don't get the dramatic view of Mont Blanc as you go through the Trou, and you go up the very steep slope, instead of down it – a question of choice. (Incidentally, 'Le Trou de la Mouche' means 'the fly hole'!)

It is said that there is gold to be found in the Aravis, although the gold seekers who came in 1914 left again shortly after, having looked in vain, although there is an interesting local legend concerning goldmines. It is said that in the evenings a man would often pass the chalet of Paccaly-d'en-Haut from the direction of the Combe de Tardevant. Heavily laden, it seemed he had struck gold, but no one knew where his mine was to be found as he put his shoes on back to front to confuse pursuers. Years later, having made his fortune, he returned to La Clusaz from Paris and confided the whereabouts of the mine to two of his friends. Armed with a plan they set off for the

Combe de Tardevant. Unfortunately, on the way they drank too much 'eau de vie' and lost the directions – the site was never discovered.

Access (from Geneva)

Take the Chamonix motorway and exit at No. 16 Bonneville/La Clusaz. Then follow the N203, signposted St-Pierre-en-Faucigny/La Clusaz and shortly after turn left on the D6A, direction St-Pierre-en-Faucigny. At the roundabout in the village continue on the D6 over the railway line, and then turn right on the D12, signposted La Clusaz. This takes you up the Borne river valley, a narrow, twisting road through the villages of Petit-Bornand and Entremont. At St-Jean-de-Sixt take the D909 to La Clusaz. In La Clusaz follow a sign Lac des Confins onto a narrow road. After about 10mins (4.5km) you pass through Les Confins, where there is a little lake, and continue to the end of the road where there is a large car park called L'Arpette.

The Route

(1) Take the narrow tarmac road out of the car park, signposted Alt. 1466m Paccaly/La Bombardellaz/Le Planet. It deteriorates into a jeep track after a large farm on a bend to the right (Crêt Pollet) which sells Reblochon cheese (see Savoyard Food and Drink in the introduction). The track passes another farm called La Lanchette and reaches a further signpost on the right (10mins).

(2) Turn right to Combe du Grand Crêt. This is the real start of the walk, on a defined path over open grassy hillside, climbing steadily and often steeply, becoming rocky in places. Over on the right are dramatic slabs of fissured rock which look like a series of waterfalls. Follow the infrequent red arrows on

Walking towards Le Trou de la Mouche (photo by Colin Mitchell)

Looking through Le Trou de la Mouche

the rocks marking the path. You come to a large rock and a small sign, Trou de la Mouche (1hr).

(3) Take the path right marked Chemin des Paturages – this is a gentler path winding round the mountain. (**Note** Straight up will also take you to the Trou, but you must turn right at some ruins which are not easy to see, and you could make the same mistake as we did the first time and find yourself on a steep slope of scree.)

To the left is the Paré de Joux mountain, a towering rock 2167m high. At the foot of the rock face there is a large cave in front of which stands a sort of open stone coffin (sarcophagus). It looks as if it should house an Egyptian mummy, but has been converted as a watering trough for cows instead! It is worth taking about 5mins to walk over and see this.

The path makes a wide detour left towards Mont Rachais, alt. 2300m, on the other side of the Combe du Grand Crêt. It then winds back over steep pasture and zigzags upwards till it goes by some ruins (1hr 20mins). (**Note** It is easy to walk straight past these ruins. All that remains is the stone outline at grass level, which is only clearly visible from above. However, it does not really matter, as you just continue up the path all the way.) You will eventually see ahead the Trou de la Mouche, which tunnels through the gigantic Roche Perfia. It looks as if there are two holes from below, but in fact there is only one. The last part up to the hole is across a sort of wide stony shoulder where there is some grass.

Careful – try to keep to the path and the occasional red arrows which are not always easy to follow. This is a

139

steep path which it is also muddy and slippery in wet weather. Down on the right is an imposing valley of scree which should be avoided. Just before you get to the top, keep to the left where it is less steep. The long, steep haul to the top is worth it when you pass through the dramatic arched hole in the solid rock. (There is a sobering plaque to Mathieu Meugnot of the 27ème BCA army unit, who died here aged 24 on the 16 January 2002.)

On our way up we met two dear old men who later informed us proudly that they were in their seventies and had been walking all their lives – one of them had climbed Mont Blanc in 1936. They knew every peak on the horizon and their estimate of how long it would take to reach the Trou, and their advice to keep to the left at the top, were spot on. Although starting after us, they nipped down the steep centre of the combe on the way back and were well ahead. One cannot but admire these incredible 'men of the mountains'.

The view is magnificent. Straight ahead is the continuation of the Aravis range, terminating in the regal peak of the Pointe Percée, alt. 2750m. To the right is the nearby snow-covered Mont Blanc range in all its glory, and further right in the background are the Grande Casse and other mountains of the Vanoise. Below is the Val d'Arly with the road going through Mégève to join the Arve

140

valley – this is one of the most extensive and breathtaking views in the whole region (3hrs).

(4) The path down from the Trou is marked on the map with little blue dots, and not without reason, as it is indeed steep and very exposed. **This is not a path for anyone suffering from vertigo and should not be done in wet weather.** Pick your way down carefully (on the map it is called the Passage du Père). Sheep tend to congregate here in the summer, and if they are blocking the path, gently insist on your right of way, rather than going round them, as they are certainly more sure-footed than you.

It takes about 20mins to get down this steep slope following the infrequent red markings. There is an incredible wall of rock to the right which culminates in the Tête de Paccaly, alt. 2467m. The rock face is fissured with narrow black lines and looks completely unscalable. As you make your way gingerly down the slope, your voice echoes, along with the sinister cry of the alpine choughs that circle around the rocky summit. It is a relief to arrive at the ridge, alt. 2355m. If you are lucky you may also spot a large bird of prey with white markings on its wings – this is the gypaète barbu (bearded vulture – see Wildlife in the introduction), reintroduced into the area a few years ago (3hrs 20mins).

The path goes down on the left, but for a really good airy view keep to the top of the ridge. Look back and you will get an impressive view of the Trou, which already seems a long way above.

(5) After the ridge follow the path ahead down the Combe de Paccaly, crossing stones, rocks and shale – be particularly careful on the shale as these small stones move very easily. The path becomes steep and alternates between rock, scree and grass, so you have to pick your way down and really concentrate! After about 1hr it gets easier. There are red splashes from time to time on the rocks. The view of the valley is impressive, with La Clusaz at the end and mountain peaks straight ahead, including the Pic de Jallouvre and the Aiguille Verte, which dominates Lac de Lessy.

The path is clearly defined with red markings on the rocks, going steadily down the combe dominated by the precipitous slopes of the Rochers de la Salla, alt. 2217m, on the right and the Paré de Joux, alt. 2167m, to the left. After about 30mins

you come to the first stunted fir trees and some bushy vegetation and, not long after, a small wooden hut with a number of signposts, alt. 1674m. (4hrs 30mins).

(6) Follow the signpost left marked La Clusaz (straight on is the Combe and Lac de Tardevant). The little hut seems puzzling at first, until you realise it used to be the outhouse of the Paccaly-d'en-Haut chalet, which is round the corner and marked on the map. The path is still well defined and less steep, the vegetation getting more varied, with stunted birch amongst the firs and pines. You arrive at the café/restaurant of Chalet de Paccaly (5hrs).

(7) Take the jeep track left in front of the chalet (the right fork is signposted Gramusset, which is the refuge at the foot of the Pointe Percée). This track meets a narrow road which you walk along for 15mins, past La Bottière chalet on the right, till you reach the car park (5hrs 30mins).

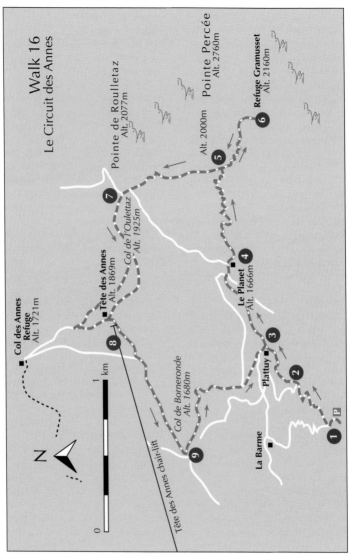

Walk 16
Le Circuit des Annes

Pointe de Roulletaz
Alt. 2077m

Pointe Percée
Alt. 2760m

Refuge Gramusset
Alt. 2160m

Alt. 2000m

Col de l'Oulettaz
Alt. 1925m

Tête des Annes
Alt. 1869m

Le Planet
Alt. 1666m

Col des Annes Refuge
Alt. 1721m

Plattuy

Col de Borneronde
Alt. 1680m

La Barme

Tête des Annes chair-lift

N

km

0

WALK 16

Le Circuit des Annes
Alt. 2162m (La Clusaz area)

Difficulty	Difficult/medium – considerable altitude gain, but nothing technical
Time	5hrs 15mins
Height gain	912m
Maps	Editions Didier & Richard IGN No. 8 Massifs du Mont Blanc/Beaufortain 1:50,000
	Cartes IGN 3430 ET Top 25 La Clusaz/Grand-Bornand 1:25,000
Depart from	Les Troncs (Grand-Bornand) – 1250m
Signposting	Excellent – old wooden signs and new white signposts; yellow/red splashes (many of them now plastic), posts with green arrows

This is a delightful day's hike, though you have to be reasonably fit. The Pointe Percée is a very popular mountain, one of the highest in the area and a challenge for serious walkers, so it is best to avoid busy summer weekends. In autumn there are lots of interesting fungi in the woods, including the distinctive red ones with white spots.

Access (from Geneva)

Take the motorway, direction Chamonix, and exit at No. 16 Bonneville/La Clusaz. Follow the N203 St-Pierre-en-Faucigny/La Clusaz. Go straight at a roundabout and shortly after turn left on the D6A, direction St-Pierre-en-Faucigny. At the roundabout in the village continue on the D6 across the railway line and then turn right on the D12, signposted Le Petit-Bornand/St-Jean-de-Sixt/La Clusaz. This takes you up the Borne river valley on a narrow, twisting road through the villages of Petit-Bornand and Entremont. At the end of the valley bear left on the D224, which leads onto the D4 where you turn left again towards Grand-Bornand. In the village of Grand-Bornand follow a sign down to the right to the Vallée de Bouchet/Les Plans. Bear right at the little chapel in the hamlet of Les Plans and continue for 3kms, past Le Centre Nordique on the left and through the hamlet of Les Troncs, to the end of the road where there is a large car park (the last 100 yards is a rough jeep track).

The Route

(1) Go to the end of the car park where there is a big noticeboard with a map of the region. Take the path up through the woods signposted Col des Annes/Refuge de Gramusset. The path crosses a riverbed. Shortly after go straight on at a second sign to the Refuge de Gramusset (left to La Barme). The path is well defined and rocky, winding up quite steeply through open beech wood and tall firs at the side of a gully with a stream running through it. After 10mins bear left (straight on is a dead end) and then a few minutes later go left again where the sign indicates Toutes Directions. Cross a stream on a rather primitive wooden bridge and continue to reach a T-junction (35mins).

(2) Turn right – the wooden sign indicating Refuge de Gramusset is on a tree further on (left is signposted Barme). Continue on up out of the woods into open pastureland to further signs.

(3) Go straight on, ignoring the sign left to Borne Ronde/Col des Annes (this is where you will come back). Continue over a low rocky rise to a further sign saying you are at Chalet de Plattuy alt. 1540m (it actually says 1640m on the sign, which is wrong according to the map and altimeter).

You can see the chalet down on your right. Follow directions to Le Gramusset (50mins).

The path goes up along the side of an attractive, open, grassy valley to reach a T-junction (signs). Here you go right (left is a shorter way to the Col des Annes) to the big old farm of Le Planay, built 1813, alt. 1666m (Le Planay on the signs, but Le Planet on the map!), which is decorated with colourful geraniums in summer (1hr 10mins).

(4) Bear right behind the chalet (more signs) and then steeply up through a small chimney where a bit of scrambling is involved. At the top of the chimney bear left (post) and continue up the side of the slope. This is the start of a long, tough haul up, but it is compensated for by a lovely view back down the valley to the hamlet of Les Troncs. (Before you get out onto the slope, look out for a cairn and a pale turquoise arrow on the right, pointing to a primitive little shrine hewn out of the rock with a bright-blue grille in front.) From the path you can see a cable on the right which is used to haul up supplies to the refuge. There are red/yellow splashes all the way up. You start to climb in earnest on a well-defined path, after the shrine, but take time to look back at the impressive Tournette mountain which dominates Lake Annecy. You reach a junction and further signs at alt. 2000m (2hrs 10mins).

Pointe Percée from Refuge de Gramusset

(5) Go right, signposted Refuge de Gramusset (straight on goes to Col des Annes – you will be coming back this way, so those who do not wish to make the steep climb to the refuge can continue straight). The path winds up steeply over rock and scree to reach the refuge at alt. 2160m. Ahead is the towering rocky peak of the Pointe Percée (2hrs 30mins).

(6) Although the surroundings of the hut are bleak and rocky, this is a popular refuge as it is the start for all climbs to the Pointe Percée. Although it is possible to walk to the summit, it is a steep and difficult climb, and much nicer to sit on the terrace and watch the people toiling up (you can see the successful climbers silhouetted on the summit!).

Retrace your steps to the signpost, No. 5 on the map, and turn right to the Col des Annes. The track goes down around the mountain at the end of the valley with some splendid views. It is fairly steep and some of the rocks you clamber over may be slippery – follow the red/yellow splashes carefully. (A few minutes after the signpost, behind a rope barricade, there is a large, deep hole in the rocks with snow at the bottom at

Refuge de Gramusset, 74450 Le Grand-Bornand, tel 0450.02.40.90 (belonging to the French Alpine Club). For reservations telephone M Buguet on 0450.27.02.56. Refreshments and meals available. Accommodation in dormitories for 60 people. Overnight stay 13.50 Euros, demi-pension 33.50 Euros. Open 22 June to 22 September (depending on climatic conditions).

all times of the year.) The path drops down quite steeply and then goes up again to reach signposts at the Col de l'Oulettaz, alt. 1925m. Look back from the col and you will see the path you came up from the farm of Le Planay. There is also an impressive view into the Arve valley with the Roc d'Enfer on the skyline (3hrs 25mins).

(7) At the signpost indicating Col d'l'Oulettaz, turn left and follow a path along the ridge (there is a short stretch of chain here, but it is not difficult). There is a fork where you can either continue along the path beneath the ridge (less airy!) or turn left to the top path which is more dramatic. From the next fork keep up on the ridge and follow red/yellow splashes, making for the chair-lift you can see at the Tête des Annes. The path undulates along the ridge through alpenrose and bilberry bushes towards a pile of rocks, alt. 1950m. Before you reach the rocks the path goes down steeply, traversing the side of the hill for 100m to reach a signpost at alt.1869m, just before the chair-lift (4hrs).

Alternative You can take the bottom path, which you can see going down to the Col des Annes, alt. 1721m, a group of large barns where cattle are housed (there are usually big herds around and the noise of the bells can be quite deafening!). Here you can buy Reblochon cheese which is made on the premises, and there is a

bar/restaurant (Frederic) which is open only in season. However, there may be lots of people and cars as the col can be reached by road. To return to the main walk, follow the sign to the Tête des Annes. (It was at this spot that we saw two magnificent *gypaète barbu* (bearded vultures) gliding majestically and slowly towards the Pointe Percée (see Wildlife in the introduction).)

(8) At the Tête des Annes signpost, continue straight to the Col de Borneronde. At a further sign keep to the top path (the path right goes to the Col des Annes). You are now walking along a bushy ridge, initially with the chair-lift on your right, and there are beautiful views down into the valley. Keep to the main path, which can be quite slippery and muddy if there has been wet weather, to reach a large crossroads at the Col de Borneronde, alt. 1680m (4hrs 30mins).

(9) Go down left in the direction of Le Plattuy. The path is fairly flat for a while as it winds back round the mountain. After 10mins go straight down at a junction (the path to the left says Gramusset) on a wide path through coniferous woods. You lose height fairly rapidly until you arrive at the signposts you went by on the way up (No. 3 on the map), just before the Chalet de Plattuy. Retrace your steps, following the signs to Les Troncs to reach the car park (5hrs 15mins).

WALK 17

Boucle du Lac de Lessy
Alt. 2045m (La Clusaz area)

Difficulty	Medium/difficult – a switchback walk, going up and down three times
Time	4hrs 35mins
Height gain	244m, 729m and 214m
Maps	Editions Didier & Richard IGN No. 3 Massifs du Chablais Faucigny & Genevois 1:50.000
	Cartes IGN 343O ET Top 25 La Clusaz/Grand-Bornand 1:25,000
	(**Note** The tourist bureau in the centre of Grand-Bornand sells a very good map showing the various walks in the region, including the Sentier de Découverte mentioned at No. 2 in the route instructions. It also offers helpful notes in English.)
Depart from	Vieux Chinaillon – 1308m
Signposting	Very good as it has been recently redone; large noticeboards at various locations

This is probably the best signposted walk in this region and it would be difficult to take the wrong way. I would call it a good family hike, provided all members are fit, as there is lots of variety. There are usually crowds of people on sunny weekends in July and August.

Access (from Geneva)

Take the motorway, direction Chamonix, and exit at No. 16 Bonneville/La Clusaz. Follow the N203, signposted St-Pierre-en-FaucignyLa Clusaz, and then turn left on the D6A, direction St-Pierre-en-Faucigny. At the roundabout in the village continue on the D6 over the railway line and then turn right on the D12, signposted La Clusaz. This takes you up the Borne river valley, a narrow, twisting road through the villages of Petit-Bornand and Entremont. At the end of the valley bear left on the D224, which leads onto the D4 where you turn left again towards Grand-Bornand/Col de la Colombière. Go through Grand-Bornand towards Chinaillon. At the entrance to the

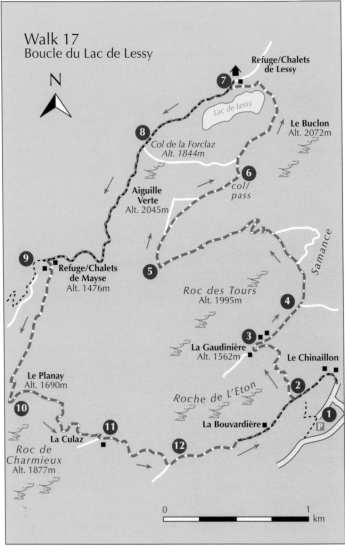

Walk 17
Boucle du Lac de Lessy

N

Refuge/Chalets
de Lessy

7

Lac de Lessy

8

Le Buclon
Alt. 2072m

Col de la Forclaz
Alt. 1844m

6

col/
pass

Aiguille
Verte
Alt. 2045m

5

Samance

9

Refuge/Chalets
de Mayse
Alt. 1476m

*Roc des Tours
Alt. 1995m*

4

3

La Gaudinière
Alt. 1562m

Le Chinaillon

2

Le Planay
Alt. 1690m

Roche de L'Eton

1

P

10

11

La Culaz

12

La Bouvardière

*Roc de
Charmieux
Alt. 1877m*

0   1 km

village take a narrow road left sign-posted Vieux Village. Go up and bear right at the signpost Lac de Lessy/La Bouvardière. Park in a small parking area on the left-hand side (this is before you get to the little church up on the right).

The Route

(1) Walk up the road for a few metres and turn left at the signpost to La Bouvardière/Lac de Lessy. Go up for 400m, passing some newly con-structed chalets, until you see a sign on the right (5mins).

(2) Take the narrow path right indicat-ing Sentier de Découverte (straight on says Lac de Lessy which is the other way round the walk). The path starts off quite steeply over open hillside

and then into scattered woodland. It becomes quite rocky as it skirts the cliff face of the Roche de l'Eton, with a number of chains to hang on to, though they are not really needed. Take a look back over Vieux Chinaillon, where many of the old chalets grouped round the church still have roofs of wooden tiles called tavaillons. You pass the first of a series of boards with the names and photos of alpine flowers to be found in the region.

You reach the top of this first climb of 244m at another board telling you about the Alpine forest. The path continues by some quaint old chalets called La Gaudinière, alt. 1562m, and further information con-cerning Flore des Chalets (the vegetation surrounding a typical

Walking towards Vieux Chinaillon

chalet). Continue on the path through the chalets (do not go off left) until you reach a T-junction (40mins)

(3) Go right, following the sign Lac de Lessy, on a wide track which narrows as you go by a large old chalet (here there is information about how a chalet is built, including the wooden tiles called *tavaillons*). Keep straight on the main track which goes down for a while and levels out as it curls round the front of the mountain. There are beautiful views of the other side of the valley, with its many ski-lifts going up to Mont Lachat. Behind is the Chaine des Aravis dominated by the majestic Pointe Percée. You reach another signpost (55mins).

(4) Continue straight, following the sign Lac de Lessy. (There is another information board here with pictures of the local fauna, such as the marmot, which you should look out for.) At this point the GR96 joins on the right from Chinaillon. (**Alternative** You could get to this point by taking the GR96 from Chinaillon.) The path undulates through open meadow called the Samance, and then bears to the left where you start to climb for the second time on a medium-steep, but well-trodden, path over Alpine pasture which is populated by brown-and-white Abondance cows in summer. As you go higher there are even better views of the Aravis range, especially as the snow-covered peak of Mont Blanc becomes visible in the

background. You can also see Chinaillon in the valley below and the road going up to Col de la Colombière. The path is heading towards the impressive end of the Roc des Tours where there is another signpost at alt. 1885m (1hr 50mins).

(5) Go right, following the sign Lac de Lessy (left is to the Roc des Tours). You can see the grassy hump of the Aiguille Verte above as you skirt up and round the mountain. (Later there is a sign left to Aiguille Verte 10mins for those with the energy to climb to the top and back!) Follow the sign Lac de Lessy with a good view in front of Le Buclon mountain, alt. 2072m. You are now on a ridge from where you get your first view down the other side to the green waters of Lac de Lessy, an attractive, kidney-shaped lake of glacial origin, nestling in a bowl in the mountains, with the dominating Buclon to the right and the white, flat mass of the Rochers de Leschaux behind. To the left is the Col de la Forclaz and, between the mountains, you can see rolling countryside as far as Lake Geneva, with the Jura range smudging the horizon. Just above the lake is a cluster of huts, including the Refuge de Lessy, which is a good place to stop for refreshment. Alternatively, stop for a picnic just beneath the ridge so that you can enjoy the beautiful views.

(6) Continue along the ridge till you reach a small col (pass). Follow the signed path which you can see going

Refuge de Lessy, tel 0450.25.98.32. Dormitory accommodation for 22 people (toilet but no shower). If you wish to stay, always telephone in advance. Overnight 8 Euros, demi-pension 27 Euros. Open from May to 15 October, depending on climatic conditions.

down towards the lake. About halfway down there is a possible short cut on a path to the left, which cuts across above the lake and meets up again at the Col de la Forclaz (this saves about 10mins). Otherwise continue to the chalets and refuge. (It is interesting to note that this is a small community in summer, and there are vegetable patches, squawking chickens and some donkeys.) (2hrs 15mins.)

(7) Just before you turn up to the refuge there is a sign left to Chalets de Mayse/Col de la Forclaz (right goes to Col de Sosay/Dent de Jallouvre). Take this wide path, which goes over a hump where you quickly lose sight of the chalets as you walk round above the lake to the col, alt. 1844m. Here you get a beautiful view below of the Nant valley and the Chalets de Mayse where you are heading. You can also see

the path you will be taking up to Le Planay (2hrs 35mins).

(8) Go straight over the col (the sign right indicates Paradis). This is a rather tiring descent of 368m down a wide, winding path which is eroded in places and can be muddy and slippery if it has been raining.

The Chalets de Mayse consists of about 12 buildings in a fold at the end of the valley, one of which is a refuge. They have a big herd of goats here and you can buy fresh goats' cheese (be careful of the geese guarding the refuge, as they are quite fierce!). From

Tanya at Lac de Lessy

the chalets you have a lovely view of the valley of the Overan from Entremont up to the Col de la Buffaz, flanked by the rugged Rochers de Traversiers on the left and the Montagne des Auges on the right (3hrs).

Refuge de Mayse, proprietor Philippe Bibollet, tel. 0450.22. 47.15.

Dormitory for 19 people. Overnight 6 Euros, demi-pension 22 Euros. Open from May to 15 October depending on climatic conditions.

(9) Follow the signpost left to Le Planay/Le Chinaillon (right goes to La Ville). Walk down a jeep track for a few minutes and then go up left by another signpost indicating Le Planay. This is where you leave the GR96 which continues down the valley. It is also the start of the third climb, which is 214m up a steep slope towards the Roc de Charmieux. At first the path is through open meadowland, and then it steepens to reach four big fir trees at a crest where you can have a rest before going down and round the flank of the mountain through alder bushes and woodland. The path steepens again, becoming rocky and tricky for a short distance as it skirts the end of the Roc de Charmieux, up to Le Planay, alt. 1690m (3hrs 35mins).

(10) At Le Planay you are now on the other side of the mountain. Above you on the left rears the impressive square

rock face of the Roc des Tours, alt.1995m. It is a great relief to go gently downwards on a delightful path, past some chalets with the Roc des Tours on the left and Mont Lachat in front. After a signpost you start dropping down the mountainside in earnest on a stony path through coniferous forest. Lower down you go round the contour of the hill and into open pastureland. At the bottom of the slope there is a signpost right to the Parking de la Cula and left to Chinaillon (4hrs).

(11) Go left along an easy path that meanders around the bottom of the mountain, initially with an old stone wall on one side, past the chalets of La Cula down below and La Mazerie. Take a pause to appreciate the lovely rolling Alpine country on your right and the rocky mass of the Roc des Tours on your left. The path widens and bears up left before you go down right, signposted Chinaillon, on a narrow path through intermittent tall fir trees to a T-junction (4hrs 15mins).

(12) Turn left towards Chinaillon on a narrow, unsurfaced road which goes underneath electricity wires. The path is very attractive as it meanders through woods and then open meadowland, past a little shrine on the right with a cross, before reaching the chalets of La Bouvardière. Walk down the road, past the turning you took on your outward journey, to the village where your car is parked (4hrs 35mins).

WALK 18

Boucle de St-Jean-de-Sixt
Alt. 960m (La Clusaz area)

Difficulty	Easy undulating walk
Time	2hrs 45mins
Height gain	Up and down – from 960m to 1080m, and then down to 752m and up again to 960m
Maps	Editions Didier & Richard IGN No. 2 Massifs des Bornes-Bauges 1:50,000
	Cartes IGN 3430 ET Top 25 La Clusaz/Grand-Bornand 1:25,000
Depart from	St-Jean-de-Sixt – 960m
Signposting	Good in parts

A delightfully easy stroll within the capabilities of all walkers. Much of the walk is on tarmac road, but there is little traffic (except for the 10mins on the main road). The countryside is beautiful, quiet and pastoral. This is the place to come if you want to see old authentic Savoyard farms and a way of life which is fast disappearing.

Access (from Geneva)

Take the motorway, direction Chamonix, and exit at No. 16 Bonneville/La Clusaz. Follow the N203, signposted St-Pierre-en-Faucigny/La Clusaz. Go straight at a roundabout and shortly after turn left on the D6A, direction St-Pierre-en-Faucigny. At the roundabout in the village continue following the D6 across the railway line and then turn right on the D12, signposted Le Petit-Bornand/St-Jean-de-Sixt/La Clusaz. This takes you up the Borne river valley, a dramatic, twisting road, through the villages of Petit-

Bornand and Entremont. Continue on the D12 to St-Jean-de-Sixt and park your car in the centre of the village in front of the *bureau de tourisme* or in a larger parking area behind the church.

The Route

(1) From the roundabout walk back down the road you drove in by (signposted Le Grand-Bornand/Bonneville) and after 150m take the second turning left where there are a number of signs, including Camping/Caravaning Municipale, and a big old chalet on the left. The road goes gently up,

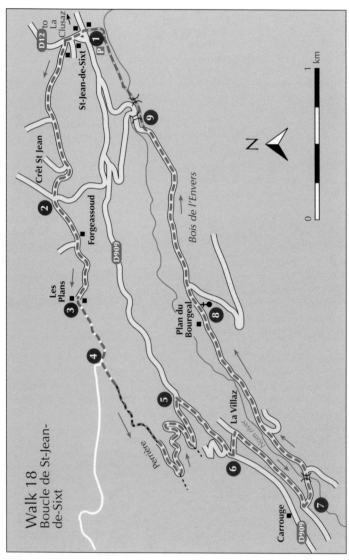

Walk 18
Boucle de St-Jean-de-Sixt

then levels off at Crêt St-Jean, alt. 1000m, and goes down. There are beautiful views into the Thônes valley with Mont Lachat on your right, the Aravis range on your left and La Tournette ahead. You reach a cross-roads with a telephone box on the right (15mins).

(2) Continue straight, direction Les Plans. You are in the hamlet of Forgeassoud and all along this road there are some very attractive chalets, some old, some new. You pass a pretty little chapel, built in 1631 but recently renovated. Continue till the road peters out at a typical old Savoyard farm called Les Plans, where there is a new building called 'Milk et Bouse' (*bouse* meaning cowdung!) where you can buy Reblochon and goats' cheese (30mins).

(3) Follow the road left which goes between the farm and the new building (gate here) towards a smart new chalet ahead. After 100m there is a sign right indicating Mont Lachat/Le Suet. Go right, climbing up the meadow, and then left at a sign Mont Lachat/Chalet de la Mare. You are walking along a narrow path through the edge of the woods to reach a wide stony track at a T-junction (40mins).

(4) Go down left (up right goes to Mont Lachat) on a wide balcony path along the side of the hill, through some deciduous woodland, but with more lovely open views down to the Thônes valley on your left, backed by the rearing peak of La Tournette. The track becomes a tarmac road and then gets wider as it winds all the way down to the valley floor. You are on the Route

View towards La Tournette from St-Jean-de-Sixt

de Perrière where there are a number of authentic old Savoyard chalets and farms. This road joins the D909 from St-Jean-de-Sixt to Thônes (1hr 10ins).

(5) Turn right and walk along the main road for about 10mins towards the hamlet of La Villaz.

(6) At the beginning of La Villaz turn down left at the crossroads (no sign). There is a telephone box over on the right and a sign to Praz Cornet. A few minutes later bear right at a T-junction and continue on a narrow road through some prosperous new houses till you come to the hamlet of Carrouge and a shrine to the Virgin Mary on the left (1hr 30mins).

This is a very Catholic part of France and there are numerous shrines in the region. If you recite three Hail Marys in front of this statue you get 100 days' indulgence in purgatory.

(7) Turn left here, signposted St Jean par l'Envers/Le Plan 1.5km, and cross the bridge over the Nom river. Turn left again and walk along a pleasant road with the river on your left. This takes you to the hamlet of Plan du Bourgeal, where there is an old fountain dated 1840 and another little chapel built in 1839 (1hr 50mins).

(8) Continue on the road towards St-Jean-de-Sixt, through picturesque meadows with ancient fruit trees and some really lovely old Savoyard farmhouses, complete with balconies bright with flowering geraniums, and flourishing vegetable gardens. You enter majestic beech and fir woods (called the Bois de l'Envers), with the river Nom flowing down on the left in a narrow gorge.

(9) Just before you reach a new bridge with green railings follow a sign right indicating Circuit de Nom and cross an older bridge called La Paserelle where the stream is a rushing torrent (this was the original road). Then go straight up some steep wooden steps, signposted St-Jean-de-Sixt par les Tennis, and continue upwards on a narrow path with the river down on the right. The path suddenly emerges by tennis courts, behind the tourist office and church in the centre of the village (2hrs 45mins).

THÔNES AREA

WALK 19

La Pointe d'Orsière
Alt. 1750m (Thônes area)

Difficulty	Difficult/medium – goes steeply up to start, and it is also steep if you do not keep to the official path to the summit
Time	4hrs
Height gain	790m
Maps	Editions Didier & Richard IGN No. 8 Massifs du Mont Blanc/Beaufortain 1:50,000
	Cartes IGN 3531 OT Top 25 Megève Col des Aravis1:25,000
Depart from	La Gutary (Manigod) – 960m
Signposting	(**Note** Although called La Pointe d'Orsière on the map, on the signposts is is called La Pointe Orcière.)
	Wooden signposts and No. 38 signs – the yellow diamonds and orange splashes have often been painted over with grey; there are new plastic signs nailed to trees; do not follow Circuit d'Orcière signs from the summit (see remarks below)

A beautiful walk in an unspoiled region. There are wonderful views of the Chaine des Aravis, Mont Charvin and nearby Sulens mountain. Since this walk was originally done the Manigod tourist office has had the entire region re-signposted and changed the original circular walks. I have not followed their Circuit d'Orcière, as there is a long, difficult descent into another valley, plus a lengthy stretch down a road, which would make it rather tedious. Also, it impinges on the Tour de la Tulle itinerary (Walk Number 20). My personal feeling is that they have overdone the signs and made directions more confusing. A map is available at the Manigod tourist office (explanations in French only). Fungi enthusiasts should do this walk in autumn when they are abundant in the woods.

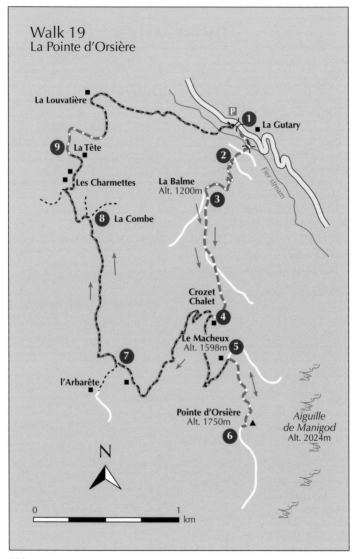

Walk 19
La Pointe d'Orsière

La Louvatière

La Gutary

La Tête

La Balme
Alt. 1200m

Flier stream

Les Charmettes

La Combe

Crozet
Chalet

Le Macheux
Alt. 1598m

l'Arbarête

Pointe d'Orsière
Alt. 1750m

Aiguille
de Manigod
Alt. 2024m

N

0   1
⊢――――――――――――⊣ km

Access (from Geneva)

Take the motorway, direction Chamonix, and exit at No. 16 Bonneville/La Clusaz. Follow the N203 signposted St-Pierre-en-Faucigny/La Clusaz and shortly after turn left on the D6A to St-Pierre-en-Faucigny. At the roundabout in the village continue on the D6 over the railway line and then turn right on the D12, signposted La Clusaz. This road takes you up the Borne river valley, a narrow, twisting road through the villages of Petit-Bornand and Entremont. Continue on the D12 to St-Jean-de-Sixt and then take the D909 direction Thônes. Instructions continue from the first paragraph after 'Alternative', below.

Alternative if Using the Geneva Ring Road

Take the N201 direction Annecy, which goes through the new Bardonnex customs (bypassing St-Julien-en-Genevois). Take the first exit (signposted St-Julien-en-Genevois/Annecy) and at the roundabout follow the road signposted Cruseilles/Annecy. You are now back on the original N201 to Annecy. Go through Cruseilles, cross by the spectacular Pont de la Caille bridge, and at Pringy, just before Annecy, follow signs to Thônes, taking a left turn onto the D16. (**Note** D16 is not marked on the signpost.) This is a newly built road, bypassing Annecy, and there are a number of roundabouts with the road number changing to N203, then to D916, before finally

going back to D16. Basically, just follow all signs to Thônes.

Soon after entering Thônes, turn right by the church on the D12, direction Serraval. After 1km bear left on the D16 to Manigod. In front of the church at Manigod take the turning down to the right, signposted Tournance/La Charmette, which goes into the narrow Fier valley. Follow all signs to La Charmette, through the hamlets of Choseaux, Joux and Tournance. **Careful** – do not stop at the first cement bridge, which also has a shrine, but continue. Just before the hamlet of La Gutary you come to another bridge (sign La Gutary at the bridge) and beyond on the left is a large blue-and-white shrine in a rock. At the bridge are various signposts, including one saying Circuit d'Orcière No. 38. Park on the left just before the bridge (3.5km from the church at Manigod).

The Route

(1) Take the narrow path to the right of the bridge going down into the woods, signposted Circuit du Banc/Circuit de Freu/Circuit d'Orcière. At first the path follows the river on the right, then goes over a bridge to a crossroads where you bear up right and continue on a wide track (5mins).

(2) **Careful** – a few minutes later look for a wooden sign on the track indicating Circuit du Banc/Circuit d'Orcière/Circuit du Freu up right. (**Note** When we did the walk someone

had turned the sign around and we went straight on.) Take this narrower track, which contours round the rocky hill on a steep path through beech and tall coniferous woods. There are faded yellow diamonds and orange splashes on rocks and trees (in places they have tried to overpaint them with grey). After 20mins you come to a stone commemorating the accidental death of Francis Avettand on 31 January 1944 at the age of 36. (Whether he fell or was shot by the Germans is anyone's guess.) Keep straight on the zigzag path.

At wooden signs the path comes out into beautiful, open meadowland and, a few minutes later, you reach the Chalet de la Balme, alt. 1200m. Here you get a marvellous view of the surrounding peaks, including the nearby Tulle and Montagne de Sulens (Walk Numbers 20 and 21) (30mins).

(3) Following signs to L'Arbarête and La Louvatière, go up a jeep track to reach a T-junction. Turn left, following the sign Circuit du Banc/Circuit d'Orcière and then, after the first corner, go up right for about 50m. Then turn left (signs here) on a narrow track which goes up steeply through woods and round the mountain for about 30mins, with occasional steep drops down one side – the faded yellow diamonds and orange splashes have been painted out and replaced by plastic numbers on trees. The path meets a jeep track (1hr 10mins).

(4) Turn up left and out into open meadowland again with the Crozet

Summit of Pointe d'Orsière

chalet, alt. 1406m, on your left. Here there is a good view of the narrow valley below, and the Parmelan mountain behind, which dominates the northern end of Lake Annecy.

In early spring the surrounding slopes are covered with narcissi, alpine daffodils and trumpet gentians.

Continue on the jeep track, curving gently uphill round the mountain to the chalet of Le Macheux, alt. 1598m, where there are lots of smelly goats! (1hr 40mins).

(5) Turn up right, signposted Circuit d'Orcière – you can see the signposts at the summit of the mountain 150m higher up. Keep left on the ill-defined track, which is quite eroded in places but there are some posts and splashes. (It is possible to make your own way up the open hillside to the summit but it is quite steep.) You arrive at the pointe, alt. 1750m, which has a signpost at the top saying Circuit d'Orcière (2hrs).

(6) There are glorious views all round, and particularly of the Chaine des Aravis from the L'Etale to Mont Charvin peaks (one does not often see them from this angle). In front is the impressive L'Aiguille de Manigod (Manigod needle), which seems part of the mountain chain itself, but looks more needle-like from a lower level.

Although the official Circuit d'Orcière path continues across the ridge (see introduction to this walk), retrace your steps back to Le Macheux chalet at No. 5. On the way down there is a good view of the ski installations at the Col de Merdassier, part of the La Clusaz complex (2hrs 15mins).

Turn left at the chalet down the same jeep track and continue past the Crozet chalet and the path in the woods you came up. The track goes down through open Alpine pastures and occasional coniferous trees, past a big tumbledown barn on the right and another chalet to the left, to reach a junction where the chalet of L'Arbarête is up on the left (2hrs 45mins). (For this part of the walk you are on the Circuit du Banc No. 27.)

(7) Keep straight on the descending track which, 20mins later, reaches a T-junction with an old wooden chalet opposite (this has La Combe on the side, but according to the map La Combe is the chalet further down which calls itself Les Charmettes!).

(8) Turn left, following sign the Circuit de Freu No. 30. (**Note** If you go right here you will eventually get back to the Chalet da la Balme, where you can retrace your steps down through the woods.) The descending jeep track shortly reaches another T-junction at the new small chalet of Les Charmettes where you go right, following signs to La Gutary/La Tête, which you reach soon after. La Tête is

161

Goats fighting on
Pointe d'Orsière

a working farm with lots of brown-and-white cows around, and it is a refreshing change to see people living and working in an isolated environment (3hrs 25mins).

(9) Go left in front of the farmhouse, following the sign Circuit du Banc/ Circuit de Freu, on a grassy path.

Along here in autumn we saw a large display of Amanita muscaria, better known as the red toadstools with white spots which fairies sit on in childrens' books – actually they are highly poisonous.

Soon the path becomes steep, rocky and slippery as it goes down

through woods in a sort of gully, bearing right (signpost says Circuit de la Tête/Gutary), past the Chalet de la Louvatière. The path widens and is less stony as it continues downward, becoming a jeep track through meadows and woods with occasional chalets.

Cross the Fier river, where the water looks very welcoming on a hot day as it tumbles over big boulders. You are now on a wide jeep track which goes up by the river and bears left to reach the road. Turn right to the bridge where you have left your car (4hrs).

WALK 20

Tour de la Tulle
Alt. 2072m (Thônes area)

Difficulty	Strenuous rather than difficult; there is one steep descent near the end of the walk
Time	5hrs
Height gain	872m in all – from the Col des Porthets to the Chalets les Fontanettes there is a drop of 550m, then a height gain of 200m to Sur le Freu, and a further descent of about 200m to the original path
Maps	Editions Didier & Richard IGN No. 8 Massifs du Mont Blanc/Beaufortain 1:50,000
	Cartes IGN 3531 OT Top 25 Megève Col des Aravis 1:25,000
Depart from	Sous l'Aiguille (Manigod) – 1200m
Signposting	Good – follow white signposts, posts with yellow arrows and yellow splashes (**Note** Some of the old wooden signs are also still in place.)

This is a strenuous walk in unforgettable scenery with wonderful views all around, particularly of nearby Mont Charvin. If you prefer to avoid the steep descent from Sur le Freu chalet you can always do the walk in the other direction. This description follows the Tour de la Tulle circuit as it used to be, and the signs are still there for most of the way, otherwise there is new signposting.

Access (from Geneva)
Take the motorway, direction Chamonix, and exit at No. 16 Bonneville/La Clusaz. Follow the N203 signposted St-Pierre-en-Faucigny/La Clusaz and shortly after turn left on the D6A to St-Pierre-en-Faucigny. At the roundabout in the village continue on the D6 over the railway line and then turn right on the D12, signposted La Clusaz. This road takes you up the Borne river valley, a narrow, twisting road through the villages of Petit-Bornand

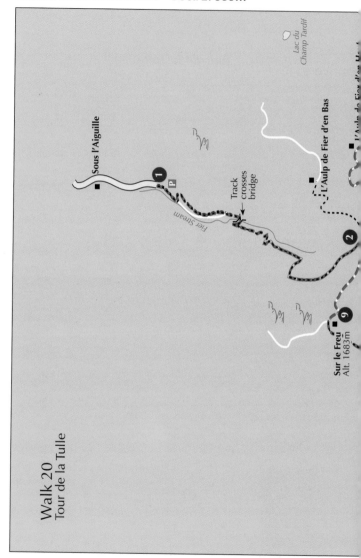

Walk 20
Tour de la Tulle

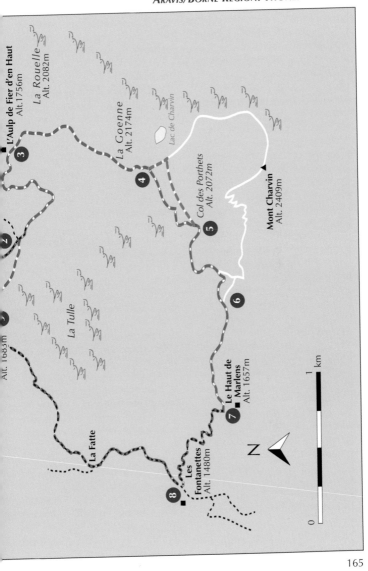

L'Aulp de Fier d'en Haut
Alt.1756m

La Rouelle
Alt. 2082m

La Goenne
Alt. 2174m

Lac de Charvin

Col des Porthets
Alt. 2072m

Mont Charvin
2409m

Alt. 1683m

La Tulle

Le Haut de Marlens
Alt. 1657m

La Fatte

Les Fontanettes
Alt. 1480m

N

1 km

0

165

and Entremont. Continue on the D12 to St-Jean-de-Sixt and then take the D909, direction Thônes. Instructions continue from the first paragraph after Alternative, below.

Alternative if Using the Geneva Ring Road

Take the N201, direction Annecy, which goes through the new Bardonnex customs (bypassing St-Julien-en-Genevois). Take the first exit (signposted St-Julien-en-Genevois/Annecy) and at the roundabout follow the road signposted Cruseilles/Annecy. You are now back on the original N201 to Annecy. Go through Cruseilles, cross by the spectacular bridge, and at Pringy, just before Annecy, follow signs to Thônes, taking a left turn onto the D16. (**Note** D16 is not marked on the signpost.) This is a newly built road bypassing Annecy, and there are a number of round-abouts with the road number changing to N203, then to D916 before finally going back to D16. Basically, just follow all signs to Thônes.

Soon after entering Thônes, turn right on the D12, direction Serraval. After 1km bear left on the D16 to Manigod. In front of the church at Manigod take the turning down to the right, signposted Tournance/La Charmette, which goes into the narrow Fier valley. Follow all signs to La Charmette and continue through the hamlets of Choseaux, Joux, Tournance, La Gutary and La Charmette to Sous l'Aiguille, which is

166

right at the end of the valley. Park your car in the parking space where the tarmac road gives way to a jeep track.

The Route

(1) At the start of a wide jeep track there is a sign saying you are at Sous l'Aiguille, alt. 1180m, with indications to Sur le Freu/Pointe d'Orcière/Lac de Charvin/Mont Charvin. Take the track which rises medium steep through light coniferous wood with the precipitous rock faces of the Orcière, La Riondaz and La Tulle ahead. You can either keep to the jeep track all the way up, or take a short cut at the first corner (marked with a yellow splash on a rock) on a narrow path along the River Fier for about 5mins, before joining the jeep track again where you bear right. The wide track crosses the river by a bridge and then, a few minutes later, a dry riverbed before passing a Tour de Sulens signpost by a small hut to the left (30mins).

Continue straight and shortly after you come out of the woods onto open Alpine pasture. You can see the path in front, curling round the Tulle mountain, and the chalets of L'Aulp de Fier d'en Bas.

(2) Ignore the steep path on the right at a signpost indicating Sur le Freu/Pointe d'Orcière/Les Fontanettes (this is the way you will return) and continue straight to L'Aulp de Fier d'en Haut/Lac de Charvin/Mont Charvin (45mins).

Careful – after a few minutes turn up right off the main jeep track (there is a post here with yellow arrows). The jeep track continues to the chalets of L'Aulp de Fier d'en Bas and Lac du Champ Tardif. The wide path climbs upwards, crossing a number of streams through a green and rocky landscape where you can see the entrances to caves above you (there are obvious short cuts if you want to take them). You arrive at the cow barns of L'Aulp de Fier en Haut, alt. 1756m. Here there are further signs indicating Lac de Charvin/Col des Porthets (1hr 20mins).

In summer you can buy Reblochon cheese made from the milk of the cows grazing on the surrounding pasture, their huge clanging bells echoing across the barren slopes.

(3) Continue past the barns on the defined, narrow path. You can see it curling up higher round the bowl of mountains to the Col des Porthets, with the peaks of La Rouelle, La Goenne and Mont Charvin, alt. 2409m, dominating the skyline. There are occasional yellow splashes to follow and a steep short cut if you want to take it.

The path winds up medium steep round the wide bowl and if you look back you can see the two groups of chalets clearly. There is a bit of a scramble over a rocky gully but the path is not difficult. You reach a signpost saying left to Lac de

Cows walking home, Fier valley, Tour de la Tulle

Charvin and straight on to Col des Porthets (2hrs).

(4) It is worthwhile to make the 15min detour to see this lovely mountain lake, even though there is quite a steep path up to the crest of the hill from where you look down onto it (it takes about another 10mins to get to the lakeside itself). It is said to be one of the prettiest of the region's Alpine lakes, and nestles in a ring of grassy mountain slopes dominated by the Goenne peak on one side and Mont Charvin on the other.

Steep descent on the Tour de la Tulle

From the crest of the hill overlooking the lake you can see a path crossing over to rejoin the one you were on to the Col des Porthets – actually there are three paths crossing over, so take your choice. If you are on the top path you traverse a scree slope for about 15mins – this is not technically difficult, but care should be taken nevertheless. If you do not go up to the lake, continue straight on a rocky path where there is less scree.

After the scree there is a short steep climb up to the Col des Porthets, where there is a gate in a fence and a sign on the rock. Look back and appreciate the path you have taken which you can see all the way to the chalets. At the Col des Porthets, alt. 2072m, you are on the other side of the ridge with the rocky Tulle mountain jutting out to your right and the Mont Charvin now on your left. Below, the path winds down to a grassy plateau and you can see the villages in the valley far below. (This is the time to take a well-earned break and picnic, as most of the rest of the walk is downhill.) (2hrs 30mins.)

(5) Take the path that goes straight down from the col (not the higher right one) and curls round the mountain. Where there is an intersection you can either go down left on a more direct path or continue straight along the side of the slope and turn left further along. Both paths meet up further down, descending quite steeply into the grassy plateau at the foot of the Tulle ridge. Way over on the left you can see woods and chalets. You pass a signpost saying you are in the Combe de Charvin (2hrs 45mins).

(6) Ignore a path off to the left, which is the way to the summit of Mont Charvin and is quite difficult. Instead continue down into the bottom of the combe. The path gets easier and less steep as you cross pleasant Alpine pastures to the Chalets le Haut de Marlens, alt. 1657m (3hrs 5mins). In season this is a café/restaurant and there is accommodation.

Refuge Haut de Marlens (privately owned), 74230 Bouchet Mont Charvin, tel 0450. 44.40.89. Open in summer only, according to climatic conditions.

(7) From the signpost, continue on a wide jeep track which curls down through pastureland (obvious short cuts) to the Chalets les Fontanettes. This is another café/restaurant, on a lovely open site, and a popular stop in summer. You reach another jeep track and a signpost Les Fontanettes, alt. 1480m (3hrs 20mins).

(8) Turn right, following indications Sur le Freu/Pointe d'Orcière. This pleasant, wide, easy track goes past the odd barn and chalet, round the front of the mountain with the rocky mass of the Tulle up on the right, passing a sign saying you are at La Fatte, alt. 1500m. There is a good view of the Orsière summit and the high grassy ridge of Mont de Sulens on the left. Continue on the jeep track, which bends to the right by a square watering hole and starts to go up (there is a height gain of around 200m between Les Fontanettes and Sur le Freu) to reach the lone large cowshed of Sur le Freu, alt. 1683m, where there is a signpost (4hrs).

(9) With the farm on your left make for the signpost you can see ahead and go right, following indication Passage du Freu 100m/Sur le Freu (left goes to Pointe d'Orcière/La Balme). The path takes you to the edge of the ridge where you can see a clear path down into the valley you came up originally. **Careful** – this is a vertiginous path and can be slippery after rainfall. You cross some dry water courses with scree, and further down the path becomes rocky with long grass – follow the yellow splashes all the way. When you get to the bottom you are on your original path at No. 2 on the map (4hrs 30mins). Retrace your steps back to the car (5hrs).

WALK 21

Tour de Sulens
Alt. 1615m (Thônes area)

Difficulty	Easy/medium jeep track most of the way – one medium-steep ascent
Time	3hrs 45mins
Height gain	316m
Maps	Editions Didier & Richard IGN No. 2 Massifs des Bornes-Bauges 1:50,000
	Cartes IGN 3531 OT Top 25 Megève Col des Aravis 1:25,000
Depart from	Col du Plan Bois – 1300m
Signposting	Excellent – lots of signposts and posts with yellow splashes on green background

There is something very satisfying about walking round a mountain instead of going up and down it! However, you do have an option to go to the top if you feel more energetic. This is an easy, well-signposted circuit all the way with no worries about getting lost. The views of the surrounding countryside and mountains (Parmelan, La Tournette, Chaine des Aravis, Mont Charvin amongst the many peaks) are really outstanding. This is real farming country (no nasty ski-lifts to be seen), and there are lots of brown-and-white Abondance cows feeding in the lush meadows, plus herds of goats, not to mention the chickens, ducks and geese scratching round the farms. This walk is best done in spring or early autumn as there is little shade on a hot day. Because of the rich soil the flowers are particularly abundant, and the rare lady's slipper orchid can be found here, though its exact whereabouts are a well-kept secret.

Access (from Geneva)

Take the motorway, direction Chamonix, and exit at No. 16 Bonneville/La Clusaz. Follow the N203 signposted St-Pierre-en- Faucigny/La Clusaz and shortly after turn left on the D6A to St-Pierre-en-Faucigny. At the roundabout in the village continue on the D6 over the railway line and then turn right on the D12, signposted La Clusaz. This road takes you up the Borne river valley, a narrow, twisting road through the villages of Petit-Bornand and Entremont. Continue on the D12 to St-Jean-de-Sixt and then take the D909, direction Thônes. Instructions continue at the first paragraph after 'Alternative', below.

Alternative if Using the Geneva Ring Road

Take the N201 direction Annecy which goes through the new Bardonnex customs (bypassing St-Julien-en-Genevois). Take the first exit (signposted St-Julien-en-Genevois/ Annecy) and at the roundabout follow the road signposted Cruseilles/ Annecy. You are now back on the original N201 to Annecy. Go through Cruseilles, cross by the spectacular bridge, and at Pringy, just before Annecy, follow signs to Thônes, taking a left turn onto the D16. (**Note** D16 is not marked on the signpost.) This is a newly built road bypassing Annecy, and there are a number of round-abouts with the road number changing to N203, then to D916, before finally going back to D16. Basically, follow all signs to Thônes.

Soon after entering Thônes, turn right on the D12, direction Serraval, and then be careful to take a small road to the left, about 2km later, sign-posted Les Clefs. At the entrance to the village bear back sharp right on a narrow road and follow all signs to Col du Plan Bois. This is a winding road uphill for about 6km. The Col du Plan Bois, alt. 1300m, consists of a café/restaurant with a parking area in front just before the road starts to wind down again to Manigod.

The Route

(1) Start walking in the direction you came up by car. Do not take the first sign left, which says Sommet de Sulens 1hr 50mins, but continue down the paved road for about 500m. As you walk down you have an uninterrupted view of the vertical cliffs of the Parmelan mountain behind Annecy and, to the left, the majestic Tournette peak, alt. 2351m. Ignore the second turning left to the hamlet of La Frasse, consisting of farm buildings and an attractive little chapel, but shortly after take the next one signposted La Frasse alt.1230m to Col de la Botte (10mins).

(2) This wide track undulates gently through forest, open fields and the barns of Les Rottes and Les Gay (now renovated). At a sign indicating Les Bancs left keep on the main track and continue to reach a fork and a post with yellow splashes (45mins).

(3) Go left following the sign to Col de la Botte (do not go downhill to Le Mont). At a further junction a few minutes later keep on the main path following the sign Col de la Botte, and do not take the path left indicat-ing Sommet de Sulens. Ten minutes later you pass a new barn on the right. Ignore a stony track to the left shortly

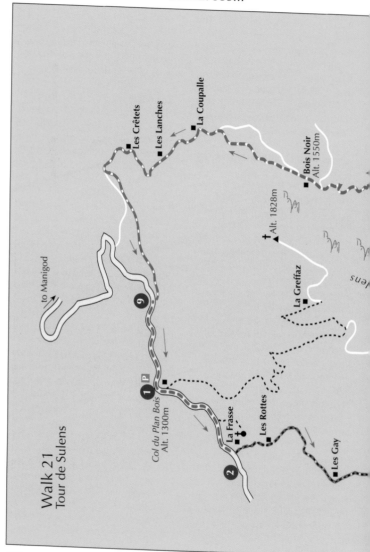

Walk 21
Tour de Sulens

to Manigod

Les Crêtets
Les Lanches
La Coupalle

Bois Noir
Alt. 1550m

Alt. 1828m

La Greffaz

Col du Plan Bois
Alt. 1300m

La Frasse
Les Rottes
Les Gay

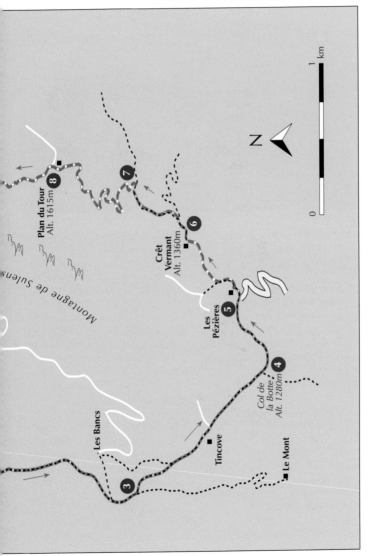

Les Pézières Farm on Mont de Sulens

after and continue onwards to reach a fork at the Col de la Botte, alt. 1280m (1hr).

(4) Go left, following the sign Les Pézières/Plan du Tour/Le Freu (you are now on the GR de Pays Tournette Aravis red/yellow route, which you follow to the road where it goes off to the right). There are lovely open views as you walk down. Over on the right are farms and hamlets nestling in an unspoilt valley with mountains behind, and straight ahead is an impressive view of Mont Charvin, alt. 2409m, and the Aravis chain of peaks, including La Tulle (Walk Number 20). On the left are the grass-covered slopes of Mont de Sulens. This path meets a paved road and a signpost (1hr 10mins).

(5) Turn up left to reach a typical large Savoyard farm called Les Pézières. (At

174

this farm you can not only buy local Reblochon cheese, you can also watch the farmer making it.) Follow the stony jeep track round the back of the farm, and then bear right (post and yellow/red splashes) on a wide, grassy path which goes alongside a fence on the left for a short while, with continuing splashes and yellow arrows, so you can't go wrong. You can see a large barn ahead at the Crêt Vermant, alt. 1360m, where you reach another jeep track.

(6) Follow the jeep track with the barn on your left (signs here again) and then go left at the next fork following yellow arrows on a tree (don't go down right).

(7) Later, turn off the main jeep track, following the sign Plan du Tour 50mins, on a wide, stony track winding up the mountain quite steeply (this can be quite exhausting in the middle of a hot day) towards an ugly cowshed at the top. There are sweeping views all round, especially of the Chaines des Aravis mountain range, with the nearby fearsome mass of Mont Charvin. Just before you reach the cowshed (follow yellow arrows) you reach a dip in the mountain at the Col du Plan du Tour, alt. 1615m, which is the highest point of the walk. On the left is the long grassy Sulens ridge, with its rather curious indentations, and on the other side is a low hill with some trees (2hrs 20mins).

(8) The path starts to go down to the left, signposted Bois Noir/Sous Sulens (right is up to the cowshed), and after 15mins you come to a big barn left, marked on the map as Bois Noir, alt. 1550m. Far above on a ridge is a cross – the highest point of the Sulens

mountain, alt. 1878m, which is really a long shoulder culminating at this point. Continue following yellow arrows to a T-junction where you bear left (post) past the barns of La Coupalle, Les Lanches and Les Crêtets, with magnificent views over the lush, farm-dotted countryside. You can see down to the valley and the village of Manigod, dominated by its church with a high steeple. You are now walking round the front of the mountain and the rocky cliff of the Parmelan swings into view again. You can also see across to the Col de Plan Bois where you have left your car. The path becomes more wooded as you get lower and then hits a tarmac road (3hrs 30mins).

(9) Turn left and walk back up the road past some old working farms to the col (3hrs 45mins).

Birdseye primrose on Mont de Sulens

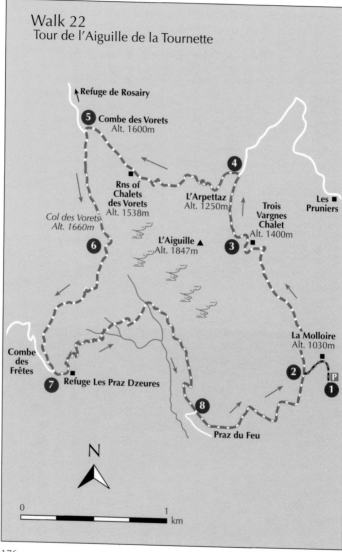

Walk 22
Tour de l'Aiguille de la Tournette

↑Refuge de Rosairy

5 Combe des Vorets
Alt. 1600m

4

Les Pruniers ■

Rns of
Chalets
des Vorets
Alt. 1538m

L'Arpettaz
Alt. 1250m

Trois
Vargnes
Chalet
Alt. 1400m

Col des Vorets
Alt. 1660m

L'Aiguille ▲
Alt. 1847m

3

6

La Molloire
Alt. 1030m

Combe
des
Frêtes

7 Refuge Les Praz Dzeures

2

1 P

8

Praz du Feu

N

0   1
km

WALK 22

Tour de l'Aiguille de la Tournette
Alt. 1739m (Thônes area)

Difficulty	Strenuous rather than difficult – somewhat vertiginous in places
Time	5hrs 10mins
Height gain	689m
Maps	Editions Didier & Richard IGN No. 2 Massifs des Bornes-Bauges 1:50,000
	Cartes IGN 3431 OT Top 25 Lac d'Annecy 1:25,000
Depart from	La Molloire (Serraval) – 1030m
Signposting	White signposts and posts with yellow arrows on green background; also faded yellow and red splashes, yellow diamonds on trees (this is the old signposting which has been erased where possible – the new signposting is not always evident, so at times one is grateful for the faded splashes)

This is a fairly tough but rewarding walk, though personally I find the Aiguille ('needle') a rather daunting-looking mountain. Although it is right next door to the magnificent La Tournette peak, which is so popular with walkers, it has the advantage of being less known and is therefore uncrowded during the summer months. You must be fit and prepared for precipitous downward slopes as well as climbing. However, the walk is not technically difficult and has lots of variety, e.g. woodlands, flowers, rock, scree and open meadows. It is well signposted all the way round, but do keep your eyes peeled for the yellow splashes and posts.

Access (from Geneva)
Take the motorway, direction Chamonix, and exit at No. 16 Bonneville/La Clusaz. Follow the N203, signposted St-Pierre-en-Faucigny/La Clusaz, and shortly after turn left on the D6A to St-Pierre-en-Faucigny. At the roundabout in the village continue on the D6 over the railway line and then turn right on the D12 signposted La Clusaz. This takes you up the Borne river valley, a narrow, twisting road through the villages of Petit-Bornand and Entremont.

Continue on the D12 to St-Jean-de-Sixt and then take the D909, direction Thônes. Instructions continue at the first paragraph after Alternative, below.

Alternative if Using the Geneva Ring Road

Take the N201, direction Annecy, which goes through the new Bardonnex customs (bypassing St-Julien-en-Genevois). Take the first exit (signposted St-Julien-en-Genevois/Annecy) and at the roundabout follow the road signposted Cruseilles/Annecy. You are now on the original N201 to Annecy. Go through Cruseilles, cross by the spectacular bridge, and at Pringy, just before Annecy, follow signs to Thônes, taking a left turn onto the D16. (**Note** D16 is not marked on the signpost.) This is a newly built road bypassing Annecy, and there are a number of roundabouts with the road number changing to N203, then to D916, before finally going back to D16. Basically, follow all signs to Thônes.

Soon after entering Thônes turn right on the D12, direction Serraval. Approximately 9kms from Thônes and 1km after the Col de Marais, take a right turn to L'Ermite/Montaubert. Follow this road, which climbs for 600m to Les Hermites. At L'Ermite keep right, direction Montaubert (Les Hermites is to the left), and then, just after a bend where Montaubert comes into view, take a narrow, stony track signposted Le Cernay/La Molloire/

178

Tour de L'Aiguille (**careful** – it is easy to miss!). The road is stony and rutted to Le Cernay, but afterwards it is tarmacked to La Molloire (2kms from turnoff). Watch for a parking area to the left on a bend below the farm where there are signposts indicating you are at La Molloire, alt. 1030m.

The Route

(1) Go out of the parking area and up left towards the farm, following the sign Les Trois Vargnes/Col des Vorets/Refuge les Praz Dzeures/La Tournette. Here you get your first view of the dramatically austere L'Aiguille mountain. La Molloire used to be a delightfully dilapidated Savoyard farm when I first did this walk, but has now been smartened up and reroofed. However, it still has its yapping dogs and a majestic billy goat. Go into the farmyard with the house on the right, and through a fence to reach a stony jeep track which climbs up fairly steeply through meadowland to reach a signpost (10mins).

(2) Continue straight, following the sign Trois Vargnes/Col des Vorets (to the left is where you come in at the end of the walk) into woodland and round the flank of the mountain. Keep on the main track, climbing quite steeply most of the time. The path veers round to the left and then to the right, getting narrower and going into open pastureland to reach the Trois Vargnes chalet, alt. 1400m, which is new and rather ugly (Trois Vargnes means 'three fir trees'). Continue past the chalet towards coniferous trees but, before you reach them, look for a sign over on the right by a fence saying Trois Vargnes alt.1400m (55mins).

(3) The track undulates down through woods for a few minutes and then crosses some scree before becoming rocky and passing below two huge slabs of rock. **Careful** – there is a yellow right-angled sign which means you go right – it is easy to miss (1hr 12mins).

The rocky path continues down to the Clairière de l'Arpettaz, alt. 1250m (*clairière* means a clearing). This is a delightful spot in springtime as it is full of marsh marigolds, orchids and lily of the valley. There is also meant to be a *source* (spring), but we couldn't find it.

(4) Ignore the path to the right leading to the hamlet of Les Pruniers (post but no sign) and continue. The narrow path goes through beech and coniferous woods, zigzagging up round the flank of the L'Aiguille mountain and then steepening as the vegetation changes to stunted bushes sprinkled with an abundance of flowers in season. You reach further signposts where you continue straight to Chalets des Vorets/Col des Vorets (right goes to Parking Les Grangettes/Parking de Belchamp). Continue round and up into open

rocky terrain sprinkled with bushes. The Aiguille mountain, with a cross on the summit, is now behind you as the path zigzags steeply up and then flattens out (there is a good view here of Thônes on the right in the valley), before reaching the ruins of the Chalets des Vorets, alt. 1538m (1hr 55mins).

Continue past the ruins, following a yellow arrow on the wall. At first the path is level and seems to be going in the wrong direction, but after about 20mins it turns sharply left as it steepens again. At this stage watch carefully for the yellow markings till you come to further signposts at the Combe des Vorets, alt. 1660m, in a shallow valley with a rocky wall ahead (2hrs 15mins).

(5) Bear left to Col des Vorets/Praz Dzeures (right goes to the Refuge de Rosairy and the summit of La Tournette). You still have 100m to gain and the track climbs up and goes sharply right up the left-hand side of the rocky combe. You come to a low ridge, but you are not at the col, and the path continues through the attractive grassy combe for about 20mins till you climb another low ridge to reach the top of the pass (2hrs 45mins).

(6) There is a sign on a rock saying Col des Vorets, alt. 1739m/Refuge les Praz Dzeures/Les Molloires. You now have an extended view down the other side of the mountain, so you know you are half way, which is encouraging! Go straight and follow the path, which you can see curving down round the slope to the right, towards the buildings of the Refuge de Praz Dzeures. This is not too steep at first and there is an impressive view of the other side of the Col d'Aiguille, with precipitous rock slopes terminating in what looks like a row of caves, then scree and finally woods, to the rocky bed of the mountain stream. Take care when the path starts to go down more steeply as there are steep drops on the left-hand side (in one place there is a chain to hang on to).

Follow the yellow arrows carefully as the way then starts to climb up steeply on a path which is near to the edge of the mountain. Finally you arrive at the top at a rock where there are chains to help you get round (not at all difficult). You are 60m higher than you were at the col (3hrs 20mins).

The path then continues round the contour of the slope to reach another signpost at the Combe des Frêtes, alt. 1750m, indicating straight to Refuge de Praz Dzeures/La Molloire (right goes to La Tournette). A few minutes later you reach two huts which house a flock of goats, and a small building where the goatherd lives. Go behind the huts and down to the refuge (3hrs 40mins). Here is a chance to have welcome refreshment, and to admire the view to the valley below, where you can even see your car parked near La Molloire.

Gite d'Alpage les Praz Dzeures, tel 0611.49.71.21.

Accommodation for 19 people (two rooms with four beds and dormitory for 11 people). Half-pension 24 Euros (adults), 18 Euros for children under 10. Open 15 June to 15 September.

(7) Continue downwards on the path, which is initially quite steep, crossing a number of streambeds, one with an attractive waterfall. Lower down the track is bordered by stunted alder bushes, and becomes wider with a stream flowing down on the right. The path crosses a wide, stony streambed coming down from the left and continues round the contour of the hill through woods and open country, losing height rapidly. You pass a pulley which takes supplies to the refuge you can just see high above, and there is also a dramatic view of the nearby Tournette mountain. The path reaches a signpost at a fork (4hrs 30mins)

(8) Go up left, following the sign La Molloire which takes you through old beech woods and past two chalets hidden in the trees. Follow the posts with yellow splashes as the path continues down round the hill through continuous beech wood and over a number of streambeds to reach the signpost at No. 2 on the map (5hrs).

Retrace your steps past the farm and down the road to the car park (5hrs 10mins).

WALK 23

Boucle des Tervelles
Alt. 1850m (Thônes area)

Difficulty	Difficult, but only because of the height gain – a hard slog up through woods for 752m to start and then a further height gain of around 200m from the refuge
Time	4hrs 45mins
Height gain	1070m
Maps	Editions Didier & Richard IGN No. 8 Massifs du Mont Blanc/Beaufortain 1:50,000
	Cartes IGN 3431 OT Top 25 Lac d'Annecy 1:25,000
Depart from	Montremont, near Thônes – 780m
Signposting	Good new signposting – follow Crêt / Boucle des Tervelles and red/yellow markings on green plastic background

After the long slog up through the woods, it seems a pity to go back down again (another slog) a few hours later (although of course it is possible to stay overnight in the Refuge de Larrieux – telephone first to make a reservation). Nevertheless, this is a wonderfully satisfying walk in a beautifully unspoilt area where you do not see a single ski-lift all day. The views over Lake Annecy and La Tournette are spectacular.

Access (from Geneva)

Take the motorway, direction Chamonix, and exit at No. 16 Bonneville/La Clusaz. Follow the N203, signposted St-Pierre-en-Faucigny/La Clusaz, and shortly after turn left on the D6A to St-Pierre-en-Faucigny. At the roundabout in the village continue on the D6 over the railway line and then turn right on the D12, signposted La Clusaz. This road takes you up the Borne river valley, a narrow, twisting road through the villages of Petit-Bornand and Entremont. Continue on the D12 to St-Jean-de-Sixt and then take the D909, direction Thônes. Instructions continue at the first paragraph after Alternative, below.

Alternative if Using Geneva Ring Road

Take the N201, direction Annecy, which goes through the new Bardonnex customs (bypassing St-Julien-en-Genevois). Take the first exit (signposted St-Julien-en-Genevois/

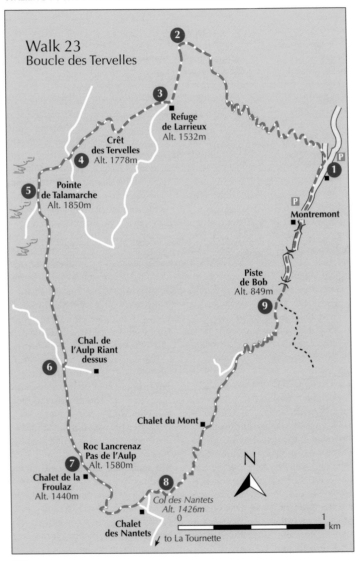

Walk 23
Boucle des Tervelles

2

3

■ **Refuge de Larrieux**
Alt. 1532m

Crêt des Tervelles
Alt. 1778m **4**

Pointe de Talamarche
Alt. 1850m **5**

1 ■ **P**

P Montremont

Piste de Bob
Alt. 849m
9

Chal. de l'Aulp Riant dessus ■

6

Chalet du Mont ■

Roc Lancrenaz
Pas de l'Aulp
Alt. 1580m
7

Chalet de la Froulaz ■
Alt. 1440m

8

Col des Nantets
Alt. 1426m

N

Chalet des Nantets ■

0   1
km

↓ to La Tournette

Annecy) and at the roundabout follow the road signposted Cruseilles/Annecy. You are now back on the original N201 to Annecy. Go through Cruseilles, cross by the spectacular bridge, and at Pringy, just before Annecy, follow signs to Thônes, taking a left turn onto the D16. (**Note** D16 is not marked on the signpost.) This is a newly built road bypassing Annecy and there are a number of roundabouts with the road number changing to N203, then to D916, before finally going back to D16. Basically, follow all signs to Thônes.

Just before Thônes centre take a right turn, signposted Montremont/ Gendarmerie/Aire de Loisirs. Follow this road for about 5kms and park just before the hamlet of Montremont on the left side of the road, opposite signposts Montremont alt. 782m, and a narrow road going off to the right. (**Note** If this parking area is full there is official parking 400m up the road.)

The Route

(1) The signs say Crêt des Tervelles (3hrs 20mins)/Refuge de Larrieux (2hrs 30mins) and other directions, with numbers which correspond to a map sold at the tourist office. Go up the road to the right, then turn off on to a stony path which goes up steeply through light beech and coniferous wood, with some nice views of the narrow valley below and the end of Mont Lachat behind Thônes. Follow a sign to the right saying Boucle des Tervelles (30mins).

The path is marked by red and yellow splashes and gets narrower and steeper as it winds up through beech woods for about 750m. It is quite a long, painful climb, but the shade of the trees is very welcome on a hot summer's day. The path is well defined all the way, so you can't go wrong, and you pass a big sign saying Fôret Domaniale de Thônes. After 1hr 10mins you come out of the woods and are rewarded with a magnificent view of the Chaine des Aravis ahead with the Pointe Percée rearing above at the end. The path continues through intermittent woodland and crosses a stream. (The water from this stream tastes delicious, but that may be the result of climbing up steeply for over 700m!) After the stream the path goes up over Alpine pasture to a signpost (1hr 20mins).

(2) Go left towards Larrieux, cross a dry streambed and follow the yellow/red markings over a low rise to the Refuge de Larrieux, alt. 1532m. Just before the refuge there is a small memorial stone dedicated to Alpagiste Frank Hofer (guardian of the hut from 1976 to1989), with the inscription 'he has made Larrieux a meeting place, of which he was the warm and kind guardian'. The building looks smart (restored in 1976), with a green galvanised roof and little wooden troughs with beautiful flowers and tables for picnickers (all rather twee). There are also glorious views of the surrounding mountains (1hr 35mins).

Refuge de Larrieux (privately owned), tel. 0450.02.19.52.

30 places in two dormitories (telephone ahead if you require a meal). 27 Euros half-board, 7 Euros night only. Open in season (May to end September).

(3) At the refuge follow the sign right to Crêt des Tervelles and Chalet du Lindion (do not take the Circuit de Larrieux No. 21). Further up there is another signpost to Col de Nantets/ Boucle de Lindion No. 19. You are climbing round a delightful, green Alpine bowl in the mountains where, in autumn, there are lots of fringed gentians and crocuses (you can see that the Circuit de Larrieux is a path round this). Straight ahead of you is a beautiful view of La Tournette, one of the highest peaks in the region at alt. 2351m.

Follow the red/yellow markings carefully. The climb is medium steep and quite rocky, giving lovely views back down into the grassy green bowl, with the refuge and the Chaine des Aravis behind. You come to a ridge at the top and find there is quite a drop on the other side down to an ugly, square, manmade watering place for cattle, lined with blue plastic. There is a sign saying Boucle de Lindion No. 19. The path goes left behind the hump of the Crêt des Tervelles, alt. 1778m, and then down to a col where there are new signposts (2hrs 10mins).

(4) Go straight on up the slope, indicated Crêt des Tervelles/Pointe de Talamarche. The path to the right goes down into a shallow valley, where you can see three ugly blue plastic ponds, to Lindion/ Morette; the path on the left (Boucle de Lindion) goes to the Ruines de Talamarche. (This is quite an important crossroads, where the GR96 and the Tour du Massif Tournette Aravis path comes up from Le Lindion and stays with you to the Col des Nantets, though there are no signs to indicate this).

There is now a climb of about 150m to the Pointe de Talamarche, part of Les Grandes Lanches ridge. Follow the white/red GR signs, which are not always easy to see. Go left at a T-junction (2hrs 20mins) – there is a white/red cross to the right which means **do not** go that way. You are now on the bumpy, wide, rocky ridge of the Pointe de Talamarche, alt. 1850m, with dramatic views straight down to the refuge. Go straight on down into a short, shallow depression and then up again. Through the trees to the right you catch your first glimpse of Lake Annecy and the jagged peaks of the Dents de Lanfon (*dents* meaning 'teeth', and they really do look like them), before arriving at the ridge of the Pointe de Talamarche.

Here are more extensive views, including La Tournette, the Chaine des Aravis and Mont Blanc to the east. As you leave the top and go round the corner you look down the other side into an attractive, long, wide Alpine

La Tournette from the Pointe de Talamarche, Boucle des Tervelles

valley with the Chalets de l'Aulp Riant Dessus in the middle. Beyond is the Pas de l'Aulp which you have to cross on the way down to the Col des Nantets (2hrs 35mins).

(5) Careful – be sure to turn left at a white/red GR splash down into the valley – it is easy to miss this path. Do not go straight ahead along the ridge as it gets increasingly narrower and steeper, though if you do it is a good perch for a picnic!

Walk down into the valley following the white/red GR splashes towards the signposts you can see opposite the chalets where another path goes off to the right (2hrs 50mins).

(6) Follow the signpost which says Boucle des Tervelles/Pas de l'Aulp/Col des Nantets. Shortly after you are on a jeep track to the Chalets de l'Aulp Riant Dessus where in summer there is a big herd of cows.

Careful – 5mins later, just before a corner which leads down to the barns, go straight on a narrow, grassy path where there is a GR mark on a rock. Look back for a view of the Pointe de Talamarche and the path you have taken through the valley. You are on an open, grassy path which goes upwards, through a fence, and then up and around the side of the Roc Lancrenaz. This is quite a tricky rocky path and care should be taken as you pick your way down and round the impressive rock face. (On one occasion we were accompanied by a large herd of goats which made the going more difficult as they tried to push us out of the way, looking for food in our rucksacks!) You reach the Pas de l'Aulp, alt. 1580m (3hrs 15mins).

(7) From this col there is an impressive view of the southern end of Lake Annecy and the surrounding mountains, especially of the nearby

185

Boucle des Tervelles

Tournette. The path then winds steeply down through meadowland and scattered firs to the chalets far below, with spectacular views on the way. Still following the GR red/white splashes, the path drops 150m to the Chalet de la Froulaz, alt. 1440m, where drinks and food are available, and then goes above the Chalets des Nantets towards a low hump with an iron cross on top and a signpost beyond. This is the Col des Nantets, alt. 1426m, where there are signposts (3hrs 30mins).

(8) Go straight, following signs Boucle des Tervelles and Montremont, on a wide stony track. You are now leaving the GR96, which continues right to the Chalets de l'Aulp (one of the starting points for climbing La Tournette) and on to the Col de la Forclaz. Up ahead on the left you can see the Refuge de Larrieux, which shows you have made a long semicircle. Now follow the stony track down through a gate, high scrub and then light beech and coniferous wood until you arrive at the

Chalet du Mont, which is set in an attractive open meadow signposted Sentier du Col des Nantets (3hrs 55mins).

Continue through meadowland with a fence to the right, and then the path becomes sunken with high banks as you go down a wide shoulder with tree-covered ravines to left and right. As the woodland thickens, the path gets narrower and steeper, seemingly winding down forever (you can hear a stream down on the right) to reach a big barn at signs Piste de Bob, alt. 849m (4hrs 25mins).

(9) Turn down left at the sign to Montremont 15mins/Tronchine/ Thônes (right goes to Abri des Varos/Col des Frêtes/Chalet de Rosairy) and after a few minutes you reach the tarmac road. Follow the road down, crossing the river twice and passing the hamlet of Montremont up on the left. You pass the official car park before reaching the smaller parking area (4hrs 45mins).

NEAR LA ROCHE-SUR-FORON

WALK 24

La Roche Parnal
Alt. 1896m (Near La Roche-sur-Foron)

Difficulty	Difficult – there is one spot where you have to climb round a rock face hanging on to a chain, putting your feet on iron spikes; not for anyone suffering from vertigo
Time	4hrs (plus 50mins if you go to the summit and return the same way)
Height gain	522m (724m if you go to the summit)
Maps	Editions Didier & Richard IGN No. 3 Massifs du Chablais Faucigny & Genevois 1:50,000
	Cartes IGN 3430 ET Top 25 La Clusaz/Grand-Bornand 1:25,000
Depart from	Le Chesnet (Orange) – 1172m
Signposting	Inadequate – a few signposts and posts with yellow arrows, but not sufficient (they seem to have removed all the former signposting and not yet replaced it, including at the start)

In summer this is a popular spot, though most people go no further than the meadows around the Chalets de la Balme. The sweeping views of the Alps, the lake and surrounding countryside are unsurpassed (because this area is of rocky limestone formation it has not been disfigured by ugly ski-lifts!). The Roche Parnal is quite exposed, with little shade, so on a very hot day this walk is not recommended. However, watch out for patches of snow which linger on the north side. The spring flowers, especially on the south side, are abundant. This walk can be done in either direction – some people prefer to go up the rock on the iron bars rather than down, the advantage being better visibility.

Access (from Geneva)
Take the motorway, direction Chamonix, and then the A41 direction Annecy, exiting La Roche-sur-Foron (first exit).

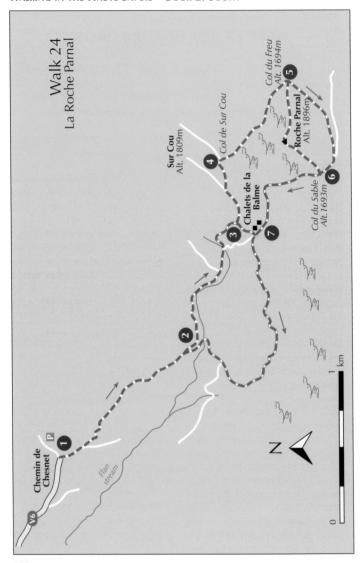

Walk 24
La Roche Parnal

(**Alternative** Exit Annemasse and take the D2, direction Reignier/ La Roche sur Foron.) At La Roche-sur-Foron follow signs to the centre of the town and look for the D2, direction Thôrens/Orange (there is no D2 sign at the turning itself). Do not turn left into the village of Orange, but continue straight on the V6 Chemin de Chesnet (also signposted Chalets de la Balme) and continue on till the road ends at a car park.

The Route

(1) No sign at the start. Take the wide, stony jeep track going steeply up through fir and deciduous wood (some faded yellow splashes), and ignore any paths branching off. The path flattens out where there has been a lot of tree felling and you get a beautiful view on the right of the impressive rock wall of the Montagne de Sous-Dine.

(2) After about 20mins go up left at a fork (the track going down to the right is where you will return), following a wooden sign on a tree which says Balme. The path narrows and goes in and out of the woods on the side of a ravine, with the Flan river rushing below. Keep to the main path, which crosses streambeds and goes through a fence to emerge onto the open hillside. To the right is the Sous-Dine, to the left the rocky edifice of the Sur Cou, alt. 1809m, and ahead is the Roche Parnal, alt. 1896m, looking rather formidable! Just before you reach the chalets there is a sign indicating Cables straight ahead (this is the way up over the chains) Sous-Dine left (55mins).

These rocky limestone mountains, the first range of the Alps rising abruptly from the fertile Geneva plain, are particularly impressive – the pitted, light-grey rocks make a sharp contrast to the intense green of the woods and fields.

(3) Go left up a steep, grassy hill (straight if you wish to do the walk the other way round and go up the cables instead of down). At the top you go through a stile and onto the Col de Sur Cou. Take time to admire the numerous peaks you can see from this viewpoint: (from left to right) the solitary Môle, the Pic de Marcelly above Taninges and, on the horizon, between the Pointe d'Andey and the nearby towering cliffs of the Rochers de Leschaux, the serrated, teeth-like peaks of the Dents du Midi – an unforgettable panorama.

(4) Bear up to the right (no sign) towards the sheer, smooth rock face of the Roche Parnal. At first the path goes through fir trees, and is somewhat boggy if it has been raining, but it later becomes defined and rocky as it curls round the base of the mountain.

There is an iron cross nailed to the rock which commemorates a young lad who fell here on 8 January 1938. It makes one reflect on the risks

189

Walking round La Roche Parnal

people take – at that time of year the path was probably covered in snow and it would certainly have been a dangerous walk to undertake.

There are red/white GR signs on the rock face, which is sheer with black granite veins scaling the surface. As you start to climb to the Col du Freu, the path becomes steep and rocky – at times you have to watch your footholds and you need both hands to grip the rocks. It is not technically difficult, though it can be quite slippery after rainfall. You reach a stile at the Col du Freu, alt. 1694m (1hr 45mins).

(5) When you go through the stile at the Col du Freu there is a glorious view down into the unspoilt Champ Laitier valley, with the long, tree-covered

hump of the Montagne des Frêtes, part of the famous Plateau des Glières. Beyond are the jagged peaks of the Chaine des Aravis, culminating in the Pointe Percée and the Mont Blanc range on the horizon.

Detour (Add around 50mins.) Although not marked on the map, there is a path to the right of the col which goes up to the top and a borne (reference marker), alt. 1896m. It is quite steep and airy, but worth the effort as the panoramic view from the summit is supreme – to the south the entire Alps, and to the north the Geneva plain, the lake, and the Jura range on the horizon. In the Arve valley below is the town of Bonneville. Return the same way and then cut across right when you see the path going round the base of the hill to the Col du Sable. (**Note** Instead of returning the same way, it is possible to take the path going over the top and down to the Col du Sable – there is a defined path, but it is airy! This is, of course, a faster way back.)

If not taking the detour, follow the defined, narrow path which curls round the south side of the mountain to the Col du Sable (do not take the one you can see going straight on round the base of the Sous-Dine). Just before you reach the col the path over the top of the mountain comes in from the right (2hrs 15mins).

In springtime the flowers are particularly striking, and include yellow, vanilla and early purple orchids, alpine daffodils, trumpet gentians, clumps of pansies, harebells, forget-me-nots and creamy pasque anemones.

(6) At the Col du Sable go through a fence and you are now back round to the north face of the Roche Parnal. You are rewarded with a beautiful view right over the end of the lake, with the Salève in the foreground and the Jura beyond. Go down on a narrow path and, at a fork, bear right to reach a chain around a large rock with iron bars to put your feet on – there is quite a precipitous drop. This gives confidence for people who do not suffer from vertigo, but it is not difficult. The only scary thing is that you cannot see in advance where to put your feet and at one spot there is rather a long gap between the iron bars (long legs help!). If you do not like it, retrace your steps back round the mountain.

After going round the rock continue on the path which you can see going down to the Chalets de la Balme, passing a small hut which used to be a refuge but has now fallen into disrepair. At the chalets is a welcome café where you can get drinks and a snack (only open in the high season). (3hrs.)

(7) Pass in front of the chalets and take the jeep track down. The going is steep and stony in places, through intermittent woodland initially, and passing a memorial stone, on the right, dedicated to one François Chappot, who died 11 June 1989 (one wonders how, as this is not at a dangerous spot). Further down the woods become denser and you cross some streams.

Keep straight (do not take turnings left) till you join the original path, No. 2 on the map, where you turn left back to the car park (4hrs).

Looking towards the Sous-Dine from the summit of La Roche Parnal

WALK 25

Montagne de Sous-Dine
Alt. 2004m (Near La Roche-sur-Foron)

Difficulty	Difficult and airy in places – there is a chain at one spot for scrambling round a rock face
Time	5hrs 45mins
Height gain	1000m
Depart from	Les Cheneviers (La Roche-sur-Foron) – 1090m
Maps	Editions Didier & Richard IGN No. 3 Massifs du Chablais Faucigny & Genevois 1:50,000
	Cartes IGN 3430 ET Top 25 La Clusaz/Grand-Bornand 1:25,000
Signposting	Adequate – new signposts and posts with yellow arrows on green background in some places (they were starting to put these up in 2004); otherwise follow yellow and red splashes, though not always obvious due to logging

This is one of my favourite walks as the views are so extensive. The first range of Chablais mountains, rising out of the Lac Léman plain, give contrasting views of undulating green fields and the lake, stretching from Geneva to the start of the Rhône valley, with the long line of Jura mountains on one side and the varied jagged peaks of the Alps on the other. It is probably best to do this walk in spring or autumn, as once out of the woods there is little shade and no streams where you can quench your thirst. This is a good area for seeing bouquetins (ibex), the agile alpine goats with their long serrated horns. The Sous-Dine is a limestone mountain, pitted with rocks and crevices, not unlike the Parmelan near Annecy. The difference is that it is not so well known and even at the height of the summer season you will see few people.

Access (from Geneva)

Take the motorway, direction Chamonix, and then the A41 direction Annecy, exiting at No. 19 La Roche-sur-Foron (first exit). (**Alternative** Sortie Annemasse and take the D2 direction Reignier/La Roche-sur-Foron). At La Roche follow signs to the centre of the town and at a roundabout turn right on the D2, signposted to Orange (the road number is not marked till after you have turned). Do not turn left towards the village of Orange but continue, and then take the C16 left to Mont Piton/Les Cheneviers. Drive through the hamlet of Les Cheneviers and go to the the end of the road where there is a large parking area.

The Route

(1) At the parking area there is a signpost Les Cheneviers, alt. 1090m, indicating Circuit de Champ Laitier/Circuit de Sous-Dine/Col des Glières. Go straight (not right), fairly steeply up a stony jeep track under shady deciduous and coniferous trees. After a few minutes follow a sign right to Circuit de Sous-Dine (post and a yellow splash on a tree).

After 5mins, turn right at a T-junction (post with yellow arrows) and continue on a wider jeep track where there are yellow splashes. Cross a forestry road (post) and continue straight (30mins). (**Note** The white blobs with a red line through them are the signs for the woodcutters only – they are not directional signs. There is a lot of forestry and construction of new roads in this area, so some yellow splashes may disappear in the future.)

At a fork (no post, though there might be one shortly) you can go left or right because they join up a few minutes later. You reach signposts at La Croisée, alt. 1377m, indicating Sous-Dine par le Monthieu up to the left and Sous-Dine par le Trou de la Pierre up to the right. Continue straight for a few metres to reach a large intersection (why they couldn't put the sign here is a puzzle) (45mins).

(2) Go left on a wide track which contours the mountain on a delightfully flat balcony path (go round the iron barrier across the track) through tall coniferous trees. To the left are tantilising views, through breaks in the trees, of the Geneva plain with the lake beyond. You reach a second clearing (1hr 10mins).

(3) Go up right, following the sign Monthieu Sous-Dine. The track climbs through woodland, bearing left, and becomes a wide logging track. Follow this main track where many of the trees have been cut down (there are occasional red splashes), ignoring paths diverging off. The wide track ends abruptly and you bear up left on a narrower path (splashes here). (**Note** Due to logging activities the wide track could continue, but hopefully there will be signposting.)

You come across a very high ant hill by the side of the path, crawling with ants going about their business. Ant hills are fairly unusual in the Alps, but are common in the nearby Jura mountains.

193

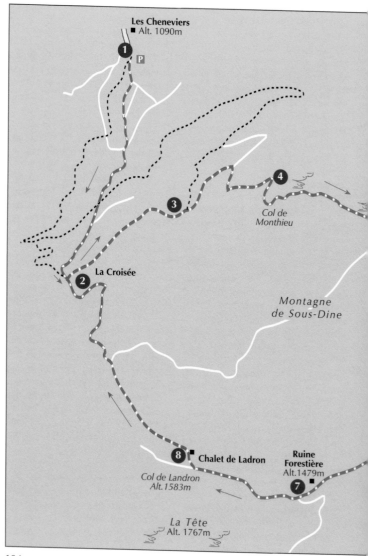

Les Cheneviers
■ Alt. 1090m

Col de Monthieu

Montagne de Sous-Dine

La Croisée

Chalet de Ladron

Col de Landron
Alt.1583m

Ruine Forestière
Alt.1479m

La Tête
Alt. 1767m

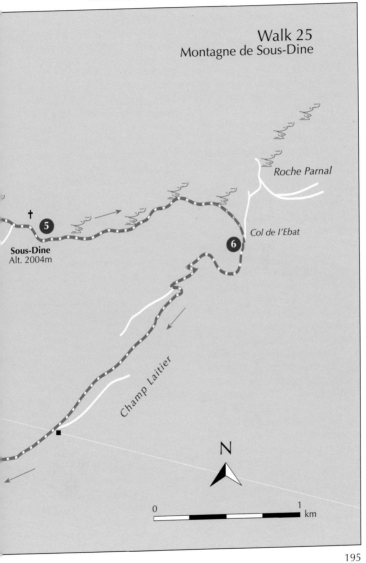

Walk 25
Montagne de Sous-Dine

Roche Parnal

5

Col de l'Ebat

Sous-Dine
Alt. 2004m

6

Champ Laitier

N

0   1 km

The path bears round over scree, and you have open views again with the rocky crests of Sous-Dine up on the right. Suddenly you come to an exposed corner where, if you went straight on, you would go over the edge! Take time here to admire the plain below, the grassy Sur Cou ahead and the rocky peak of the adjacent Roche Parnal mountain. Beyond are the peaks of the Chablais region (1hr 40mins).

(4) The path bears round to the right and becomes narrow and rocky as it starts to climb quite steeply up the open mountainside – this is not for anyone suffering from vertigo, as sometimes you need both hands to clamber over the rocks. The path goes through a narrow rocky gully to the Col de Monthieu, and then slackens off as you walk through knee-high vegetation and lovely mountain flowers in a fold in the hillside, before going up the shoulder and along a crest with a dramatic drop on one side (happily not always visible from where you are walking). The path undulates over grassy terrain with occasional stunted firs, lots of boulders and flat limestone rocks. At one place there is a sunken area on the left surrounded by boulders. The Sous-Dine is a flattish, rock-pitted, limestone mountain, so there is no dramatic summit.

You reach a wide grassy area where there is a yellow arrow on a flat grey rock, pointing back the way you have come, and a red arrow pointing

down the other side saying Landron (this is an alternative path off the mountain – not done by the author).

(5) Continue upwards for 5mins to a small stone cairn and a cross (dated 1996), which is on the edge of the mountain. You are at the highest point of the Sous-Dine, alt. 2004m, with one of the best views in the region. The Geneva plain, the lake and the Jura range are to the north, the Alps to the south, and the Thorens-Glières plateau on the immediate left (2hrs 30mins).

Walk along the ridge crest on the path, which is sometimes indistinct with occasional red markings. The crest is rocky and indented, undulating up and down, and the path sometimes goes quite near to the rocky cliff edge. There is another rocky hole to the right.

If it is a clear day you get a wonderful view of Mont Blanc and surrounding peaks as you walk along. If you are lucky one of the almost tame ibex will position itself in front of you for a magnificent photograph!

The path becomes more difficult as you start picking your way down over small crevices and large rocks into a narrow, rocky defile. At one stage there is a drop down a rock face with a short ladder.

Continue following the red splashes downwards. The path is not technically difficult, but you are negotiating round large boulders, so care is needed. Finally you have to lower yourself across a sheer rock face by a chain. The best way to do it is to grab hold of the chain, face into the rock and move your feet along the cracks, like rappelling. These chains are only about 3m long and there is no steep drop below. After this the worst is over and you can see the track in the valley below coming from the Col de l'Ebat. Take the narrow path going down the slope till it peters out and make your way to the jeep track (3hrs 35mins).

(6) Turn right at the bottom and you walk into a gloriously unspoilt valley called the Champ Laitier. The coniferous trees on the hillside to the left seem to sweep right down to the valley floor, the dark forest green giving way to the emerald green of the Alpine pastures. A stream meanders through and there are no ugly buildings to mar the tranquil scene. On the right are the dramatic rocky slopes of the Sous-Dine.

This lovely valley of Champ Laitier has known death and destruction, however. The reason there are so few farms here is because the Germans burned them down during the Second World War. This is one of the famous Thoren-Glières valleys where the last of the gallant French Resistance bands held out against the enemy. On the forest-covered

Ibex on the summit of the Sous-Dine

hillside are hidden bunkers and caves where the soldiers were relentlessly hunted out over many months and at great cost of life.

The path goes gently down and then flattens out as it skirts the valley side. You get a good view of the Parmelan mountain which dominates Annecy; on the horizon to the left is the dramatic summit of the Tournette, the highest peak in the area.

There is an isolated farm/chalet along the path (being renovated in 2002). When open, kindly shepherds will let you renew your water supplies, as there is little shade on this hike and, being a limestone mountain, all the streams run underground.

If you walk down this valley in mid-August you will notice that the slopes are covered with glorious purple thistles. The track later passes another solitary chalet (Office National des Fôrets) and reaches a signpost at Ruine Forestière, alt. 1479m (4hrs 15mins).

(7) Go up right (left goes to the Champ Laitier chalet and further to the famous Resistance Monument), passing a ruin to the left where there is a plaque, and further on a barn set back on the right. It is then a short grind to the Col de Landron, alt. 1583m, and further signs (4hrs 30mins).

(8) Follow the sign straight to Les Cheneviers. To the left is an interesting peak called La Tête, alt. 1767m, and you get your first views of the coastal plain again, as you have walked right round the mountain. The path continues through open spaces and woodland – there is a big sign announcing that you are in the protected area of the Fôret Dom de la Haute Filière and, just after the sign, a path up to your right which says Sous-Dine. This is the shorter way down from the red arrow at the top. Way over, down on the left, you can see the road up to the Plateau des Glières.

The path passes a high rock face and gets stonier and wider as it goes down fairly steeply through cool forest, passing a sign at Ancien Chemin. Keep to the main path till you get back to the first clearing (La Croisée), where you take the right fork down to signs Sous-Dine par l'Enclave/Sous-Dine par le Monthieu. Continue down the same way as you came up (5hrs 45mins).

WALK 26

Plateau des Glières
Alt. 1440m (Near La Roche-sur-Foron)

Difficulty	**Walk 1** Easy historical walk on the plateau
	Walk 2 Medium/more challenging – it includes the historical walk, then descends to a valley and climbs back up to the plateau
Time	**Walk 1** 1hr 45mins (slowly and reading the historical notices)
	Walk 2 3hrs 45mins
Height gain	**Walk 1** Negligible
	Walk 2 300m down and up
Maps	Editions Didier & Richard IGN No. 3 Massifs du Chablais Faucigny & Genevois 1:50,000
	Cartes IGN 3430 ET Top 25 La Clusaz/Grand-Bornand 1:25,000
Depart from	Parking on Plateau des Glières
Signposting	**Walk 1** Good
	Walk 2 Lacking in places, though well signed where it joins the Sentier Tom Morel and Sentier de l'Attaque (see below)

The Plateau des Glières, alt. 1500m, is a typical 'hanging valley'. You have to go up a long, winding road to reach this flat upland area, once remote and unheard of. Now it is lodged in the annals of history, as it is here that the French Resistance movement held out against the German army in the Second World War (see section on Thônes in the introduction). Due to the courage of a few hundred men, many of whom were subsequently killed in the fighting, the Haute Savoie region was liberated a few months later. A dramatic monument was designed by the architect Emile Gilioli and inaugurated by the culture minister and writer André Malraux on 2 September 1973. It is in the form of a sun between two wings, one of which is cut off. It symbolises the desire for freedom immortalized in the words used by the Resistance: *'Vivre libre ou mourir'* ('live free or die'). There are noticeboards

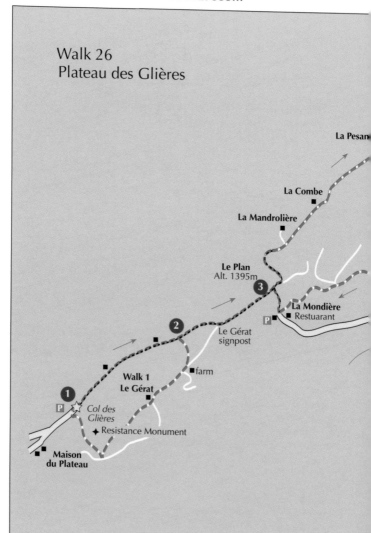

Walk 26
Plateau des Glières

La Pesan

La Combe

La Mandrolière

Le Plan
Alt. 1395m
3

La Mondière
■ Restuarant

Le Gérat
signpost

2

P

■ farm

Walk 1
Le Gérat

1

P ☆ *Col des Glières*

✦ Resistance Monument

Maison du Plateau

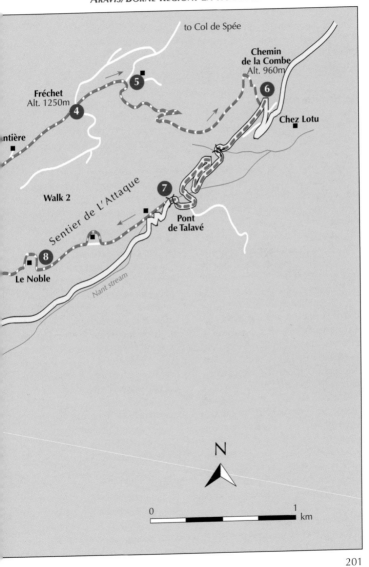

to Col de Spée

Chemin de la Combe
Alt. 960m

6

Chez Lotu

Fréchet
Alt. 1250m

4

5

ntière

Walk 2

Sentier de L'Attaque

7

Pont de Talavé

8

Le Noble

Nant stream

N

0   1
km

along the path (with explanations in English) giving information about the invasion and the names of the commanders who fought and died defending their country. There is also an information centre at the start of the walk, open from 1 June to 30 September.

Access (from Geneva)

Take the motorway, direction Chamonix, exit at No. 19 (La Roche-sur-Foron) and take the direction Annecy on the N203. Continue until you see a sign left to Thorens-Glières on the D2. * Continue on the D2 to the village of Thorens-Glières and then follow all signs to Plateau des Glières on the D55. The road winds up for another 12km. Keep straight (do not take a turning right) until you reach a large parking area at the end of the road where there is a *chalet d'accueil* (welcome centre).

Alternative road Take the N201 direction Annecy, which goes through the Bardonnex customs (bypassing St-Julien-en-Genevois). Take the first exit (signposted St-Julien-en Genevois/Annecy) and at the roundabout follow the road signposted Cruseilles/Annecy. You are now back on the original N201 to Annecy. Go through Cruseilles and cross the Pont de Caille. Continue through the village of Allonzier-la-Caille and, at the entrance to the motorway, look for a turning to the left on the D2 signposted Thorens-Glières 12km. Continue from *above.

The Route (for both walks)

(1) Read the noticeboard describing the role the Resistance played during

the Second World War on the Plateau des Glières, and then go to the end of the parking area where there are two observation tables with maps and names of the surrounding peaks. You also have a good view here of the impressive concrete monument commemorating the Resistance (see above). Take the obvious signposted path along the grassy plateau, passing the first notice called Le Monument.

You pass a further notice saying you are at the Chalet of Marie des Bossons, one of the inhabitants who sheltered and fed the soldiers. Continue past another large chalet where it is explained that this chalet has been rebuilt on the ruins of the *poste de commandement* (command post) of Tom Morel, the first leader of the Resistance, and his successor, Captain Maurice Anjot, both of whom were killed. Nearby is a small pond which supplied the troops with much-needed water. Continue on and watch for a provisional sign right saying Le Monument (25mins).

Walk 1

(2) Go right through a small fir wood and then through about three electric fences – the path turns right near the jeep track to the farm and continues through open meadowland. (**Careful**

– this part of the walk could be changed depending which part of the meadow the cattle are grazing on.)

You reach a further noticeboard by a chalet. This was used by the Scouts Skiers Platoon and by Tom Morel, the first leader of the Maquis (Resistance). The path turns to the left between electric fences and then goes back on the jeep track (going to the farm). Here is another notice saying that the chalet was built on the ruins of the infirmary, which was burnt to the ground by the Germans on 26 March 1944. This is now also part of a nature walk; there are more signs describing the life of the inhabitants of the plateau in earlier times, the making of local cheeses, and descriptions of vegetation and flowers. Another notice indicates the site of the main arms and ammunition depot, which is now a grass-covered dip where the chalet was blown up.

Take the wooden slats across the meadow to the monument.

It is worth going inside to see a small gold replica of the monument and to read the moving story of how 465 young men and women held out for two months, aided and abetted by the local inhabitants, from 31 January to March 1944 under their young commander Tom Morel and, when he was killed, his successor Capitaine Anjot. When German forces parachuted onto the plateau, 121 of them were killed and more were deported. The plateau was finally liberated by the Allies in August 1944.

Follow the obvious slatted wooden path across the meadows to the parking area (1hr 45mins).

Walk 2

(2) Continue on past the provisional sign right saying Le Monument (you will take this on the return). The path reaches a signpost at Le Gérat, alt. 1390m, where the sign right indicates that it is a Chemin Privée/Passage Interdit, and you are not allowed to go that way. (In other words, the farmers do want tourists walking through their meadows where there are cattle in summer, so the path has been re-routed.) Continue straight past another noticeboard, Les Espagnols, explaining that 56 Spanish refugees joined the Resistance and set up two platoons – 11 of them were subsequently killed. The path reaches a T-junction at Le Plan, alt. 1395m (35mins).

(3) Turn left towards La Mandrolière/Chez Lotu/Les Lignières/Col de Spée on a wide jeep track, passing a large chalet to the left called Chez Constance at La Mandrolière. Continue on between electric fences past the odd chalet, and through wide-open pastures full of wild flowers in spring and summer. There is a lovely view ahead of the high rocky cliffs of the Monts Leschaux. The jeep track starts to lose height to reach another chalet with a cross up on the right, and further signposts at Fréchet, alt. 1250m (left goes to the Col de Spée) (1hr).

(4) Go straight, following the sign to Chez Lotu, on a grassy path which continues to descend and enters woodland. At a fork where there is a post, stay on the path, continuing downwards – you can see a chalet ahead (1hr 15mins).

(5) Careful – about 100m before you reach another chalet (it seems to have three names, La Combe, Chalet de Bonheur and La Paradise!), take the path to the right (no signpost). The path continues down the side of the hill (you can see the chalet up on the left) through beech wood, becoming wider and more defined as it zigzags down with a tree-covered gorge on the right. Cross a new wooden bridge to eventually reach a road and signposts at Chemin de la Combe, alt. 960m (1hr 45min).

(6) Turn right (left goes to Chez Lotu) up the road, which zigzags fairly steeply for 30mins to reach further signposts. Continue straight, sign-posted Monument de la Resistance 1hr 35mins (a path left goes to Montièvran/Les Plans). A few minutes later you reach more signs at a parking area. Cross a bridge with green railings where there are red/white GR splashes. Shortly after there are further signposts at Pont de Talavé, alt. 1150m (2hrs 10mins).

(7) Go off right up a steep, narrow path through woodland where you can see the road down on the left. You reach a jeep track where you go straight up ahead on a grassy path, hugging the side of the wood with a large chalet up on the right (the road is down on the left). You pass another chalet as you continue climbing medium steep and then a third (all these chalets look exactly the same), called Le Noble, where there are signposts. You are on the Sentier de l'Attaque, alt. 1390m, the path the Germans walked up to attack the French troops (2hrs 50mins).

(8) The way becomes somewhat undefined as it goes behind the chalet and comes to a post with yellow arrows. Follow the path through open meadows (in the spring there are covered in wild flowers, including a variety of interesting orchids such as the red and white helleborine, butterfly and spotted). You are finally back on the plateau again and there is a lovely view across the upland meadows – on the right is the rocky limestone ridge of the Sous-Dine. The track reaches the Restaurant la Mondière where there is a parking area (Chez la Jode on the official map) and then continues to the original T-junction at No. 3.

The track passes Le Gérat signpost (the forbidden junction is to the left) and then reaches the provisional sign to the monument on the left. To see the monument more closely and finish the historical part of the walk, take the left path and continue the short walk from No. 2. If not, continue back to the parking area (3hrs 45mins).

LAKE ANNECY AREA

WALK 27

Le Parmelan
Alt. 1835m (Lake Annecy area)

Difficulty	Medium/difficult; do not go up the Grand Montoir if there is snow, as there is an easier way round
Time	4hrs
Height gain	635m
Maps	Editions Didier & Richard IGN No. 2 Massifs des Bornes-Bauges 1:50,000
	Cartes IGN 3430 OT Top 25 Mont Salève 1:25,000
Depart from	Above the village of Villaz – 1200m
Signposting	Excellent all the way round – follow yellow splashes

There are two ways up this mountain, one from the forestry road beyond the village of Villaz and the other from above the village of La Blonnière. I have chosen the way up from Villaz as it is easier to find, there is more parking space and the path is less steep. This walk is a classic, simply a must if you are staying in the Annecy region as the panoramic views are breathtaking. It is extremely popular with the local population, who love to come up at weekends and picnic at the top by the refuge, so beware weekends in high summer, as you will find the mountain swarming with people. If you have time, stay at the refuge and watch the sun rise at dawn, but remember you are unlikely to be alone.

Access (from Geneva)

Take the motorway, direction Chamonix, exit at No. 19 (La Roche-sur-Foron) and take the direction Annecy on the N203. Continue on this road for about 22km and then turn left on the D175 to Villaz. Go through the village up to the D5, where you turn left, and then shortly after right up a small road, the C101, signposted Parmelan. The road goes on for 5km before ending in a parking area.

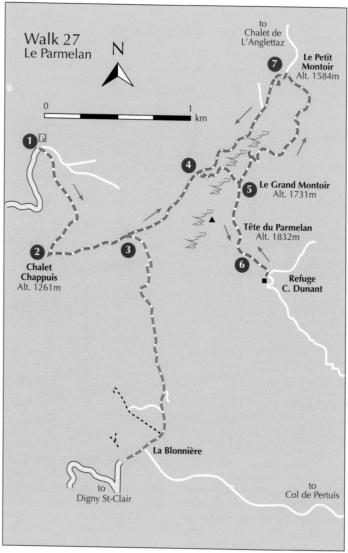

Walk 27
Le Parmelan

N

0   1 km

1 P

to
Chalet de
L'Anglettaz

7 Le Petit
Montoir
Alt. 1584m

4

5 Le Grand Montoir
Alt. 1731m

Tête du Parmelan
Alt. 1832m

2
Chalet
Chappuis
Alt. 1261m

3

6

Refuge
C. Dunant

La Blonnière

to
Digny St-Clair

to
Col de Pertuis

The Route

(1) At the end of the parking area there is a sign saying Tête du Parmelan 2hrs. Take the wide, stony track beside it bearing upwards through tall firs. After 5mins turn right at a sign on a tree to Chalet Chappuis, and continue on a wide, fairly flattish path, winding round the base of the mountain to the Chalet Chappuis. (**Note** If you do not wish to go to the chalet there is a path up left along here signposted Tête du Parmelan par Sentier des Vaches (not done by the author).)

The Chalet Chappuis serves drinks and snacks and is splendidly situated in an open area which juts out of the mountain. You get a magnificent view straight down the Thônes valley, framed by the mountains around Lake Annecy. It is a delightful place, a popular spot to linger and enjoy the surroundings before continuing (5mins).

(2) Follow the sign Boucle du Parmelan on a narrow path, still going upwards through woods. After 5mins you come to a T-junction where you go right. Keep on the path, parallel to a fence, and at a second T-junction turn right again and continue to further signposts (30mins).

(3) Turn up left, following the sign Refuge C Dunant, which also indicates straight on to Parking La Blonnière (this is an alternative way up – see above). You reach a wider track where you turn up right and, a few minutes later,

bear left following a sign Parmelan and yellow splashes. The path curls round the mountain, becoming wider, and then narrows again. A few minutes later you have your first close view of the high cliff face of the Parmelan and you may wonder how you are ever going to get up it. Still in shady woodland, you arrive at the intersection of the Petit Montoir and the Grand Montoir (50mins).

(4) Straight ahead is the Petit Montoir, an easy path following the contour of the mountain, or you can go right up the Grand Montoir, which goes steeply up the face of the mountain. It is not technically difficult, and there are chains or an iron rail to hang on to, but it is not for anyone who suffers from vertigo. (**Note** There is a sign here saying it is dangerous to take this path if it is covered in snow.) If you are not afraid of heights, take this way, as it is an exciting climb up the rock face. The going is rocky but well trodden and there is a steep, treeless drop on one side. Where it seems to descend slightly, keep going and do not take any short cuts. After 20mins of climbing you reach the shoulder at a signpost indicating that you have rejoined the path via the Petit Montoir (1hr 30mins).

(5) Turn right and continue up the shoulder. You now appreciate that the top of this mountain is an incredible limestone plateau of long, corrugated rock fissures, dotted with stunted firs and crisscrossed by narrow, deep crevices and cavernous holes. This is a weird, lunar landscape which was a glacier thousands of years ago, and it is dangerous to walk over if you do not stick to the paths or if fog comes down. On the horizon rises the glistening Mont Blanc range, with the Plateau des Glières in the foreground, where the last of the French Resistance fighters held out in the Second World War (see Walk Number 26). Behind is the Annecy valley, with the Pont de Caille bridge clearly visible, and Lac Léman and the Jura mountains in the background.

Continue on the well-trodden rocky path and suddenly, over a slight rise, you come to the Refuge Camille Dunant, alt. 1825m, belonging to the French Alpine Club. Built in 1883 it is large and rather ugly, with a corrugated-iron roof. There are actually two buildings, the newer one being an annexe with additional dormitory accommodation.

Refuge du Parmelan (Club Alpin Français), tel. 0450.27.29.45. For reservations telephone M.Basilio on 0450.02.11.14.
    The refuge serves a variety of food and drink and can accommodate 50 people in three dormitories. Open from 26 June to 15 September (weekends until 10 October).

The real summit is back up on the right, above the hut (2hrs).

There is a breathtaking panoramic view over the town of Annecy and the mountains surrounding the lake, with a glimpse of the end of the lake through the Col de Bluffy. Straight ahead are the serrated, teeth-like cliffs of the Dents de Lanfon, with the high peak of the Tournette rearing up beyond. Over on the left are the snow-covered peaks of the Mont Blanc range and below is the winding, green Thônes valley – no wonder it is crowded with people on summer weekends.

Further on from the refuge there is a sign to La Blonnière par le Col de Pertuis 3hrs/Grotte de l'Enfer/Chalet de l'Anglette/Villaz. La Blonnière par le Col de Pertuis is a longer way round to the alternative start of this walk. I have not done it, but am told it is quite difficult. If you have time, take this path and then branch off after about 10mins towards the Grotte de l'Enfer (clearly marked). The Grotte de l'Enfer is difficult to find and the path, though clear at first, gets tricky further on. However, if you persevere along the path for about 15mins you get a good idea of the glacial terrain and you can peer into the awesome limestone holes and crevices. In spring and summer there is an abundance of wild flowers in the patches of fertile soil between the rocks. It is then wiser to retrace your steps to the refuge.

(6) Retrace your steps to the signpost Grand Montoir/Petit Montoir Facile (meaning easy) and go straight

Going up the Grand Montoir, Parmelan

towards Petit Montoir on a stony path round the back of the mountain. It is attractive and well defined, snaking through the serrated rocks and fissures of this limestone region, dotted with shrubs and small fir trees, but watch your feet in places. This path is longer than the Grand Montoir as it goes right round the Parmelan cliffs.

(7) At a sign to Chalet de l'Anglette right and Villaz straight, go straight on over the col when you will see the Annecy valley again and the path ahead going right along the hill.

Continue along the front of the mountain, with the daunting, rocky face of the Parmelan on your left and the valley down on your right. It is a delightful, undulating path and a wel-come change from the steep haul up the rock face, though there are occasional steep drops where the mountain falls away on your right. There are numerous hidden caves in the rock face, and at one spot you notice a complete change of temperature (more noticeable on a hot day), presumably due to cold air emanating from the deep rock fissures. The path goes into cool fir woods back to the signpost indicating left up to the Grand Montoir (3hrs). You are now on the path you came up. Ignore a sign down right to Refuge du Parmelan par Sentier des Vaches and continue down. Be careful to take the right fork to Chalet Chappuis (not left to La Blonnière) and continue back to the car park (4hrs).

WALK 28

Cascade d'Angon
Alt. 781m (Lake Annecy area)

Difficulty	Easy, though there is a short, steep path to start
Time	2hrs 45mins
Height gain	300m
Maps	Editions Didier & Richard IGN No. 2 Massifs des Bornes-Bauges 1:50,000
	Cartes IGN 3431 OT Top 25 Lac d'Annecy 1:25,000
Depart from	Talloires on Lake Annecy
Signposting	Good – new white signposts as well as the original wooden ones; some posts with yellow arrows on green background

Although this walk is short, it is well worth doing and perfect for taking visitors and children, who will enjoy the dramatic waterfalls. The contrast between woodland and meadows is delightful and makes this a very satisfying expedition – the views of Lake Annecy and surrounding peaks are spectacular, especially in early spring when the leaves are off the trees. It is worth going into the charming village of Talloires afterwards and sitting at one of the lakeside restaurants – some of them very upmarket. (**Note** The road through the village is one way.)

Access (from Geneva)

Take the motorway, direction Chamonix, and then the A41 signposted Annecy/Grenoble/Lyon. Exit Annecy centre and follow all signs to the D909 Veyrier Le Lac/Talloires, which will lead you to the road along the eastern shore of the lake. (**Alternative** Take the N201 direction Annecy, which goes through the new Bardonnex customs (bypassing St-Julien-en-Genevois). Follow all signs to Annecy and the D909 as above.) Continue on the lake road, direction Talloires, but keep to the road above the village. At a roundabout, go straight, direction Angon/Balmette, and almost immediately after the school at the roundabout park in the official parking area to the right where there is a sign Cascade d'Angon. (If you pass tennis courts further on you know you have gone too far.)

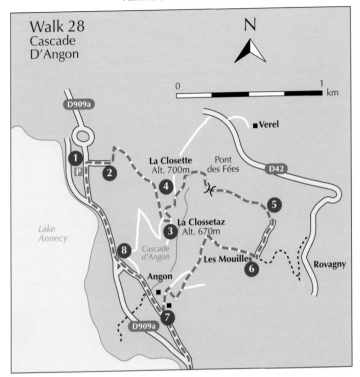

The Route

(1) Following the white sign Cascade d'Angon, go out of the car park and turn left. Almost immediately turn up right on the Route de Vivier where there is a large sign Domaine de l'Hermitage. Walk up the road passing the L'Hermitage, which used to be a hotel but is now a smart apartment block.

(2) About 100m further on take a wide, stony track to the left, signposted Pont des Fées and St-Germain. The rocky track goes up steeply at first through delightful beech woods, and then levels off as it bears round the contour of the hill.

(3) You reach more signposts at La Clossetaz, alt. 670m, where you continue straight to Cascade d'Angon/ Rovagny (ignore the path going down right signposted Angon). A few minutes later you reach an iron barrier which is the start of the walk along

211

the side of the gorge to the waterfalls (45mins).

Go through the barrier on a defined path which goes along the edge of a deep, wooded gully. There is an iron railing on one side for protection, as you often have to bend under the overhanging rock of the cliff face on the other side. There are two beautiful waterfalls. The first is smaller and the path goes underneath it, which can be a rather watery experience if there has been lots of rain. It continues to the second waterfall, which is very dramatic, as it falls straight off the cliff into the narrow, rocky gully far below. The last few metres to the waterfall is tricky as the path goes up over slippery rocks, although there is a chain and a barrier. As you walk around the gully

there are lovely views back over the end of the lake.

Retrace your steps to the gate and the wide track (No. 3 on the map) where you turn right and continue upwards. There is a lovely view to the left here of the château on the promontory jutting out from the village of Duingt across the lake. You reach further signs at La Closette, alt. 700m (1hr 15mins).

(4) Go right, signposted Pont des Fées and Rovagny (if you go straight you reach Vérel where there is a *buvette*). You cross over the two streams above the waterfalls, the first one on a slatted wooden bridge where the water flows enticingly over small rocks. The second one, the Pont des Fées ('fairy bridge'), is 5mins further on, up round

The Taillefer ridge with Le Roc des Boeufs behind from the waterfall walk

a corner. The bridge is more substantial, with the river flowing fiercely below through a deep gully.

After the bridges, turn up left (right goes to the edge of the gorge) where the path comes out into beautiful meadowland which in springtime is a carpet of flowers amid long, waving grass – purple wild geraniums, bright-blue cornflowers, yellow vetch, golden buttercups, tall white daisies and fluffy cow parsley, creating a kaleidoscope of colour – a natural place to stop and take refreshment while you admire the colour and scenery. You can see Lake Annecy through the trees and the Taillefer ridge with the Roc des Boeufs behind (Walk Number 30). Continue upwards past another field on the left.

(5) A few minutes later you come to the road to Les Mouilles and Rovagny. Turn right (do not go straight up where there is a wooden post) and continue till you come to a corner at Chemin les Mouilles with a sign left to Rovagny (1hr 40mins).

(6) Turn sharp right, following a wooden sign indicating Angon/Talloires. Follow the defined path, which has a tiny stream flowing on the right before it goes through delightful meadowland. Make for a clump of trees in the centre of the field and then go across into woodland where there is a rocky path with faded red splashes. (**Note** In summer the track across the field becomes undefined amid the waving grass and flowers.) The path is rocky, going down fairly steeply through attractive beech woods on the other side of the waterfall gorge (be careful if it has been raining, as the rocks are slippery). Keep to the main path all the way down.

(7) The track comes out at the village of Angon (there is a big building in front which is being renovated). Turn right and cross the 'waterfall' river (proper name Grenant but it doesn't sound so nice!). (Look at the huge stone mill wheel to the left, rather spoilt by a new house built beside it.) You pass another track to the right, signposted Pont des Fées, which is another way up the hill.

(8) The road meets the D909 where you turn right and walk back to your car along the lakeside – this is very pretty much of the way back, on a little path right beside the water. Retrace steps to car (2hrs 45mins).

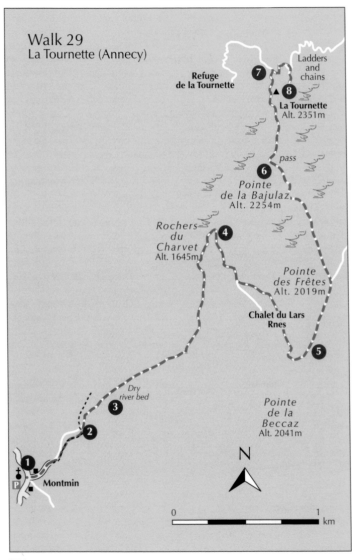

WALK 29

La Tournette
Alt. 2351m (Lake Annecy area)

Difficulty	Difficult – a challenging walk, as there is a vertiginous scree slope to cross, and then a chain plus two ladders to negotiate to reach the final summit (nevertheless, hundreds of walkers do it every year)
Time	6hrs 30mins
Height gain	1024m
Maps	Editions Didier & Richard IGN No. 2 Massifs des Bornes-Bauges 1:50,000
	Cartes IGN 3431 OT Top 25 Lac d'Annecy 1:25,000
Depart from	Montmin – 1094m
Signposting	Excellent – follow green splashes; the path is defined all the way and you can't go wrong

La Tournette is the highest peak in the Annecy region and very popular with more experienced walkers. If you look at the map you can see that the summit can be reached from various starting points, and it is possible to do a two-day circle staying in one of the refuges (see end of the route for list). This is a tough walk, but within the capabilities of any fit person not suffering from vertigo. It is worth the effort as the view from the summit is unforgettable. There is something very satisfying about completing a challenging walk, especially as many people are hesitant to hang on to chains and clamber up ladders, but are thrilled when they have done so. The fact that in summer there are often queues to get to the *fauteuil* shows that this is one of the popular Alpine classics. If you want to do this walk and be relatively alone, it is better to go on a weekday outside the busy months of July and August.

Access (from Geneva)

Take the motorway, direction Chamonix, and then the A41 signposted Annecy/Grenoble/Lyon. Exit Annecy Centre and follow all signs to the D909 Veyrier le Lac/Talloires which will lead you to the lake road. Just before Talloires, look for the D42 to the left, which is a narrow, rather windy road going over the Col de la Forclaz (a popular spot for tourists in summer as the view down the Annecy lake is magical) and on to the village of Montmin. At Montmin park your car beside the church.

Alternative Take the N201, direction Annecy, which goes through the new Bardonnex customs (bypassing St-Julien-en-Genevois). Take the first exit (signposted St-Julien-en-Genevois/Annecy) and at the roundabout follow the road signposted Cruseilles/Annecy. You are now back on the original N201 to Annecy. Follow all signs to Annecy and the D909 Veyrier le Lac/Talloires and proceed as described above.

The Route

(1) Near the church there is a sign on a *lavoir* ('wash trough') which says La Tournette Circuit No. 14 – 4 hrs. Cross the village street and go up the tarmac road as indicated between two old houses. It degenerates into a jeep track, rather like an English country lane, with steep banks of vegetation and occasional chalets. Keep on the main track. As you walk up you can see down left into the valley and over to the Col de la Forclaz. Continue till you come to a signpost (10mins).

(2) Go up right, signposted Tournette, following the green splashes which accompany you to the summit. You pass through a gate on to a pleasant

216

stony path going up medium steep through intermittent woodland, getting rockier as you climb higher, with steepish wooded slopes of beech and fir on either side. In front there are daunting views of the massive La Tournette mountain. The path comes out of the woodland and crosses a dry riverbed (35mins)

(3) It levels out for a short while before going back into stunted beech woods and climbing again medium steep. As you come of out the woods for the last time you can see way over on the right the huge cliffs of the Pointe de la Beccaz, and on the left the Pointe de la Bajulaz with La Tournette behind. The path becomes stonier and then rockier as you pass a small cave (55mins).

When we walked here in October we saw a group of three female bouquetins (ibex) on the mountainside opposite underneath some rocks – they did not seem the slightest bit concerned to see four humans crashing up the path.

After meandering through a wide rocky gully and over a stile (presumably to keep the sheep in and not the *bouquetins*), the path starts to steepen again, going up in zigzags and becoming rockier. Look carefully for the cairns and green splashes as you approach the Rochers du Charvet, alt. 1645m (1hr 30mins).

(4) This is a grassy hump and lookout point with a good view back the way you have come, and down to the village and church of Montmin where you left the car. You can see the path going right up to the col – it almost doubles back along the gully higher up the mountain, steepening as you climb to the ridge, crossing a dry riverbed and passing through stunted alder bushes. Down on the right are the ruins of the Chalet du Lars, which look as if they are now being used as sheep pens. Here you get your first view of Lake Annecy in the distance and you feel you have come a long way. The path reaches a grassy ridge, alt. 1899m (2hrs).

(5) From the ridge there is a good view of the other side of the mountain with the valley going towards the town of Thônes. The Pointe de la Beccaz towers to the right, but turn left along the ridge towards the Pointe de la Bajulaz. The path is airy but not difficult or steep, culminating in the Pointe des Frêtes, alt. 2019m. There is a turning right to a refuge far down in the valley below and a sign on a rock indicating Serraval (2hrs 30mins).

There is an imposing wall of rock straight ahead, but you can see the path bearing round to the left and going up over the ridge. Care should be taken here because, although the path is defined, it goes across a rather rocky slope followed by scree for about 15mins. You have to pick your way along fairly meticulously so that you do not slip.

(6) You reach a col between the Pointe de la Bajulaz and La Tournette (3hrs).

Lake Annecy from the summit of La Tournette

Now the green splashes you have been following diligently are joined by brown markings. The col is rather desolate and rocky, and there is still another 160m to another col and the climb to the top. Take time to appreciate the view of Lake Annecy with, on the other side of the water, the smudged outlines of the Taillefer ridge, Roc des Boeufs and the Semnoz ridge beyond, the latter extending all the way along the lake to the town of Annecy. You can also see down to the Chalets de l'Aulp and the path winding up the mountain. (This is one of the alternative ways to the summit and halfway up is the French Alpine Club Refuge de la Tournette.) Continue, following the green splashes, along a defined path which curls upwards round the mountain through a jumble of magnificent rocks with numerous small crevices, caves and holes. In some places there are precipitous drops on the left, but thankfully not too near the path! The track reaches a T-junction (3hrs 15mins).

In the autumn we saw mottled, brown-and-white ptarmigan picking industriously at something tasty on the rocks but, like the bouquetins, they did not seem concerned by our approach.

(7) Turn right (the left path is the alternative way down). You continue through a rocky area and then follow the arrows round the bottom of the Tournette cliffs.

There is a cross on the rock face dedicated to Jeanne-Pierre Dufour, who died here on 16 August 1962 at the age of 22 years. You come across such monuments to walkers who have tragically fallen on just about every altitude walk in the Haute Savoie. It is a tragic reminder that walking in the mountains can be a dangerous activity should the weather turn bad, or there is a moment of inattention.

A few metres on there is a chain across a rock face, about 50m in length, but not tricky to negotiate as there are plenty of footholds. It leads into a narrow chimney where there are two ladders (25 rungs on the second one) up to a flattish rocky area with a cross at the end – you have reached the summit.

(8) This is the obvious place to stop and have a picnic while admiring the fantastic mountain ranges in all directions and the whole of Lake Annecy (4hrs). There is no other way off this summit but to return down the ladders which, I read with interest, were installed in 1968. Retrace your steps the same way back to the car (6hrs 30mins).

Refuges
Refuge de la Tournette (French Alpine Club), tel 0450.68.52.30; Refuge/Hôtel La Rosairy (privately owned), tel 0450.02. 00.26; Refuge Le Casset (privately owned), tel 0450.68.54.11

WALK 30

Taillefer Ridge and Le Roc des Boeufs
Alt. 1335m (Lake Annecy area)

Difficulty	Difficult/medium, with some rocky scrambling as far as Entrevernes and then a steep climb to the Col de la Cochette
Time	6hrs 15mins
Height gain	885m
Maps	Editions Didier & Richard IGN No. 2 Massifs des Bornes-Bauges 1:50,000
	Cartes IGN 3431 OT Top 25 Lac d'Annecy 1:25,000
Depart from	Duingt (on Lake Annecy) – 450m
Signposting	Good – new signposts plus posts with yellow arrows on a green background; blue splashes on the Roc des Boeufs

One of my favourite walks, as it has one of the most beautiful views in the whole region. It also has a Mediterranean feel about it, mainly due to the stunted oak and juniper bushes on the Taillefer ridge. It is lovely on a hot summer's day, as there is plenty of shade, but you get better views of the surrounding peaks if you walk when the leaves are off the trees. However, you will not be disappointed at any time of the year, as it is one of the most charming and beautiful walks in the Annecy region. The second part of the walk, namely up to the Roc des Boeufs, is steep though not difficult, but less enthusiastic walkers can go as far as Entrevernes and either return by road or back along the Taillefer ridge.

Access (from Geneva)

Take the motorway, direction Chamonix, and then the A41 motorway signposted Annecy/Grenoble/Lyon. Exit Annecy Sud (No. 16) and follow all signs to Albertville. Take the N508 which goes along the western shore of the lake till you get to the village of Duingt, which is three-quarters of the way down, where the lake narrows, with Talloires on the opposite shore. There is an attractive small château jutting out into the water. In the village take the first turning to the right after the church (there is a sign saying Grotte du Notre Dame du

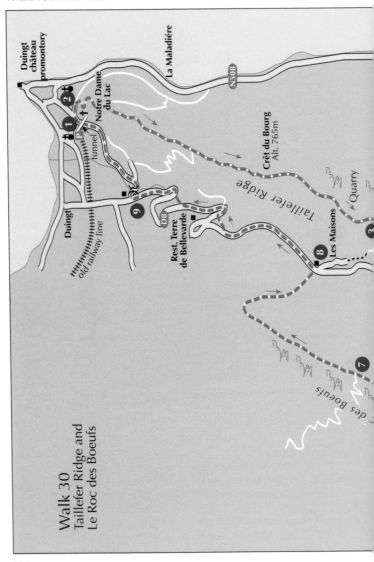

Walk 30
Taillefer Ridge and
Le Roc des Boeufs

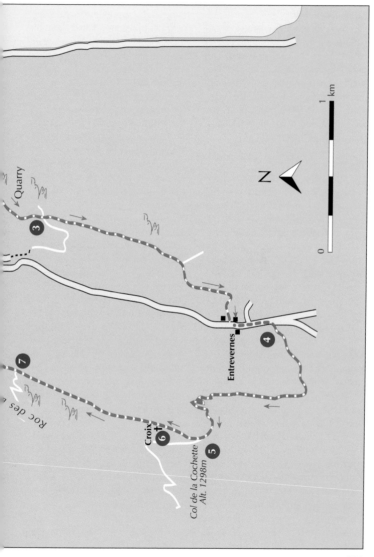

Lac/Taillefer). Follow this narrow road for above 200m till you come to a car park on the right and a sign to Grotte Notre Dame du Lac. Park your car here. Above the bank in front of the small car park you can see the start of a tunnel. It is fairly long and was originally a railway tunnel which has recently been restored and converted into a bicycle track.

The Route
(1) Following a post with yellow arrows, walk left up the road from the car park and shortly you will see a number of wooden signs up on the right to Taillefer Panorama 45mins/ Circuit Entrevernes 2hrs/Grotte du Notre Dame du Lac/ Belvedere Saint Michel. (**Note** This sign was not there when the author last did the walk in 2004, but is sure to be replaced by the new white signposts which are going up all over France.)

This is the start of a pilgrimage to the grotto and on the right is the first of the stone shrines depicting the Five Joyful, Sorrowful and Glorious Mysteries of the Life of Christ. It is interesting to look at these shrines, and at the same time to admire the glorious view down to Duingt and over Lake Annecy, as you follow the cemented path, obviously well used by pilgrims over the years. After the shrines the path goes up left, but continue straight on for a few metres to the huge grotto hewn out of the rock, called Notre Dame du Lac. Standing lonely amongst the boulders is a

rather sad statue of the Virgin Mary, with lots of plaques dotted about the rocks thanking Our Lady for favours granted. There is also an inscription asking for protection against the enemy, dated 24 June 1940.

The building of grottoes to the Virgin Mary was very popular at the turn of the century, and you will find them scattered about the Savoie area which has always been a bastion of Catholicism, in contrast to the Calvinism of its northern neighbour, Geneva.

(2) Go back down and take the path (which is now on your right) where there are signs to Crêt du Bourg 765m/Les Maisons/Entrevenes/ Duingt. This is an easy, well- defined, medium-steep climb through a reserve of Corsican pines and larches. After about 5mins of twisting path you come to a small circular glade with an imposing statue of the Archangel Michael crushing the devil with his foot. From here there is an impressive view down the lake all the way to the town of Annecy.

I think the devil looks more interesting than St Michael, whose face seems rather smug, with eyes hooded and peering over the lake, rather than at the devil whom he is meant to be killing!

Keep to the main track going upwards through stunted woodland.

Soon after you reach another viewpoint, where there is a bench and a magnificent panorama to the left of the Dents de Lanfon with the Col des Frêtes and La Tournette (Walk Number 29) on the other side of the lake. You are now walking along the wide Taillefer ridge which juts out into the lake, so at the start there are impressive watery views on both sides if the trees have shed their leaves. You reach a signpost at alt. 590m (25mins).

Follow the sign straight to Entrevernes (left goes down to La Maladière on the lake) towards a clearing and a squat concrete *borne* (marker), where there are further benches from which to enjoy the view. Following a post with yellow arrows, continue on through woodland past another signpost at alt. 648m, indicating right to Duingt (this is another alternative way back for those preferring a shorter walk). The path becomes rockier with stunted vegetation, mainly juniper and oak. As you go higher you get even more extended views as you are exactly opposite the imposing La Tournette mountain, alt. 2351m, which dominates the southern end of the lake. The Col des Frêtes and the Dents de Lanfon are visible again, and also the

Parmelan overlooking Annecy with, on a clear day, the Jura mountains in the background. In the foreground below is the little château on its promontory, like an island in the sparkling water. As views go, this one is breathtaking.

You go over the Crêt du Bourg, alt. 765m, though there is no sign to say you are there, so you don't really know when you have reached it. The path gets rockier and you start clambering upwards over boulders – you are still going along the ridge with the end of Lake Annecy in view to the

The summit and view – Roc des Boeufs

left, but to the right is now a narrow, green valley which looks gloriously unspoiled, apart from a road through it to the villages of Les Maisons and Entrevernes. After a short, rocky climb you pass a large rock to the right followed by two short railings. You are reaching the area of a huge disused quarry which was recently in full operation. A few minutes later the path reaches a corner where you have a view of the quarry ahead which, from far off, makes a huge and unsightly gash in the mountainside (1hr 10mins).

Careful – at the viewpoint bear right following a post with yellow arrows (this too was missing in 2004) to reach a large notice Carrière de Lathuile et Duingt. There is a wire across the path ahead, so go right again (no sign here) on a steep, rocky path which goes down, skirting the quarry, and then up to the ridge again. You come to a yellow arrow where you bear left uphill, direction Entrevernes (again there was once a signpost which has done a disappearing act!). Down to the right is an overgrown path which goes to Les Maisons (1hr 35mins).

(3) A few minutes later, after a bit of a rock scramble and a walk through woodland, there is another group of signposts called Le Taillefer, alt. 760m, at a jeep track. Cross the track and continue up again (right is Les Maisons). (If you are tired at this stage, take the right track down to Les

Maisons and at the village take the road back to Duingt.) The path becomes easier with thicker pine woods on each side. At a further sign bear right, direction Entrevernes. The path continues through woodland and starts to descend.

If you do this walk in autumn you will see a variety of fungi along this path. Some are quaintly conical, others with a sinister, watery blue tinge, and of course the colourful 'picture book' variety – bright red with white spots. It is an art to know your fungi, as some are deadly poisonous, and you should never pick them unless you know they are edible. To make sure, take them to any pharmacie ('chemist') who will examine them for you

At a T-junction follow the sign right to the village of Entrevernes. The path goes down, skirting a field (post with yellow arrow here) and along the side of a hill with a stream down on the right. You come into a lane where you follow the little river down. Leaving the stream on the right, the path then goes up into the village by a restored farm and the old village bakery (2hrs 15mins). (**Note** If you want to take a rest here go right to reach the war memorial in a little square (toilets available).

A quaint Savoyard village, renovated tastefully so that it looks spruce, but retaining an old world charm. When

looking down on it from the other side we noticed that most of the roofing was new and there was not a single dilapidated building.
Whenever I have done this walk I have never met anyone in the village – perhaps they are all working in Annecy!

(4) When you reach the main street turn left and walk along for a few metres to a signpost indicating right to the Col de la Cochette (this signpost is hidden by the wall of the bakery, but La Cochette is written on the wall). From the village to the col is a 450m steepish climb and seems endless (it says 1hr 45mins at the start, but it normally takes a bit less). At first the path takes you along the hillside, parallel to the village which is long and straggly with the church down on the right, through an ancient orchard, the stunted, gnarled trees covered in lichen.

After the orchard follow the path round to the left (post here) through meadows with stately chestnut and walnut trees. After passing a small barn you enter woodland again and almost immediately there is a fork. Go up left on a stony slope and you will see a pink splash. **From here to the Col de la Cochette follow intermittent pink splashes**. The path veers to the left and you feel you are going in the wrong direction. The gradient is steep and at times the path is not well defined, though from time to time there are pink splashes. The track

finally swings back to the right and becomes stony, winding upwards. If you look back you have a good view of the Taillefer ridge you walked along on the other side of the valley, with the lake beyond. The path gets steeper as it approaches the cliff face of the col, and crosses under the high-tension wires of a long line of electricity pylons to reach the woody ridge of the Col de la Cochette, alt. 1298m (3hrs 45mins).

(5) At the col take the signpost up to the right saying Duingt. (If you go straight you will go down the other side of the ridge and eventually reach St Eustache in the next valley.) The path goes again under the high-tension wires as you go up to the ridge and along a rocky, wooded, undulating path following blue splashes.

Careful – do not to miss this next bit, which is only for those who like a short, steep scramble. After about 10mins you see a red and blue splash on a large rock to your left. Go to the end of the rock and, if you can manage it, clamber up a narrow steep cleft (some chains to help you) to reach a small rocky summit where there is a large iron cross dated 1994. It is a dramatic spot for a picnic, as you have an uninterrupted view of all the surrounding mountains, including the Bauges and Beaufortain ranges southwards, and all the way to the Jura in the north with the lake and town of Annecy. It is one of the most beautiful views in the whole region (4hrs).

(6) The path becomes rocky with lovely open areas. (If you have not managed to scramble up the rock, there is a lovely picnic area a few minutes further on where you can see back to the cross.) Follow the blue splashes carefully, as they are not always obvious, along the wooded rocky ridge which now starts to go down gently. You arrive at a clearing with a medley of signs (4hrs 35mins).

(7) Go straight towards Les Maisons/Duingt (left indicates St Jorioz, which is a village north of Duingt). The path gets wider and the trees taller as you start descending, at first gently and then later medium steep. After 15mins, if you watch out on your left, you will see a large flat area. This is a jump-off point for para-penters, but it is also a good spot to stop and rest, with a chance to admire the views again.

The path bears round to the right and winds down the front of the mountain. There are some flat rocky places, so care should be taken, especially if the ground is wet. Near the bottom the path skirts a field to arrive at a T-junction where you turn right. Continue down past other fields to meet the road at the hamlet of Les Maisons at a signpost (5hrs 30mins).

(8) Turn left and walk down the valley. The narrow road descends in wide bends but there are a couple of short cuts. (A few new houses have been built along here which could have altered the paths.)

You reach a welcome restaurant/ *gîte* (Terre de Bellevarde) on the left, opposite a cross from which you have a stunning view of the château on the lake. At the cross there is a short cut cutting off a wide bend. The road continues down past some old houses and you can see another château on your right with an original slate-tiled roof topped with a weather vane (6hrs).

(9) Turn right, before you reach the château, down a narrow, walled road (Route des Viviers) and continue down, crossing a bridge over a stream with a small waterfall splashing over mossy hummocks. Walk down this charming road which follows a stream flowing left. The road passes a large cross and then goes under the old railway bridge to the car park (6hrs 15mins).

APPENDIX 1

Maps Used in the Guide

The maps used in this guidebook are as follows.

1:25,000 (1cm = 250m)

These show the paths clearly.

    Cartes IGN 3430 OT Top 25 Mont Salève

    Cartes IGN 3429 ET Top 25 Bonneville/Cluses

    Cartes IGN 3530 ET Top 25 Samoëns/Haut Giffre

    Cartes IGN 3430 ET Top 25 La Clusaz/Grand-Bornand

    Cartes IGN 3531 OT Top 25 Megève Col des Aravis

    Cartes IGN 3431 OT Top 25 Lac d'Annecy

1:50,000 (1cm = 500m)

These give a more general view.

    Editions Didier & Richard IGN No.3 Massifs du Chablais Faucigny & Genevois

    Editions Didier & Richard IGN No. 2 Massifs des Bornes-Bauges

    Editions Didier & Richard IGN No. 8 Massifs du Mont Blanc/Beaufortain.

These maps are being phased out and are difficult to find. They have been replaced by IGN Serie Orange, also difficult to find but available on the internet (see below).

Also available:

Cartes IGN 01 Léman (Rives du Léman, Genevois, Pays de Gex, Chablais, Faucigny, Giffre) 1:60,000, and a useful map showing the whole area is Cartes IGN No. 45 Annecy/Lausanne-Parc Naturel Régional du Haut-Jura, Série Verte 1:1000. These maps can be bought locally and sometimes the French supermarkets sell them cheaper. Maps are more expensive if bought in Geneva.

The above maps should be available in the travel section of larger English bookshops or they can be ordered from specialist shops

The Map Shop
15 High Street
Upton- upon-Severn
Worcs WR8 OHJ
Tel 01684 593 146 (Freephone 0800 085 4080)
Email themapshop@btinternet.com
Website **www.themapshop.uk**

Stanfords
12–14 Long Acre
Convent Garden
London WC2E 9LP
Tel 020 7836 1321 Fax 020 7836 0189
Website **www.stanfordsmaps.com**

Websites where IGN maps can be ordered and sent: **www.map-world.co.uk**, **www.maps2anywhere.com**, **www.ign.fr** (this is the official French IGN website)

APPENDIX 2

Tourist Offices and
Syndicats d'Initiative in the Haute Savoie

Meaning of symbols for tourist offices:

**** A main tourist office offering a wide range of information. Normally employs qualified personnel able to speak several languages. Open all the year round. Last minute hotel reservations possible.

*** As above but without hotel reservations.

** Offers regional and local information with a bilingual (usually English) employee. Open all the year round.

* Local information only with no guarantee of someone speaking English. Open in season only but with answering service all the year round.

Syndicats d'initiative are the equivalent of tourist offices but are situated in the smaller villages. They are only open in the season – some of them have an answering service but this is not guaranteed.

Please note that when phoning tourist offices from Great Britain you dial 0033 and then leave off the 0 before the 4, e.g. 0033.450.51.32.31.

For general information on the Haute Savoie Department.

**** Agence Touristique de la Haute Savoie,
56 Rue Sommeiller BP 348
74012 Annecy Cedex
Tel 0450.51.32.31
Fax 0450.45.81.99
E-mail tourisme@cdt-hautesavoie.fr
Website **www.savoiehautesavoie.com**

* Bonneville (Faucigny/Haut Giffre)
23 Rue de Carroz
74130 Haute Savoie
Tel 0450.97.38.37
E-mail officetourismebonneville@wanadoo.fr

* Brasses (Les) (Faucigny/Haut Giffre)
74490 Haute Savoie
Tel 0450.35.91.83
Website **www.alpesduleman.com**
Includes villages of Bogève, Megevette, Onnion, Viuz-en-Sallaz and St-Jeoire-en-Faucigny.

** Cluses (Faucigny/Haut Giffre)
Chalet Savoyard
Place des Allobroges
74300 Haute Savoie
Tel 50.98.31.79
Website **www.cluses.com**

Duingt (Annecy region), syndicat d'initiative in the mairie
74410 Haute Savoie
Tel 0450.68.67.07
Website **www.lac-annecy.com**

*** Flaine (Faucigny/Haut Giffre)
74300 Haute Savoie
Tel 0450.90.80.01
Website **www.flaine.com**

*** Grand-Bornand (Le) (Aravis/Borne)
74450 Haute Savoie
Tel 0450.02.78.00
Website **www.legrandbornand.com**

** Manigod (Aravis/Borne)
74230 Haute Savoie
Tel 0450.44.92.44
Website **www.manigod.com**

* Marignier (Faucigny/Haut Giffre)
74970 Haute Savoie
Tel 0450.34.60.22

* Menthon-Saint-Bernard (Aravis/Borne)
74290 Haute Savoie
Tel 0450.60.14.30
Website **www.lac-annecy.com**

* Mieussy/Sommand (Faucigny/Haut Giffre)
74440 Haute Savoie
Tel 0450.43.02.72
Website **www.mieussy-sommand.com**

* Montriond-Le-Lac (Faucigny/Haut Giffre)
74110 Haute Savoie
Tel 0450.79.12.81
Website **www.montriond-portesdu-soleil.com**

* Mont Saxonnex (Faucigny/Haut Giffre)
74130 Haute Savoie
Tel 0450.96.97.27
Website **www.mont-saconnex.fr**

** Passy/Le Plateau d'Assy/Plaines Joux
Ave. du Dr. Arnaud Le Plateau d'Assy
74480–74190 Haute Savoie
Tel 0450.58.80.52
Website **www.ot-passy.com**

* Petit-Bornand (Le)/Les Glières (Aravis/Bornes)
74130 Haute Savoie
Tel 0450.03.52.38
Website **www.petit-bornand-les-glieres**

* Reposoir (Le) Syndicat d'Initiative (Faucigny/Haut Giffre)
74950 Haute Savoie
Tel 0450.98.18.01

** Roche-sur-Foron (La) (Aravis/Borne)
Place Andrevetan
74800 Haute Savoie
Tel 0450.03.36.68
Website **www.larochesurforon.com**

* Saint-Jean-d'Aulps (Faucigny/Haut Giffre)
74430 Haute Savoie
Tel 0450.79.65.09
Website **www.saintjeandaulps.com**

** St-Jean-de-Sixt (Aravis/Borne)
74450 Haute Savoie.
Tel 0450.02.70.14
Website **www.saintjeandesixt.com**

*** Samoëns (Faucigny/Haut Giffre)
Gare Routière
74340 Haute Savoie
Tel 0450.34.40.28
Website **www.samoens.com**

* Sixt-Fer-à-Cheval (Faucigny/Haut Giffre)
74740 Haute Savoie
Tel 0450.34.49.36
Website **www.sixtferacheval.com**

** Talloires (Annecy region)
Place de la Mairie
74290 Haute Savoie.
Tel 0450.60.70.64
Website **www.talloires.fr**

* Taninges/Praz de Lys (Faucigny/Haut Giffre)
74440 Haute Savoie
Tel 0450.34.25.05
Website **www.taninges.com**

*** Thônes (Aravis/Borne)
Place Avet
74230 Haute Savoie
Tel 0450.02.00.26
Website **www.thones-tourisme.com**

* Thorens-Glières (Aravis/Bornes)
74570 Haute Savoie
Tel 0450.22.40.31
E-mail ot.thorens@infonie.fr

* Villards-sur-Thônes (Les) (Aravis/Bornes)
74230 Haute Savoie
Tel 0450.02.07.88
Website **www.villards-sur-thones.com**

APPENDIX 3
Market Days

Below is a list of the market days in the towns and villages mentioned in the book. They mainly start early and finish around 13.00. There are three types of market – *marché traditional*, which is a normal market offering a wide range of goods and produce; *marché paysan*, where the local farmers sell their home-grown produce; and *marché nocturne*, held in the tourist season with more arts and crafts and geared to the holiday maker. There are also *foires* in the larger towns, which are trade fairs with a range of farming and industrial equipment. The larger ones include the exhibiting and judging of livestock and often have a fairground. Very popular are markets with a theme, such as *Foire aux vins et huitres* (wine and oysters), *Foire aux bestiaux* (livestock), *Foire aux livres* (books), *Foire brochante* (bric-a-brac), and so on. For information regarding these specific markets telephone the local tourist office.

Traditional Markets in the Haute Savoie

Monday — La Clusaz, Cluses (town centre), Seyssel, Thonon, Viuz-en-Sallaz.

Tuesday — Annecy – food only in the old quarter and general market, Place des Romains. Annemasse, Boëge, Bonneville, Evian.

Wednesday — Annecy le Vieux, Châtel, Frangy, Grand-Bornand, Morzine, Plateau d'Assy, Samoëns, Thorens.

Thursday — Annecy (Novel), Cluses-Sardagne (afternoon), Cruseilles, Les Gets, Lullin, La Roche-sur-Foron, Taninges, Thonon.

Friday — Annecy (old quarter), Annemasse, Chapelle d'Abondance, Bonneville, Evian, Marignier (afternoon), St Jeoire-en-Faucigny, St Julien-en-Genevois.

Saturday — Annecy (Bd Taine), St Pierre-en-Faucigny, Reignier, Sixt (summer only), Thônes, Mieussy (afternoon).

Sunday — Abondance, Annecy (old town).

APPENDIX 4
Glossary of Useful French Words

Au bout de	at the end of (something)
L'aigle	eagle
L'aiguille	needle (summit of a mountain)
L'arbre	tree
L'arête	ridge
L'auberge de jeunesse	youth hostel
Bas	low
La borne	boundary marker (usually concrete)
La boucle	circle or loop (used to describe a round trip)
Le buisson	bush
Le boulet	type of mushroom
Le bourg	market town (borough)
Le bouquetin	ibex
Le brouillard	fog
La buvette	café
Les cailloux	stones, rocks
La canne	walking stick
Le carrefour	crossroads
La carte	map
La cascade	waterfall
La chambre d'hôte	bed and breakfast
La chapelle	chapel
Le champignon	mushroom
Le chemin	path
Le cheval	horse
La chèvre	goat
La chute de pierre	rockfall
Le ciel	sky
La clairière	clearing, glade
Le col	pass
La combe	shallow valley
La commune	district (small)
La corniche	overhanging mass of hardened snow at the end of a precipice
Le couloir	corridor (in mountain terms, a narrow passway through rocks)
Le coup de soleil	sunstroke
La crête	top or ridge
La croix	cross
Le danger (dangereux)	danger (dangerous)
Descendre	to go down
L'église	church
Entrée interdite	no entry
L'est	east
L'étang	pond
La falaise	cliff
La ferme	farm
La foudre	lightning
La fleur	flower
Le gîte	refuge
Le gouffre	large hole, chasm
La grotte	grotto
Haut/e	high
Le hameau	hamlet
Là-bas	down there
Là-haut	up there
Le lac	lake
Le lièvre	hare
Marcher (se promener)	

	to walk
La mairie	village hall (literally means mayor's house)
La montagne	mountain
Monter	to go up
La moraine	debris (rocks) carried down by a glacier
Le moulin	mill
Le mouton	sheep
La neige	snow
Le nord	north
Les névés	glacier-snow – treacherous snow patches
Le nuage (nuageux)	cloud (cloudy)
L'oiseau	bird
L'orage	thunderstorm
L'oratoire	wayside shrine
L'ouest	west
Le papillon	butterfly
Le parcours vita	exercise route (usually in woods)
Le pèlerin	pilgrim
La pente	slope, gradient
Le pic	peak or summit (e.g. Pic des Mémises); also means woodpecker
La pierre	stone
La piste	track (usually meaning a man-made path for skiers)
Plagne, plan	mountain term for small plain or plateau
Le plateau	plain, plateau, upland
La pluie	rain
La pointe	point or head (e.g. Pointe de la Gay)
Le pont	bridge

Le poteau (indicateur)	signpost
Le pré/praz	field, meadow
La randonnée	long walk (ride)
Le ravin	ravine, gully
Le réfuge	mountain refuge (hut)
Le renard	fox
La rivière	river
Le rocher	rock
La route	road
Le ruisseau	stream or rivulet
Le sac de couchage	sleeping bag
Le sac à dos	rucksack
Le sanctuaire	sanctuary
Le sapin	fir tree
L'herbe	grass
Le sentier	marked path
Le serpent	snake
Le soleil	sun
Le sommet	summit
La source	spring (water)
Le sud	south
Le taureau	bull
Le télécabine	cable car
Le télésiège	chair-lift
Le téléski	drag, tow or pommel lift
Le temps	weather
La tempête	thunderstorm
Le terrain privé (propriété privée)	private property
Le trou	hole
Le tonnerre	thunder
La vache	cow
La vallée	valley
Le versant	side (of a mountain)

NOTES

NOTES

LISTING OF CICERONE GUIDES

NORTHERN ENGLAND
LONG-DISTANCE TRAILS
The Dales Way
The Reiver's Way
The Alternative Coast to Coast
The Coast to Coast Walk
The Pennine Way
Hadrian's Wall Path
The Teesdale Way

FOR COLLECTORS OF SUMMITS
The Relative Hills of Britain
Mts England & Wales Vol 2 – England
Mts England & Wales Vol 1 – Wales

BRITISH CYCLE GUIDES
The Cumbria Cycle Way
Lands End to John O'Groats – Cycle Guide
On the Ruffstuff: 84 Bike Rides in North England
Rural Rides No.1 – West Surrey
Rural Rides No.2 – East Surrey
South Lakeland Cycle Rides
Border Country Cycle Routes
Lancashire Cycle Way

CANOE GUIDES
Canoeist's Guide to the North-East

LAKE DISTRICT AND MORECAMBE BAY
Coniston Copper Mines
Scrambles in the Lake District
More Scrambles in the Lake District
Walks in Silverdale and Arnside AONB
Short Walks in Lakeland 1 – South
Short Walks in Lakeland 2 – North
Short Walks in Lakeland 3 – West
The Tarns of Lakeland Vol 1 – West
The Tarns of Lakeland Vol 2 – East
The Cumbria Way & Allerdale Ramble
Winter Climbs in the Lake District
Roads and Tracks of the Lake District
The Lake District Angler's Guide
Rain or Shine – Walking in the Lake District
Rocky Rambler's Wild Walks
An Atlas of the English Lakes

NORTH-WEST ENGLAND
Walker's Guide to the Lancaster Canal
Walking in Cheshire
Family Walks in the Forest Of Bowland
Walks in Ribble Country
Historic Walks in Cheshire
Walking in Lancashire
Walks in Lancashire Witch Country
The Ribble Way

THE ISLE OF MAN
Walking on the Isle of Man
The Isle of Man Coastal Path

PENNINES AND NORTH-EAST ENGLAND
Walks in the Yorkshire Dales – Vol 1
Walking in the South Pennines
Walking in the North Pennines
The Yorkshire Dales
Walks in the North York Moors – Vol 1
Walks in the North York Moors – Vol 2
Walking in the Wolds
Waterfall Walks – Teesdale and High Pennines
Walking in County Durham
Yorkshire Dales Angler's Guide
Backpacker's Britain – Northern England
Walks in Dales Country
Historic Walks in North Yorkshire
South Pennine Walks
Walking in Northumberland

DERBYSHIRE, PEAK DISTRICT, EAST MIDLANDS
High Peak Walks
White Peak Walks Northern Dales
White Peak Walks Southern Dales
White Peak Way
The Viking Way
Star Family Walks Peak District & South Yorkshire
Walking In Peakland
Historic Walks in Derbyshire

WALES AND WELSH BORDERS
Ascent of Snowdon
Welsh Winter Climbs
Hillwalking in Wales – Vol 1
Hillwalking in Wales – Vol 2
Scrambles in Snowdonia
Hillwalking in Snowdonia
The Ridges of Snowdonia
Hereford & the Wye Valley
Walking Offa's Dyke Path
The Brecon Beacons
Lleyn Peninsula Coastal Path
Anglesey Coast Walks
The Shropshire Way
Spirit Paths of Wales
Glyndwr's Way
The Pembrokeshire Coastal Path
Walking in Pembrokeshire
The Shropshire Hills – A Walker's Guide
Backpacker's Britain Vol 2 – Wales

MIDLANDS
The Cotswold Way
West Midlands Rock
The Grand Union Canal Walk
Walking in Oxfordshire
Walking in Warwickshire
Walking in Worcestershire
Walking in Staffordshire
Heart of England Walks

SOUTHERN ENGLAND
The Wealdway & the Vanguard Way
Exmoor & the Quantocks
Walking in the Chilterns
Walks in Kent Book 2
Two Moors Way
Walking in Dorset
Walking in Cornwall
A Walker's Guide to the Isle of Wight
Walking in Devon
Walking in Somerset
The Thames Path
Channel Island Walks
Walking in Buckinghamshire
The Isles of Scilly
Walking in Hampshire
Walking in Bedfordshire
The Lea Valley Walk
Walking in Berkshire
The Definitive Guide to Walking in London
The Greater Ridgeway
Walking on Dartmoor
The South West Coast Path
Walking in Sussex
The North Downs Way
The South Downs Way

SCOTLAND
Scottish Glens 1 – Cairngorm Glens
Scottish Glens 2 – Atholl Glens
Scottish Glens 3 – Glens of Rannoch
Scottish Glens 4 – Glens of Trossach
Scottish Glens 5 – Glens of Argyll
Scottish Glens 6 – The Great Glen
Scottish Glens 7 – The Angus Glens
Scottish Glens 8 – Knoydart to Morvern
Scottish Glens 9 – The Glens of Ross-shire
Scrambles in Skye
The Island of Rhum
Torridon – A Walker's Guide
Ski Touring in Scotland
Walking the Galloway Hills
Walks from the West Highland Railway
Border Pubs & Inns – A Walkers' Guide
Walks in the Lammermuirs
Scrambles in Lochaber
Walking in the Hebrides
Central Highlands: 6 Long Distance Walks
Walking in the Isle Of Arran
Walking in the Lowther Hills
North to the Cape
The Border Country – A Walker's Guide
Winter Climbs – Cairngorms
The Speyside Way
Winter Climbs – Ben Nevis & Glencoe
The Isle of Skye, A Walker's Guide

The West Highland Way
Scotland's Far North
Walking the Munros Vol 1 –
  Southern, Central
Walking the Munros Vol 2 –
  Northern & Cairngorms
Scotland's Far West
Walking in the Cairngorms

IRELAND
The Mountains of Ireland
Irish Coastal Walks
The Irish Coast to Coast

INTERNATIONAL CYCLE GUIDES
The Way of St James – Le Puy to
  Santiago cyclist's guide
The Danube Cycle Way
Cycle Tours in Spain
Cycling the River Loire – The Way
  of St Martin

**WALKING AND TREKKING
  IN THE ALPS**
Grand Tour of Monte Rosa Vol 1
Grand Tour of Monte Rosa Vol 2
Walking in the Alps (all Alpine areas)
100 Hut Walks in the Alps
Chamonix to Zermatt
Tour of Mont Blanc
Alpine Ski Mountaineering
  Vol 1 Western Alps
Alpine Ski Mountaineering
  Vol 2 Eastern Alps
Snowshoeing: Techniques and Routes
  in the Western Alps
Alpine Points of View

**FRANCE, BELGIUM AND
  LUXEMBOURG**
The Tour of the Queyras
Rock Climbs in the Verdon
RLS (Robert Louis Stevenson) Trail
Walks in Volcano Country
French Rock
Walking the French Gorges
Rock Climbs Belgium & Luxembourg
Tour of the Oisans: GR54
Walking in the Tarentaise and
  Beaufortain Alps
The Brittany Coastal Path
Walking in the Haute Savoie
Walking in the Ardennes
Tour of the Vanoise
Walking in the Languedoc
GR20 Corsica – The High Level Route
The Ecrins National Park
Walking the French Alps: GR5
Walking in the Cevennes
Vanoise Ski Touring
Walking in Provence
Walking on Corsica
Mont Blanc Walks
Walking in the Cathar region
  of south west France
Walking in the Dordogne

PYRENEES AND FRANCE / SPAIN
Rock Climbs in the Pyrenees
Walks & Climbs in the Pyrenees

The GR10 Trail: Through the
  French Pyrenees
The Way of St James –
  Le Puy to the Pyrenees
The Way of St James –
  Pyrenees-Santiago-Finisterre
Through the Spanish Pyrenees GR11
The Pyrenees – World's Mountain
  Range Guide
The Pyrenean Haute Route
Walking in Andorra

SPAIN AND PORTUGAL
Picos de Europa – Walks & Climbs
Andalusian Rock Climbs
The Mountains of Central Spain
Costa Blanca Rock
Walking in Mallorca
Rock Climbs in Majorca,
  Ibiza & Tenerife
Costa Blanca Walks Vol 1
Costa Blanca Walks Vol 2
Walking in Madeira
Via de la Plata (Seville To Santiago)
Walking in the Cordillera Cantabrica
Walking in the Canary Islands 1 West
Walking in the Canary Islands 2 East
Walking in the Sierra Nevada

SWITZERLAND
The Jura: Walking the High Route &
  Ski Traverses
Walking in Ticino, Switzerland
Central Switzerland –
  A Walker's Guide
The Bernese Alps
Walking in the Valais
Alpine Pass Route
Walks in the Engadine, Switzerland

GERMANY AND AUSTRIA
Klettersteig Scrambles in
  Northern Limestone Alps
King Ludwig Way
Walking in the Salzkammergut
Walking in the Black Forest
Walking in the Harz Mountains
Walking in the Bavarian Alps
Germany's Romantic Road
Mountain Walking in Austria
Walking the River Rhine Trail
Trekking in the Stubai Alps
Trekking in the Zillertal Alps

SCANDINAVIA
Walking In Norway
The Pilgrim Road to Nidaros
  (St Olav's Way)

EASTERN EUROPE
Trekking in the Caucausus
The High Tatras
The Mountains of Romania
Walking in Hungary

CROATIA AND SLOVENIA
Walks in the Julian Alps
Walking in Croatia

ITALY
Italian Rock
Walking in the Central Italian Alps

Central Apennines of Italy
Walking in Italy's Gran Paradiso
Long Distance Walks in Italy's Gran
  Paradiso
Walking in Sicily
Shorter Walks in the Dolomites
Treks in the Dolomites
Via Ferratas of the Italian
  Dolomites Vol 1
Via Ferratas of the Italian
  Dolomites Vol 2
Walking in the Dolomites
Walking in Tuscany
Trekking in the Apennines

**OTHER MEDITERRANEAN
  COUNTRIES**
The Mountains of Greece
Climbs & Treks in the Ala Dag
  (Turkey)
The Mountains of Turkey
Treks & Climbs Wadi Rum, Jordan
Jordan – Walks, Treks, Caves etc.
Crete – The White Mountains
Walking in Palestine
Walking in Malta

AFRICA
Climbing in the Moroccan Anti-Atlas
Trekking in the Atlas Mountains
Kilimanjaro

NORTH AMERICA
The Grand Canyon &
  American South West
Walking in British Columbia
The John Muir Trail

SOUTH AMERICA
Aconcagua

HIMALAYAS – NEPAL, INDIA
Langtang, Gosainkund &
  Helambu: A Trekkers' Guide
Garhwal & Kumaon –
  A Trekkers' Guide
Kangchenjunga – A Trekkers' Guide
Manaslu – A Trekkers' Guide
Everest – A Trekkers' Guide
Annapurna – A Trekker's Guide
Bhutan – A Trekker's Guide

AUSTRALIA AND NEW ZEALAND
Classic Tramps in New Zealand

TECHNIQUES AND EDUCATION
The Adventure Alternative
Rope Techniques
Snow & Ice Techniques
Mountain Weather
Beyond Adventure
The Hillwalker's Manual
The Book of the Bivvy
Outdoor Photography
The Hillwalker's Guide to
  Mountaineering
Map and Compass

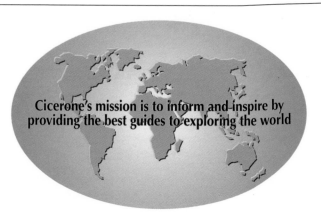

Cicerone's mission is to inform and inspire by providing the best guides to exploring the world

Since its foundation over 30 years ago, Cicerone has specialised in publishing guidebooks and has built a reputation for quality and reliability. It now publishes nearly 300 guides to the major destinations for outdoor enthusiasts, including Europe, UK and the rest of the world.

Written by leading and committed specialists, Cicerone guides are recognised as the most authoritative. They are full of information, maps and illustrations so that the user can plan and complete a successful and safe trip or expedition – be it a long face climb, a walk over Lakeland fells, an alpine traverse, a Himalayan trek or a ramble in the countryside.

With a thorough introduction to assist planning, clear diagrams, maps and colour photographs to illustrate the terrain and route, and accurate and detailed text, Cicerone guides are designed for ease of use and access to the information.

If the facts on the ground change, or there is any aspect of a guide that you think we can improve, we are always delighted to hear from you.

Cicerone Press
2 Police Square Milnthorpe Cumbria LA7 7PY
Tel:01539 562 069   Fax:01539 563 417
e-mail:info@cicerone.co.uk   web:www.cicerone.co.uk